Page 2

Edited and

with an Introduction by

FRANCIS BROWN

A NEW YORK TIMES BOOK

HOLT, RINEHART AND WINSTON

NEW YORK   CHICAGO   SAN FRANCISCO

PAGE 2

The Best of
"Speaking of Books" from
The New York Times Book Review

Library of Congress Catalog Card Number: 69-10225

Designer: Ernst Reichl

8724007
Printed in the United States of America

CONTENTS

Francis Brown
   Introduction   ix

I The Literary Scene

Saul Bellow
   Cloister Culture   3
Bernard Malamud
   Theme, Content and the "New Novel"   9
Nathalie Sarraute
   The Novel for Its Own Sake   13
Gerald Sykes
   The Changing of the Avant-Garde   17
Alan Pryce-Jones
   The Beautiful People   22
Brigid Brophy
   And Critics   25
Leon Edel
   To a Young Critic   30
Walter Allen
   Writers and Editors   33
Eleanor Clark
   The Great Divide   37
I. Bernard Cohen
   Science and the Nonscientist   43

II The Writer's Occupation

George P. Elliott
  Writers on Campus   51
M. L. Rosenthal
  Poets of Academe   55
John Knowles
  The Writer-in-Residence   58
Brian Glanville
  What Else Should Writers Do?   62
John Bowen
  Out of Experience   69
James MacGregor Burns
  Politicians as Authors   72
Howard Zinn
  Historian as Citizen   77

III The Writing Experience

Anthony Burgess
  The Seventeenth Novel   85
Alec Waugh
  The Novelist as Hero   89
V. S. Pritchett
  Writing an Autobiography   93
Edward Dahlberg
  The Writer's Plight   98
Sean O'Faolain
  And Svengali Was a Reviewer   103
John Le Carré
  The Undercover Man   109
R. K. Narayan
  Advantages of Anonymity   113
Kurt Vonnegut, Jr.
  Science Fiction   117
Andrew Sinclair
  The Dear Departed   120
J. H. Plumb
  Trials of a Biographer   125

IV   On Style and Styles

Frederic Morton
  Vhere Iss Charlotte Street?   133
Stanley Burnshaw
  Modern Hebrew Poets   138
Alan Pryce-Jones
  Difficult or Impossible   144
Robert Gorham Davis
  What's in a Name?   148
Eric Partridge
  Degraded Language   152
Ronald Gross
  Found Poetry   157
Peter Quennell
  A Matter of Style   162
Donald Hall
  An Ethic of Clarity   165
D. W. Brogan
  "Clio, a Muse"   170
Lindsay Rogers
  Metaphors   175
James A. Michener
  An Honest Account of What Transpired   180
Morris Bishop
  Limericks   186

V   Visitations

Peter Quennell
  Literary Sight-Seeing   193
Carlos Baker
  Hemingway's Italia   197
Walter Teller
  Whitman at Timber Creek   201
Helen Bevington
  The Way to Little Gidding   205
Walter Teller
  "The Outermost House"   210

VI The Experience of Literature

Carlos Baker
The Relevance of a Writer's Life 217
Harvey Swados
Writers of the Thirties 221
Brian Glanville
The Sporting Novel 226
John Bowen
The Novel As . . . 231
W. H. Auden
A Novel by Goethe 234

VII Portraits, Appraisals and Reappraisals

Carolyn Heilbrun
A Modern Among Contemporaries 241
Andrew Turnbull
Perkins's Three Generals 245
Herbert Mitgang
Carl Sandburg 251
Gore Vidal
John Horne Burns 256
Peter Quennell
Evelyn Waugh 260
Horace Gregory
Edwin Muir 264
Horace Gregory
A. D. Hope 270
Mark Harris
Alan Swallow, 1915-1966 274
Sidney Hyman
De Gaulle, Author 278
Anthony Burgess
The Politics of Graham Greene 284
Francis Steegmuller
Apollinaire and Friends 291

INTRODUCTION

SPEAKING OF BOOKS has been a rubric in The New York Times
Book Review almost since the memory of man runneth not to the
contrary. It was long associated with the by-line of J. Donald Adams
who for more than two decades wrote not only about books but about
their authors and the literary atmosphere surrounding them, speaking
sometimes in praise, often in vigorous dissent, but always speaking his
mind. He retired in 1964. Since then many voices have spoken of books.
What some of them have said has been brought together in the present
collection.

Virginia Woolf once declared that "an essay can be short or long,
serious or trifling, about God and Spinoza, or about turtles and Cheap-
side," and something of these qualities has characterized the essays
in Speaking of Books in recent years. The writers have been told, in
what has become almost a cliché, that they are being given a literary
pulpit from which they can preach any doctrine they see fit to profess
and express, with the proviso, of course, that it have some suitability
and relevance to the audience.

In a sense one could almost say that the essays have resulted from
a planned planlessness, for the authors are not only free from dicta-
tion. There has never been any set editorial scheme of so many pieces
on the novel, or on matters of style, or on whatever it might be. No
author, be he novelist or critic, poet or historian, has been favored
over another, no topic unduly preferred. Yet the façade of casualness
misleads. The very selection of authors is planning as fundamental as
the editorial decision to publish and in what sequence. Variety of
subject and diversity of style and point of view have been objectives
throughout, and from these has come the stimulus of surprise that
belongs to the unpatterned and unpredictable. The sixty essays selected

for this collection are witnesses to the variety and diversity I have been talking about.

On another occasion (in my collection "Opinions and Perspectives") I said that while the business of a book review is book reviewing, The Times Book Review does not live by reviews alone, and it is perhaps worth saying again. An essay, in its relaxed, often discursive fashion, lends perspective to the more specific discussion of particular books, can bring greater understanding and appreciation of books and the men and women who write them. An essay affords a pause, a chance to look around, or sometimes to look back, to be introduced however casually to personalities and places worth knowing and remembering. It affords the opportunity to develop a thought, to juggle ideas and, if done properly, to set out point and counterpoint with stylistic grace.

Probably every man who has anything to do with books or the business of writing has an essay within him, something major or minor that he wants to say about an experience he has had, an idea that has been itching him, or observations he believes worth sharing and wants to share. In Speaking of Books there has been an opportunity for just that sort of expression, what David Daiches may have had in mind when he described the essay as "the most self-indulgent of literary forms."

"You seem to be reviving the personal essay," someone—it may have been Leon Edel—remarked when invited to contribute to Speaking of Books. Personal essays they certainly have been, personal as opposed to the scholar's more objective treatise or literary deep-think, for the emphasis has been on this is what I believe, this is what interests me, this is how it was, all offered in the form almost of good conversation—except that probably not since the days of Dr. Johnson has there been what we like to think of as good conversation, and I sometimes wonder how good it was even then.

It is surprising how many of the essays, though written with the purpose of making some general comment on a situation of literary pertinence, are autobiographical. Of course everything any one of us writes is largely autobiographical; it reflects a period of our thinking, a working of our minds, a reflection of our concerns at the moment. When Saul Bellow spoke before the International Congress of P.E.N. on "cloister culture," he obviously had something he just had to say, and it stemmed from his knowledge and observation of the literary landscape around him. It was an important personal statement, a personal essay, a footnote to autobiography.

Without pressing the obvious too hard, I think we can see the same elements in Bernard Malamud's speech of acceptance at the 1967 National Book Awards and in Nathalie Sarraute's address to the 1966 Long Island University writers' conference. Or, in a somewhat different fashion, in Wystan Auden's appreciation of the modern translation of Goethe's novel "Elective Affinities."

When we use the word autobiographical, I suspect that we usually have in mind something less subtle and more like the familiar "all of which I saw, and some of which I was." In that mood we dine with J. H. Plumb and his host, "Earl A.," on a tiny cheese soufflé and apple in a famous house, share the freezing bed-chamber—and then breakfast on what the story books, and Plumb, describe as an English country gentleman's concept of how to start the day in proper fashion (kidneys to eggs to sausage to kippers). Or perhaps the preference is for Helen Bevington's company on her way to Little Gidding in the cold rain of an English April. Or Walter Teller's seeking out Timber Creek, with regards from Walt Whitman.

There are all sorts of ways of tackling the problem, of handling it effectively. John Knowles, in his "Writer-in-Residence," has a personal story to tell, and he makes very plain what it was like for him to be that strange bird, a writer among students, many of whom could not have cared less. In "Writers on Campus" George P. Elliott goes at the subject in quite a different style, more generalized perhaps, less specific, less self-revealing, and yet the reader is fully aware that Elliott is talking of what he has seen and of what he was.

A good many of the essays in this collection, in fact most of them, were written on invitation. A line was thrown out, and it was the author's decision whether or not to take it. Most of them did. Sometimes an invitation included the suggestion of a suitable topic, but it was no more than a suggestion. Again the writer could take it or leave it and, if the topic seemed right to him, proceed to treat it after his own fashion. Or he could, often did, offer a subject of his own, one more to his liking. Literary events, or accomplishments, are good subjects. Aware that Victor Pritchett has just completed his autobiography, "A Cab at the Door," what could be more natural than to ask him about the writing of autobiography? The result was the kind of engaging essay one associates with V. S. Pritchett.

On the whole ours is not an essay-writing age; events press upon us, the clash of controversy is loud, the time is too little for the kind of agreeable and light-hearted contemplation that produces essays. Probably that is a principal reason why so few unsolicited essays are offered Speaking of Books, and why very few that are offered pass the test. Occasionally there is an exception, to be greeted with huzzas. Such a one was James Michener's "A True Account of What Transpired."

There is an old saying that an editor should have no friends, and if anyone gives thought to the reason why, the answers are easy. Of course editors, even Book Review editors, do have friends, however perilous the course of friendship, as well as acquaintances and what for want of a better description can be described as faceless pen pals. From such relationships many a Speaking of Books essay has been drawn, not all but many.

The Indian writer R. K. Narayan and I had met, decided to continue our talk another day, and on the second occasion had lunch together. As we talked, he recalled visiting an American university in the Middle West, where he had met with a group concerned with literary matters. "Are any of your books available in English translation?" asked one of the professors, who obviously knew nothing of his guest. "I write in English," was the reply. Embarrassment. "I'm afraid I must leave now," said the questioner. "I have to catch a plane for Washington." Out of that anecdote came the obliquely related essay, "Advantages of Anonymity," in which he tells of this incident.

If I had not met Nathalie Sarraute and had a long conversation with her one evening in the Palais Royal long ago, would her essay be part of this collection? Or without the friendship of Alec Waugh, who took me to Lord's for my first cricket match, would he be represented? I cannot say for certain. But certain I am that it was Anthony Burgess's own suggestion, after being invited to join the "goodlie company," that brought us "The Politics of Graham Greene," and that Gore Vidal's appreciative essay on John Horne Burns was the writer's idea, not the editor's.

But enough of the wherefore and the how. Out of the planned planlessness and the disparity a pattern of sorts emerges. The pieces fall into place. The purpose becomes plain. The order of the collection, from the opening Literary Scene to the final Portraits, Appraisals and Reappraisals, is a procession moving from the general to the specific, playing with literary ideas and concepts as it goes along, saluting accomplishment, making room for experience. But the collection needs no gloss. As it should, it speaks for itself.

In an essay on the essay, and writing from familiarity, Virginia Woolf asserted that "the principle which controls it is simply that it should give pleasure. . . . Everything in an essay must be subdued to that end. It should lay us under a spell with its first word, and we should only wake, refreshed with its last. In the interval we may pass through the most various experiences of amusement, surprise, interest, indignation; we may soar to the heights of fantasy . . . or plunge to the depths of wisdom . . . but we must never be roused." I disagree about our not being roused; I would be for all that. But it is a provoking statement of a high ideal. I would like to believe she was not speaking in a far country.

Francis Brown

New York, February, 1968.

I
The
Literary
Scene

SAUL BELLOW
Cloister Culture

As one of the leading American novelists of the past quarter century, Saul Bellow ("Augie March," "Henderson the Rain King," "Herzog") scarcely needs an introduction. His essay is based on a 1966 address to the International Congress of the P.E.N. Club held in New York.

WE CAN'T master change. It is too vast, too swift. We'd kill ourselves trying. It is essential, however, to try to understand transformations directly affecting us. That may not be possible either, but we have no choice.

The changes on which I would like to comment are those in the relations between the writer and the public in the English-speaking countries. I shall begin with the sort of description of these relations an avant-garde writer might have given 30 years ago.

He would certainly have referred to himself as a highbrow. Not without irony, but seriously nevertheless, he would have distinguished himself from the middle-brow, the ape of culture, and from the low-brow or no-brow, that philistine hater of all that was good and beautiful in the modern tradition. This is not to say that the highbrow writer invariably loved his isolation and that he rejected the great public out of pride or decadent class-feeling. On the contrary, the division of cultures into high and low caused much bitterness and was considered by many highbrows to be dangerous to society and to civilization as a whole.

Perhaps overlooking the humiliations of the poet under patronage, the vanguardist of the thirties was often nostalgic for the 18th century and the small, refined and aristocratic public of that age of master-pieces. In his view the 19th-century public was already fully vulgarized —enthusiastic, perhaps, but coarse-grained, an audience of shop-keepers. The weaknesses of this public were aggravated by commercial exploitation, by promoters who made great fortunes in cheap novels, bringing mass culture into the world. The vanguard minority, by this vanguard account, grew smaller and smaller. The specialist now ap-peared, the technician, a new sort of intellectual with little or no understanding of art and small sympathy for the life of the mind.

Finally, in the 20th century, to state the case as it was stated by a brilliant critic and observer, the late Wyndham Lewis, an authentic highbrow, civilization cut itself in two, driving into pens and reserva-tions all that was most creative and intelligent. The vanguard artist, like the American Indian, was shut up in barren places, sequestered in the ivory tower, deprived of human contact and influence. Probably all this would end in the total liquidation of intellectuals. Only a few twilight masterpieces by men like Joyce or Paul Klee would remain, and we would reach the stage of final degradation, the era of brutal unre-lieved stupidity.

This in some ways resembles the description of the bourgeois situa-tion given by the 19th century romantic, not wholly unjustified but containing certain exaggerations. The romantic saw himself cut off from society, held in contempt by its rulers, separated from the people and longing to be reunited with them.

Wyndham Lewis was a thoughtful and original observer, but it is apparent that he made any number of wrong guesses. Intellectuals have not been liquidated. On the contrary they have increased in number and in influence. They are now spoken of with respect, even with awe, as indispensable to the government, as makers of educated opinion, as sources of symbolic legitimacy—replacing the clergy. Old Walt Whit-man, announcing, "The priest departs, the divine literatus arrives," does not sound as unhinged as he did 30 years ago.

I do not speak of the *quality* of these literati (that is another mat-ter; they are still a little remote from divinity) but of the growth of their power.

On the eve of World War II the highbrow public was indeed very small. This is no longer the case. We now have a growing class of intellectuals or near-intellectuals. There are millions of college graduates. A college degree may not mean much. It does, however, indicate exposure to high culture. And the literary culture to which these students are exposed was the creation of highbrow geniuses—disaffected, subversive, radical. The millions who go to art museums today admire there the strangely beautiful, powerful paintings of artists who worked in what Lewis called the thickening twilight of modernism. The millions who take courses in literature become acquainted with the poems and novels of men who rejected the average preferences of their contemporaries.

The minority public is no longer that handful of connoisseurs that read Transition in the twenties or discussed "significant form." We have at present a large literary community and something we can call, *faute de mieux*, a literary culture, in my opinion a very bad one.

For one thing, the universities have now embraced modern literature. Stony old pedants two generations ago refused to discuss anyone newer than Browning, but their power was broken in the thirties, and all universities permit the study of contemporary writers. Thousands of teachers turn out millions of graduates in literature. Some of these teachers, a very small minority, are quite useful; others are harmless enough, textual editors, antiquarians and fuddyduddies. Others are influential interpreters. Or misinterpreters.

It is in the universities that literary intellectuals are made, not on Grub Street, not in Bohemia. The mass media and the university-sponsored quarterlies have between them swallowed up literary journalism. The salaried professor will supply literary articles cheaply and has all but wiped out his professional competitors. Bohemia, too, has been relocated in new quarters, near to university campuses.

The university therefore is producing quantities of literary intellectuals who teach, write or go into publishing houses. So far as I can see this new group, greatly influenced by the modern classics, by Joyce, Proust, Eliot, Lawrence, Gide, Valéry, etc., have done little more than convert these classics into other forms of discourse, translating imagination into opinion, or art into cognitions. What they do is to put it all differently. They redescribe everything, usually making it less accessible. For feeling or response they substitute acts of comprehension.

Sometimes they seem to be manufacturing "intellectual history," creating a sort of subculture more congenial to them and to their stu-

dents than art itself. Sometimes I think they are trying to form a new
model of the civilized intelligence for the 20th century, an intelligence
to which a more worthy art will one day be offered—the *zeitgeist* per-
mitting. Perhaps the "dehumanization of art" of which Ortega speaks
reflects the demands made upon art by literary intellectuals. It may in
part be a result of the pressure they put upon it for meanings.

Redescription can be intriguing and useful, and succeeding generations must, like Adam and Eve in the Garden of Eden, rename their
beasts. Molière revealed the comic possibilities of this when M. Jour-
dain discovered that all his life he had been speaking prose. We
Americans take great satisfaction in this comedy of terms. We pay
psychologists to penetrate our characters and redescribe them to us
scientifically, rationalizing consciousness on the verbal level at least.
We are delighted to hear that we are introverted, fixated, have a repres-
sion here, a cathexis there, are attached to our mothers thus and so.
Such new accounts seem valuable in themselves, worth the money we
pay for them.

Yet what our literary intelligentsia does is to redescribe everything
downward, blackening the present age and denying creative scope to
their contemporaries. They assume themselves to be the only heirs of
the modern classical writers. Our most respected men of letters identify
themselves with Joyce, Proust, et cetera, and present themselves as the
distinguished representatives, indeed the only representatives of these
masters. The agents, managers or impresarios (popularizers) of James
or the French symbolists consider themselves the only successors of
these writers. Thus they enjoy a certain genteel prestige. They are the
happy few. And they are not unlike the old pretorians faithful to the
remains of poor Browning. But the scale of operations is much greater.

There are clear signs that intellectuals in what American universities
call the humanities are trying to appropriate literature for themselves,
taking it away from writers. These intellectuals are like the British
princess who said to her husband during the honeymoon, "Do the
servants do this too? Much too good for them." Literature is too good
for contemporary novelists, those poor untutored drudges.

And what do these intellectuals do with literature? Why, they talk
about it; they treasure it; they make careers of it; they become an élite
through it; they adorn themselves with it; they make discourse of it.
It is their material, their capital. They take from it what they need
for their own work in culture history, journalism or criticism of manners producing hybrid works, partly literary, sometimes interesting in

themselves, but postulating almost always the decadence or obsolescence of contemporary literature. They want to use the literature of the modern tradition to make something far better; they project a higher, more valuable mental realm, a realm of dazzling intellectuality.

Let me direct your attention to other consequences of the teaching of modern literature. In "Beyond Culture," Professor Lionel Trilling tells us that we now have a sizable group of people in the United States educated in the modern classics. He thinks they have not turned out very well. One sees his point.

They seem to have it both ways. On the one hand these teachers, editors or culture-bureaucrats have absorbed the dislike of the modern classic writers for modern civilization. They are repelled by the effrontery of power and the degradation of the urban crowd. They have made the Waste Land outlook their own. On the other hand they are very well off. They have money, position, privileges, power; they send their children to private schools; they can afford elegant dental care, jet holidays in Europe. They have stocks, bonds, houses, even yachts, and with all this, owing to their education, they enjoy a particular and intimate sympathy with the heroic artistic life. Their tastes and judgments were formed by Rimbaud and D. H. Lawrence. Could anything be neater?

Yet this may be the way things are in the modern world, a consequence perhaps of the decline in belief, or of certain doubts about the value of human actions. Thus in a short life one feels free to combine all things of value. People pursue luxury but try to keep by some means values conceived in austerity. They combine private security with rebellious attitudes, monogamy with sexual experiment, conventional family life with bohemian attitudes, the *dolce vita* with the great books. Vice presidents during the working day, they may be anarchists or utopians at cocktail time. In the higher income brackets, insulated from the dirt and danger of New York, they retain as a matter of course all the sentiments of alienation, honor-bound to be sullen, ungrateful, dissatisfied, suspicious and theoretically defiant of authority.

There is nothing very new in this. Dostoevsky observed that people who recited Schiller's odes with tears in their eyes were also very good at managing their bureaucratic careers. No wonder Professor Trilling is upset. He sees that a literary education may be a mixed blessing, and that the critics, writers and executives sent into the world by English departments have not turned out very well.

What important function might they be performing? That question is answered by Irving Kristol in a number of The Public Interest. He points out that the literary intellectuals help shape the opinions of the educated classes and play a crucial role in defining the moral quality of our society. He says, "There is surely no more important task than to question or affirm the legitimacy of a society's basic institutions, to criticize or amend the original assumptions on which political life proceeds. How well equipped are our literary intellectuals for this job? Not, it must be confessed, as well equipped as they ought to be."

This then is the situation. Critics and professors have declared themselves the true heirs and successors of the modern classic writers. They have obscured the connection between the contemporary writer and his predecessors. They have not shaped the opinions of the educated classes. They have done nothing to create a new public. They have miseducated the young. They are responsible for a great increase in what Veblen called "trained incapacity."

Furthermore, they have projected the kind of art and literature that suits them and have the power to recruit painters and novelists who will meet their requirements. Novels are written which contain attitudes, positions or fantasies pleasing to the literary intelligentsia. These are of course given serious consideration, though they may be little more than the footnotes of fashionable doctrines.

Literature is becoming important for what one can do with it. It is becoming a source of orientations, postures, life-styles, positions. These positions are made up of odds and ends of Marxism, Freudianism, existentialism, mythology, surrealism, absurdism, *undsoweiter* —the debris of modernism, with apocalyptic leftovers added.

I am speaking of educated and indeed supercivilized people who believe that a correct position makes one illusionless, that to be illusionless is more important than anything else, and that it is enlightened to expose, to disenchant, to hate and to experience disgust. Wyndham Lewis had an excellent term for this last phenomenon— he spoke of the vulgarization of once aristocratic disgust by the modern romantics. One might add that the skepticism of the Enlightenment has also been vulgarized, and that it is at present thought blessed to see through to the class origins of one's affection for one's grandfather, or to reveal the hypocritical weakness and baseness at the heart of friendships.

Nevertheless there are friendships, affinities, natural feelings, rooted norms. People do on the whole agree, for instance, that it is wrong to murder. And even if they are unable to offer rational arguments for this, they are not necessarily driven to commit gratuitous acts of violence. It seems to me that writers might really do well to start thinking about such questions again. Evidently they will have to do this without the aid of the critics. The critics are too romantic to deal with these problems.

A final word about the avant-garde. To labor to create vanguard conditions is historicism. It means that people have been reading books of culture-history and have concluded restrospectively that originality is impossible without such conditions. But genius is always, without strain, avant-garde. Its departure from tradition is not the result of caprice or of policy but of an inner necessity.

As for the highbrow public of an earlier time, it has now been assimilated by our literary culture and transformed into something else. For the time being the writer will have to do without it. He will have to believe that what he writes will evoke a public, that the new forms he creates will create a new public, summoned up by the force of his truth.

BERNARD MALAMUD
Theme, Content and the "New Novel"

The following essay is adapted from Bernard Malamud's speech of acceptance on the occasion of receiving the National Book Award for his novel "The Fixer" in March, 1967. He received the same award in 1959 for his collection of short stories, "The Magic Barrel."

ONE thinks a good deal about the subject and theme of his fiction. What can he write about that will almost of itself contribute to his book's originality, strength, distinction? Melville, who made the long journey from "Typee" to "Moby Dick," stated it in these terms: "To produce a mighty book you must choose a mighty theme." His corollary was that one couldn't write a great and enduring book about the life of a flea. I'm not so sure about that—a writer like John Barth, with his sense of comedy and profusion of metaphor, might make a go of it. However it's obvious that a mighty theme doesn't necessarily guarantee a mighty book. Some writers may chance upon a theme of this sort without knowing what they've discovered. And some who have made a study of "great themes"—indeed, keep lists of them in their billfolds—when they try to make use of one, beat a hollow drum. They may want to work with a significant theme, but it doesn't excite their experience, or speak to their talent. A god or hero appears on paper, but the visage is Rock Hudson's, and the voice is the voice of Bob Dylan.

What the matter boils down to, I think, is that a "mighty theme" is useful only when it inspires a good writer to an unusual response; when it proliferates possibilities in every thought. If a writer is, as an individual, moved by themes that may be called "mighty," obviously it will pay him to involve himself with one, a task that isn't so simple, because the mighty themes have been used again and again, and he must struggle to discover how they can be presented in such a way as to seem new. Since times change but not, essentially, man, the old themes have the force of both the contemporary and the eternal.

On the other hand, no subject or theme is *verboten*, and any theme, however slight, in the right hands may be embodied in a work of art, though the danger is that at best it may turn out to be the work of a miniaturist. And it should be said that scope, depth, breadth in the novel are not necessarily the province of genius; the writer of talent who makes the effort to educate himself may find his way to them.

Theme has an almost sensible quality—it has texture, visibility, flavor, but these differ from book to book, and of course from writer to writer. Think, for example, of the thematic quality of Melville himself, Mark Twain, Cervantes, E. M. Forster, Hemingway, Faulkner, Tolstoy. Sometimes theme seems surface deep, almost touchable. Sometimes it lies hidden in dusk, or a deeper dark, and may reveal itself as light long after the book has been read, in sudden insight; and sometimes it invisibly transfigures the very experience it seems to be not present in.

It is, of course, not an intrusion in art; how can it be if it is a formal effect of imagination? It has as much value in the art of fiction as anything else in fiction—provided that (whatever its effect on the reader) it has become an aspect of the book's form. By drawing the action close to its ultimate elucidation it helps create the art work of the novel. To achieve true style the writer must envision the essence of the work; and it is envisioned in the act of writing, as possibilities occur and the book as a form emerges.

Theme discovered—one doesn't clip it out of a book or newspaper and paste it on the page—may lead to understanding essence, hence to crystallizing style and form. If the theme, inartistically handled, hardens to exoskeleton, or drips like printer's ink from the center of the fiction—if, in other words, it has become "message"—then the failure is of the art. The existence of theme, contrary to the thinking of some who want fiction refined almost to pure form, does not contaminate the work. Theme achieves the formal value in art that only an artist can give it. It is evolved from understanding, knowledge, evaluation of experience, though the mind that invents them is not necessarily present as the inventor. History of course can be shaped to contain theme, or even be it, although then it is no longer history. It becomes, when the form is right, a part of the fabric of the fiction, as though through a process of crystallization in time, as Stendhal's branch is crystallized.

But theme, according to the latest in criticism of the novel, is meaning, "signification" imposed by interpretation, therefore *content* in fiction; and content, the argument goes, if not the outright enemy of form, interferes with its ascendancy. To subordinate content, to the highest concerns of art—to art as pure esthetic—new forms, wholly revolutionary would be the ideal, certainly different from those in traditional use, must be conceived. The traditional novel, though it may run in a path "parallel" to the "new novel," is burdened by narrative ("To tell a story has become strictly impossible"), characterization ("Our world . . . has renounced the omnipotence of the person . . ."), and an anthropomorphic view of experience ("The exclusive cult of the 'human' has given way to a larger consciousness . . ."); therefore the novel of the past must be replaced by a new novel.

The purpose of the "new novel," according to Robbe-Grillet, whom I have been quoting above, is "to construct a world more solid and more immediate" rather than "a universe of signification"—to present, in other words what is there, without interpretation, hence to invent a form "capable of expressing (or of creating) new relations between man and the world." As a writer I welcome the invention of new forms that may bring the novel to greater power, but I cannot welcome a theory of the novel that ultimately diminishes the value of a writer's experience, historical and personal, by limiting its use in fiction.

I was born just before the profuse bloodletting of World War I. I have not forgotten the bleak, hungry depression that for a decade corroded the American land. Nor how Stalin's Moscow Trials were for years passionately defended by men of intellect and goodwill. How Hitler, a fanatic with stench for a soul, came to power in Germany. A line of Jews more than a thousand miles long was gassed to death, their bodies plundered of shoes, teeth fillings, human fat for soap.

World War II, begun in a graveyard of sinking ships, ended with atomic bombs that should never have been dropped, destroying Hiroshima and Nagasaki. The cold war spawned Senator McCarthy, who turned men into cowards the length and breadth of this nation, and we're not done yet with the fear he engendered. Overnight we were fighting a new war in Korea. A young American President had the back of his head shot off into the hands of his wife. And now, in Vietnam, a small, gentle-faced people, caught between two armies, have become living torches.

After what one lives through, who runs from content? What moves me moves me to art. What moves me to art I may deal with in whatever forms, whatever means of achieving a fiction, I am able to use. To say that this is the world and it is present is hardly satisfying or sufficient. What a fool I'd be not to say what I think of the world!

Let me limit myself to a few related observations:

1. A new novel will not come as the result of a theory or program in essence reductive, incomplete, proclaiming the part for the whole. Like everything else in art, the novel is changing—but a new novel will, in all probability, appear when a single master of fiction sits down and writes it. What one gives to fiction is what he has to give, not what is prescribed. One gives all he can; he limits as art demands, not definition.

2. I welcome, as I said before, the seeking for new forms in fiction. However, no form dies; they are all eternally available to the artist to use in a manner original to him. He reinvents them as he uses them. A 19th-century form used by a 20th-century writer becomes a 20th-century form. Nothing is outdated if it creates art. The best form for an artist is that which compels him to use his greatest strength.

3. That the world is present is only a small portion of the truth available to art. In the novel the world appears in language, itself a form of interpretation. Therefore, why should it not be further valued, explained—experienced? One cannot sit on language; it moves beyond the presence of things into the absence of things, the illusion of things.

Art must interpret, or it is mindless. Mindlessness is not mystery, it is the absence of mystery. Content cannot be disinvented. Presentation of the world, or history, or society is not enough when it may be necessary to proscribe them.

4. If the world, as some say, is ultimately an esthetic phenomenon, so, too, in its way, is humanity. One might even argue that there is such a thing as an esthetic of behavior. Wasn't it Santayana who said that the purpose of love is to increase beauty? Morality may have more than one source of beauty. Art is, moreover, the invention of the human artist, not an act of God or nature. To preserve itself it must, in a variety of subtle ways, conserve the artist through sanctifying human life and freedom.

5. If one is moved by the mighty theme, he had better go find it.

NATHALIE SARRAUTE
The Novel for Its Own Sake

Nathalie Sarraute is a practitioner of the "new wave" in French fiction and has several times visited the United States as its spokesman. Her novels include "Golden Fruits" and "Portrait of a Man Unknown." This essay is based on a talk she gave at a writers' conference at Long Island University in 1966.

IT IS a happy symptom, a reassuring symptom, that the idea of revolution—indeed, of revolutions—in literature is spreading more and more. It is especially reassuring as far as the novel is concerned, since not long ago, the idea of revolution seemed to have been forgotten. After the last war, especially in France, no one spoke of the novel in terms of revolution, never mind evolution. It was a genre that seemed to be fixed in an immutable mold. Such words as research, form or technique, although used in the other arts, were not applied to the novel. Nor did one describe a novel as "traditional"; this word would have seemed pretentious, even shocking.

Indeed, what could one mean by "traditional novel"? That was what I was asked when, in 1950, I wrote an article entitled "The Age of Suspicion," in which I attacked certain forms still forced on novelists by the critics. There was no such thing as a "traditional" novel. There was only the novel as such. Everyone knew that the novel was —and should always be—simply a story with characters. It had to give us an image of life which would be, to us, reality itself; an image of life as we live it, in terms of the whole of our existence—or just one day. Such a novel could serve forever, without anyone becoming tired of it, without anyone ever wanting to renew it. Why, in fact, should one want to renew it? The only consideration of consequence is that the novel give us the most precise, faithful and just image of the reality in which we are immersed.

To renew the novel it did not seem necessary to change its form; form had no importance. It seemed enough to apply this form (that has given such brilliant proof of its efficacy) to another part of reality, another society, another country. It seemed enough to renew the *état civil* by creating new characters, by describing a society in perpetual flux. If a writer did not find a subject, it meant that he was looking for the moon. He ought to look at his own life, and describe it, and use in describing it the good old tools that had already served so well.

To make this new and original it was enough to unveil one's own experience with sincerity, with courage, with no conventional feelings of shame and modesty. Thus literature would fulfill its duty, which was to enlarge our experience, to let us partake of other existences, to let us live in other milieus, to acquaint us with people we should never have known otherwise.

The novel placed itself between documentary and art, closer to the former than to the latter. Literary periodicals at that time were very keen on these slices of life. They published, for instance, the memoirs of a prostitute, and those of a mother whose child was born with a terrible disease. But it was said that the novel must not only inform the reader; it must educate him, help solve social conflicts, foment, reform or revolutionize. And to reach this end any means were valid.

The simplest form, the form most accessible to all readers would be the most efficient, effective and therefore the best. So, for reasons apparently noble, for reasons to which it seemed immoral not to yield, the novel was gradually edged out of the domain of art. It was becoming, among the arts, a sort of Cinderella tied to domestic duties, to utilitarian tasks.

In the first quarter of this century, however, there had been movements in the novel that had altered its forms; there had been certain revolutions. One would have thought that new forms, like those of Proust or Joyce, might have made the innumerable novels written in the manner of the 19th-century novel seem "traditional," of an out-dated period. But it was not so. The traditional form had such power that it came between the reader and any new work. It was a frame the reader automatically imposed—not only on his own experience but also on all the works with which he came in contact.

After the last war, in France, Proust's star was on the wane. It was said that his work was interesting only as a critique of a social class. And his genius, like Balzac's, was revealed by the creation of undying human types. The rest of his work was considered pure "psychologizing," hair-splitting, samples of sheer bravura. Joyce, not as easily salvaged, had written a very good book, "A Portrait of the Artist." The same could be said for parts of "Ulysses." As for the remainder, it was sheer rhetoric and boredom. "Finnegans Wake" was known little or not at all. And had it been known, it would have aroused no interest.

During these years, unusual work appeared like a freak or a pass-ing trauma. It did not interfere with the peaceful course of the novelis-tic art. When a novel did not fit the established framework, it became a curiosity, an interesting little monster, an exception to prove the rule: it became an anti-novel.

Such were the most representative trends in French postwar fic-tion. But since the novel (as its history of several centuries has often shown) is not essentially a tool of social progress, or information, or entertainment, but first and foremost an art, the same thing which befalls other arts happens here: it undergoes a constant evolutionary process. Its span of life is marked by successive revolutions. In fact, as with all the arts, the novel is essentially a form which projects a cer-tain pattern of sensations. It is a form which is endowed with exist-ence, life, virtue and power, but only by the sensations of which it is composed and which it sends forth.

Whether we are dealing with Balzac, Flaubert, James, Proust or Faulkner, the entire virtue of the novelist's work is due to the fact that it is imbued with sensations intrinsic to it. These virtues come from the perfect fusion of these sensations, of this vision (however trite this word may be) and of this form. It is this fusion which gives enjoyment to the lovers of literature. Essentially, it is the same joy the other arts give to those who love and appreciate them.

The social, psychological or philosophical enlightenments that can be derived from a novel are but by-products. Isolated from the form which expresses them, they add to reality as we know it. They become elements of reality which help historians, sociologists and psychologists in their work; they help every one of us to deepen our knowledge. But when they are isolated from their form, they lose the esthetic value that only this form can impart to them, the special quality which alone enables a novel to be a work of art.

In order to acquire and keep this quality, it is necessary that the sensations to which it owes its existence should be an order of sensations that has as yet not been expressed. The entire value of the form depends on the spontaneous, virgin, intact quality of the vision which is at its origin. It is the endeavor to express something as yet unsaid, that gives and allows the form to keep forever its initial impact, its strength and its freshness.

Even centuries later, one should feel again this vibration that was felt on first contact. Conversely, if the novelist is content to work on the same level, on a plane of sensation already established by other writers—that is to say (sensation and form being inseparable) if one merely hopes to renew the novel by expanding the reader's level of experience, by widening it, so to speak, by stretching it, if one does no more than add new characters to Balzac's and sets them in another society or another period, then the result will be prefabricated, conventional, without impact or life. The novelist's art, whatever its qualities of social, educational or historical order, becomes academic art.

Novels of this kind, by writers who use traditional forms, often seem attractive when they first appear. They are situated at our level of experience. They communicate sensations to which we are accustomed and which we recognize immediately. They show us life through a lens we were taught to focus. After a while, however, they seem unreal, as deceptive as a false front.

Reality, which some of us can grasp on our own, seems more complex, denser, richer in new sensations, than novels imprisoned in the rigid frame of convention. New novelists will then create new forms to express their own sensations (as yet unexpressed but already anticipated), which traditional forms have failed to encompass. Later still, these forms will be set aside in turn by the writers of the future, to allow new sensations, new visions to come to life through new forms.

Thus, the novel follows its course like any art. Whatever was unaccustomed becomes conventional in the hands of imitators. The novel renews itself; it seeks and finds the new conventions it needs. Examine the direction taken by this movement, its constant evolution; you will find that its orientation is always the same. This orientation rids the new sensation of the conventional form that would crush it, enabling it to fit a new mold preserving its integrity and purity. Thus the sensation the novel communicates, like any art, has to undergo a kind of metapsychosis.

New, strong sensations have in the past permeated the novels of Balzac, Flaubert, Proust or more recently Céline, if we name only the French. At present, the French writers are seeking new forms. What is the quality of this pattern of sensations, and hence of these forms? It is not for us to judge; what counts is the sincerity and intensity of this search.

Whether these successive incarnations are more or less attractive, more or less enriching, is beyond our control. What is important is that the novel, in its ups and downs, must pursue its course. That this is so is my most profound conviction. The life and dignity of the novel depend on it.

GERALD SYKES
The Changing
of the Avant-Garde

Gerald Sykes has been described by the poet Stanley Kunitz as "a student of civilization and souls," and in a recent book, "The Cool Millennium," he presented some of his findings. Some of his other books: "The Hidden Remnant," "Alienation," "The Children of Light."

THE OTHER day a student said to me, "You know this death-of-God stuff doesn't mean a thing to me. But the death of the avant-garde —that really hurts." And I knew at once what he meant.

When I was in college I too believed in the avant-garde. I read Baudelaire, Flaubert, Joyce, Lawrence, Proust, and I reached the youthful conclusion that the stuffiness they attacked would some day be overcome. My confidence in the future was increased by such delights as the sculpture of Brancusi, the architecture of Wright, the painting of Picasso, the music of Stravinsky. To me it was plain that the avant-garde, as represented by them and others, would mean sooner or later an end to the business-as-usual dullness that oppressed me in the classroom, at home and nearly everywhere else.

That was a long time ago. Now I teach college students, and hear comments, such as the one I have mentioned, that mean they want to feel the same optimism I felt in an earlier day; but I have to disappoint them. In spite of their natural desire for a happy ending I have to say that the avant-garde has been taken over by the very forces it once attacked. Except for a small portion of it which daily retreats further into one private language or another (and secedes further from the cares of ordinary human beings) the avant-garde has become a label, a brand-name that helps salesmen to sell Op dresses, Boulez records and McLuhan paperbacks. In an overproductive economy where merchandising is at last more important than manufacture, the avant-garde label is needed now to embellish the consoling myth that humanity, despite its many new misgivings, is still going forward.

Idealistic youth does not like to hear that the avant-garde is no longer a promise that it can be sure will be kept. Books about Van Gogh, Schönberg, Kafka, Le Corbusier and other forerunners have led my students to expect a steady increase of cultural progress. They do not enjoy being told that Hazlitt wrote, as long ago as 1814, in "Why the Arts Are Not Progressive," that what "depends on genius or feeling soon becomes stationary, or retrograde," and only "what is mechanical . . . is progressive." Or that his grim thought has been grimly confirmed a century and a half later by the way the myth of the avant-garde is now shrewdly aimed at "culture consumers" and has become as subject to "turnover" as cars or cosmetics. A blurb for a Robbe-Grillet novel subtly asks readers to overlook its dullness because it is *littérature objective*, the newest excitement of the avant-garde in Paris. And if this kind of pitch fails for that book, it is soon used again by another publisher on another novel by another man. There is chic— and money—in the avant-garde.

When the avant-garde was born in 19th-century France its members believed in it as a way of combatting the sentimental *kitsch* that had followed the rise of industrialism. The plain people, once the anonymous creators of robust ballads, exquisite embroidery, brilliant folksongs, now preferred bad art to good—"Pamela" to "Tom Jones," Waldteufel to Wagner, rose-tinted sunsets to those of Turner. The avant-garde was a reassertion of authenticity and craftsmanship that became a way of life. Writers and other artists (scientists too, so long as they had a hard time) found a sustaining faith that nourished them during their years of rejection. A really new book, like "The Red and the Black," had necessarily to speak a new language that not many readers could expect to understand right off. In time, however, the rest of the world would catch up with the new language and begin to appreciate what it said. In Stendhal's case this occurred about half a century after he died, or at least his books were first reprinted then.

Social revolutionaries soon seized upon the avant-garde mystique and adapted it to their own purposes. They convinced themselves that the great mass of mankind was only waiting for spiritual pioneers to lead them into a new sensitivity that even the most commonplace citizens, or so Friedrich Engels believed, would acquire. Ideas would "trickle down." Naturally the avant-garde moved ahead of the regular army, but after a while, of course, the army would catch up, and all would share in a great victory. The military metaphor was no more than the right way to read history. Humanity would go forward.

Meanwhile faith in the avant-garde sustained skeptical writers, like Flaubert aand Maupassant, who did not in the least share the revolutionaries' hopes for *all* mankind. These writers quarreled inevitably about the composition of the avant-garde—who belonged to it and who did not (see the "Journals" of the Goncourt brothers)—but its value to the world seemed to them self-evident. So far as I know, none of them imagined that it would some day be appropriated by its deadliest foes. They could not foresee that its appeal, born of the loneliness of its adherents, would be converted into a political technique by demagogues and into a weapon of war by dictators. In their understandable naiveté they failed, for example, to anticipate the genocidal constructions that could be built upon the word "forward."

What is more, when war ended and peace came at last—at least to the more prosperous parts of the world—the most imaginative avant-gardiste remained unable to predict what the new postwar prosperity would do to his beloved creed. He did not see how useful it would prove to merchants of fashion, as an aid to accelerating the obsolescence not only of books and pictures but of clothes and upholstery. (See any copy of Vogue or House Beautiful.) He failed to anticipate that it would become the criterion of snobbism in our day, among those who had never opened its books, or glanced at its pictures, or turned on its music—or shared for a moment the courage that produced them, although they can talk and dress as if they did.

Why did the avant-gardiste lack the earthy insight that might have led him to foresee these present-day exploitations of his most cherished faith? First, he was so used to poverty that he could not understand prosperity. (When each new picture brought Picasso a small fortune, he still preferred to pay small bills with canvases rather than cash.) Also, the adherent's faith meant so much to him that he could not look ahead and see what soon became obvious to more practical minds: that sizeable profits could be realized on the one faith that stood unchallenged, in an age of expediency, when all other faiths, religious and secular, had been put on the defensive. He did not know that people would need a sustaining myth and that he had created one of the best.

He was still blindly in love with the avant-garde. To him it meant living in a magic world that retained its wonder and surprise, a world he could celebrate, a world not yet confused by science, business and technology. Living there meant being like a child, able to see what the emperor really had on, and able also to announce it without fear. Anyone who gave up a child's freedom, he believed, surrendered to the forces of spiritual death.

Such an attitude, rejecting any traffic with the forces that were actually reshaping the world around him, soon became *too* childlike. By the time Dada appeared in World War I, the avant-garde was already declining into a babel of private languages that said "To hell with you" to everyone who did not speak to each one of them. (Science, of course, had always had its private languages, but science might produce something useful, like antibiotics, television or the bomb.) Historically, the avant-garde declined first in France, where it began; only later did the United States experience both its rise and its fall. Now we Americans, our education hastened by our more complete technicalization, are quite as advanced in internecine esthetic strife as any other land, and for some decades have been influencing the rest of the world with our jazz, our skyscrapers, our tough-guy fiction, our action painters, our Pop Art.

Nevertheless our colleges still graduate large classes of compulsive advance-guardsmen who cling babylike to an earlier mystique and refuse to recognize its present condition. The mere sale of books is confused with reading them. (About five pages of good ones get read, a publisher tells me.) Teachers persist in plugging old causes which no longer have any meaning—for instance, the Sexual Revolution, which they will not see is now as dead as the Russian one, and serves chiefly to sell psychoanalysis, miniskirts and pills. They denounce puritanism at a time when syphilis is kept alive by post-penicillin teen-agers who never encountered a single Victorian taboo. Or they announce "the end of ideology" when pluralistic pragmatism, once the basis for avant-garde criticism of all programmatic solutions, has hardened into such a formidable and deaf ideology that it prevents us from listening to the people of Vietnam. And in the arts, against the counsels of great practicing artists like Yeats and Stravinsky, most of us cling to the bland assurance of the scientist Jacob Bronowski, who insists that in 50 years "we shall have a Renaissance that will put the Italian one to shame."

Students do not like to contemplate the changing of the avant-garde into a lucrative museum piece. They are entering an ever more competitive society that wants them to make good, and soon. To succeed, they will have to sell their best wits in a tough marketplace, and sales of that sort are not made without genuine enthusiasm. They want to believe fervently that the avant-garde is still going forward.

When they are honest, however, or imaginative enough to recognize the truth of their predicament, they see that the myth of the avant-garde is one more of many lures being used to entice them into what they all call "the rat race." They need time to recover from the shock. That is a major reason why they now rather famously prefer to "play it cool." (And why 90 per cent of them go into graduate schools.) Enormous new anxiety, about far more than the draft, has to be held at bay while eager young minds look to their own resources in a time of genuine bereavement.

It will be a healthy thing when they take stock of their own resources, rather than count any longer on a faith that, as one student said, has "gone and died." They know now that the dead faith must be replaced by an undiscovered new one that will take students, artists and scientists into a new loneliness, grimmer than any of them ever knew before. Only out of loneliness, faced without the dubious consolations of the old avant-garde, can a new one come again.

ALAN PRYCE-JONES
The Beautiful People

When Alan Pryce-Jones writes of the English past, he writes with the knowledge of an Englishman and as the former editor of the London Times Literary Supplement. He is now a resident of the United States and was a book critic for the New York Herald Tribune.

Pushing the shopping cart through supermarket crowds not obviously intellectual, worming a way down the bus past readers of James Bond in paperback, the modern writer may be excused for feeling nostalgic for what, at a safe distance, looks like better days.

Not long ago, in Newport—a city which invites nostalgia anyway—I found myself at a sale of books. Those I bought were all collections of letters written by English women at the beginning of the 19th century. As I read, the world of franks and donuts receded. In its place arose a vision of park walls and peristyles, of houses with luxurious names like Chatsworth, Bowood, Trentham, behind the windows of which innumerable loving sisters and witty cousins wrote their daily letters to one another.

And what good letters they are. Can anything be better than Lady Granville's description of Horace Walpole's friend, Miss Berry, in old age: "Sociable by habit, *exigeante* by situation and intimate by force"? Blackberry and Gooseberry, Miss Berry and her sister were named, for the age did not err by kindness.

But it was not so much the sharpness of these writing ladies which struck me as the thought that it must have been pleasant indeed to be part of a society where reading and writing and talking were treated as a relaxing skill, rather like tennis or bridge a century later.

You could still talk about "everybody" then, meaning by that term everybody who ran the country. Everybody was everybody's blood relation; everybody stayed with everybody and dined at Holland House or danced at Devonshire House or took the waters at Spa.

And then, how high was the general standard. Boredom, of course, was the one unforgivable sin, so everybody had to be diverting. Otherwise they risked the kind of rap given by another enchanting letter writer, Emily Eden: "Bingham kills me, dead; he is so tiresome, that it almost amounts to an excitement."

Must not the brilliant world in which these sparkling creatures moved, so quick, so cosmopolitan, so sure in its standards, have offered an ideal trampoline for the writers of the day? Alas, the answer is that it did nothing of the kind.

Not that these tireless women neglected books. Sometimes they even wrote them. Emily Eden herself is a delightful novelist, and each of them, in her correspondence, keeps recommending, as it might be, clever young Mr. Milman's new tragedy "Fazio" or Susan Ferrier's "Destiny." But who today remembers either? Or the once celebrated Mrs. Caroline Norton, or even Lady Caroline Lamb except as Byron's mistress?

The great writers of the day might or might not form part of a chosen circle, but they never belonged, or wished to belong, to what was certainly one of the most intelligent as well as powerful groups in the history of European society.

There is something comforting in this fact. Among the complaints raised against the modern world is that writers cannot find a compact public anywhere. The audience they address becomes yearly more invisible, more anonymous, packed as it is into movie-houses or sitting passively in front of a jumpy TV tube. Here and there, in the Zurich of 1915, the Paris of the twenties, the London of 1930, in Chicago, or Greenwich Village, groups have formed for a few years. One does not think of Gertrude Stein or Virginia Woolf or W. H. Auden as solitaries. As if huddled together for warmth, writers have clustered round a single center from time to time until a war or a depression has scattered them once more.

But it is the common lot of the writer today to be not just alone but lonely. He has certainly not had a Holland House to dine in, or Macaulay to listen to, surrounded by his peers. In parts of Europe he may possibly feel loved and wanted; he may even be addressed as "cher maître." But in the United States or England he will do well to put on the protective coloring of a business man, if not an upstate farmer; for in Anglo-Saxon lands, writers are known to be not altogether respectable.

It is partly this fact that makes them write. Their standing as outsiders saves them from the cosiness that afflicts in-groups everywhere. In the 1820's it was not Keats or Shelley who spent Christmas with Lord Spencer at his great countryhouse but the amiable and second-rate Samuel Rogers. Even the bluestocking ladies, round about 1910, who liked to add a writer or two to their weekend collections—rather as though they were investing in a rare piece of Meissen china— seldom laid hands on the first-rate. They had to make do with the nice, the funny and the smart.

Indeed, not only do writers get very little from being accepted by an in-group, they are actively harmed by the fact. For one thing, if they are imaginative writers they ought to keep free of as many obligations as possible. Suppose that, instead of dining out and weekending, Henry James had acted rashly from time to time: got drunk, hung around stage doors, explored a few side streets as well as the Bellevue Avenues of life. He might have escaped that which, for all his greatness, makes him extremely irritating at times—a kind of missishness, of overbreeding. As it is, he has an air of not wanting to offend last summer's hostesses. How much better, like Proust or Joyce, to take ultimate refuge in sickness or exile; even to turn a back to the world, like Faulkner, or invent a personal set of Hemingway masks.

The alternative is to make of niceness a refuge. I can remember Somerset Maugham dismissing more than one contemporary as "f-far too n-nice a man to be a g-good writer." And certainly the great houses of a century and more ago were full of writers who might have been better remembered had they only been nastier. If you asked Sydney Smith to stay, or Samuel Rogers, the experience was wholly enjoyable. The ladies, recounting it all later, were regularly entranced by "Mr. Rogers's good jokes and stories," and they all kept Sydney Smith's thank-you letters for the sake of his pleasantries like his opinion of fashionable society, that it is "like high table-land, very flat and cold."

Nice people, however, evaporate, along with the social life they compose. Nobody much reads Maurice Baring, Howard Sturges, Reggie Turner and their like. They were splendid guests, excellent hosts, most honorable writers, but they have never approached the reputation of the great curmudgeons, the Ibsens, the Tolstoys, the Flauberts, who had time for other people only on their own terms.

The curmudgeons realized, perhaps, that good readers are as rare as good writers; certainly they can never be concentrated into a neat little group of the elect. Those who sat round the table at Holland House and listened to Sir Walter Scott gave Scott no real audience. They were merely a group of well-dressed people who consumed his time and talent, just as they consumed the peaches on the table and the champagne in their glasses.

Even very gregarious races, like the French, would hardly deny this.

Their frauds of genius, the Cocteaus and Valèrys and Gides, leaving cards, kissing hands, talking, talking, talking, remain frauds unable to repress their genius all the time. But the genius has to slip through the interstices of living—one of the reasons, I think, why so much good French writing is in the form of notebooks or journals.

We in America—or in any Anglo-Saxon country, for that matter—are exposed to fewer temptations. There are no salons, no cafés, no disciples to address us as "maître." Genius uses the supermarket like everyone else, and even the omnivorous universities hesitate to collect our thank-you letters or annotate our jokes. If the reaction of our writers to a rising flood of congratulation is a lunge towards drink or suicide, it is often because the pressures of society on an imagination geared to loneliness are too great. The alternative—comparable on a smaller scale to the inbred hospitality of Holland House and its rivals —is something like the literary world of Boston in its heyday: contented, pleasant and not entirely first-rate.

Gibbon's friend, Lady Stanley of Alderley, was probably right when she wrote to her sister Louisa that for most people books ought to be aimed above their "middling capacities," so that "the few ideas they have may not be bothered." Regrettably, the best books in the world all come into this category; they have been dug painfully out of solitary minds. Whether it would have been pleasanter to sup with the Whigs or the Transcendentalists in warm-hearted comfort is another matter.

BRIGID BROPHY
And Critics

Brigid Brophy is one of the liveliest and most outspoken critics in London. She is also a novelist ("Flesh," "The Snowball,") and an expert on Mozart ("Mozart the Dramatist").

WHEN a review praises a book, those few members of the public who pay attention at all note down the name of the book and its author. When a review slashes a book, they note the name of the reviewer.

By this means the public constantly confirms what it is determined to believe anyway, that critics are frenzied destruction-maniacs; and one of the results is that even so forbearing a critic as myself, who have published 10 words of praise for every word of dispraise, can be regarded here and there as a literary Lizzie Borden.

Neither does the public hesitate to diagnose what has driven the critic into frenzy. A critic who, like myself, is also a "creative writer" is obviously soured by professional jealousy. A critic who, on the other hand, writes only criticism is equally obviously soured by his lack of "creativeness."

Since one or other of these prongs will catch every critic that ever was, the public can be sure, when it meets a critic at a cocktail party, that it is meeting a warped nature. This it demonstrates by starting straight in to appeal to his better nature. Bluff, decent chaps expostulate, "I've nothing against criticism, so long as it's *constructive* criticism," and dear old ladies plead, "*Must* you pick on the bad things? Can't you find *something* to praise?"

It is noticeable that the public never asks whether the prophet Jeremiah *had* to pick on the bad things in sin. A politician is not begged to keep his criticism of the opposing party "constructive." No one urges that John the Baptist should have sought something nice in his contemporaries instead of resorting to vulgar and hurtful abuse by addressing them as a generation of vipers.

The explanation, of course, is that society takes its politicians and prophets seriously, agreeing with them that politics and morals are matters of moment for which it's worth, if necessary, hurting a few feelings. Indeed, society has not yet wholly given up the primitive notion that those are matters for which it may be worth hurting people's bodies. That being so, it would be gracious of society, before it accuses critics of a destructive bent, to notice that critics make no such elementary moral mistake. It's not critics but governments who, in some countries, put authors in prison, and not critics but magistrates and customs officers who, in mentally underdeveloped countries like Great Britain, burn books. The magistrate who burns a book imposes his own opinion on the public by force and suppresses the evidence on which the public might have disagreed with him. The most flaming review in the world leaves the book physically unscathed and readers quite free to read it if they choose to disregard the reviewer's advice.

And in fact, a critic, by the very nature of his profession, has renounced trying to make his opinion prevail by any methods except argument and demonstration. Argument will take him quite a long way. The adage that there's no arguing about tastes is not immediately true, or half the pleasures of social intercourse would vanish; but it is ultimately true, and at that point the critic has simply to demonstrate what he means and toss to his readers the opportunity to make up their own minds.

A critic who merely pronounces, as in a voice from a cloud, "Mr. X writes vile prose" usurps an authority he knows he doesn't possess, because he knows he cannot prove the vileness. To claim an authority he can't sustain if challenged only makes him vulnerable. All a decent critic can do, in self-protection as well as in decency, is quote some of Mr. X's prose; he invites his readers to agree that it's vile but they, having the prose in front of them, are in a position to judge that, on the contrary, it's excellent. This is a critic's only way of being fair at once to Mr. X, the public and his own fallibility. But the public, returning unfairness for fairness, is inclined to receive it as a further mark of critical blood-lust and to suppose that the critic, having hacked up Mr. X, is now insisting on displaying the bloody gobbets.

The public is, in fact, at thorough cross-purposes with critics. It keeps calling out to them not to shoot the pianist because he's doing his best. And the critic, who has long ago renounced all wish to shoot the pianist even if the lazy fellow is *not* doing his best, keeps trying to explain to the public that, if the pianist's best is not good enough, it would imperil art itself were the critic to give his performance a good notice.

The truth at the bottom of the misunderstanding is that the public is still flippant about art (for which critics are probably to blame). Being flippant, it is sentimental. It draws a false distinction between "constructive" and "destructive" criticism which is as genteel and hypocritical as the false distinction implied by "I don't mind a dirty joke so long as it's funny as well." There is, in fact, no way of calling a book bad "constructively," except the one way which is universally affronting to authors and which no fair-minded critic ever offers— that is, to go through the author's work condescendingly "correcting" it as if it were a school exercise. Critics are not there to educate authors. (They may be there to educate the public, which is why they may be to blame for the public's backwardness.)

Being sentimental, the public thinks it is acting in the interest of sweetness and light when it asks the critic to swallow his integrity in the way that kind people swallow theirs when old Auntie Matilda invites their opinion of her new hat. Art, the public implies, is as lightweight as a hat; the world won't come to an end if the old girl gets away with it.

The critic, however, believes that the world—or the most precious part of it—may well come to an end if pretentious or incompetent works of art so regularly pass for good that civilization loses the knack of discriminating. Discrimination is the essence of art—of both creating and appreciating it. What we call creating is in fact a process both constructive and destructive. The artist, as his edifice goes up, has at each stage a choice. Creation consists as much in rejecting the wrong solutions as picking the right ones. What is called destructive criticism merely accomplishes the rejections the artist was too uncritical to perform himself.

My own 10 words of critical praise are neither more nor less "constructive" than the one word of dispraise I've uttered in proportion to them. Were it wrong in itself to dispraise, the fact that I have also praised would not avail me, any more than a murderer could excuse himself for dispatching one life by pleading he had also brought 10 children *into* the world. However, critical dispraise is markedly *not* murder, since it leaves its victim alive and available. And in fact the ratio a critic can write of praise to dispraise depends on the accident of what comes his way to criticize and the larger accident of when he lives. If, like Bernard Shaw, he is a drama critic in London at a time when the London theater is full of dross, he will have no alternative to uttering almost unadulterated growl. And it is impossible to say which was the more "creative" of Shaw's two great feats: growling the 19th-century dross out of the theaters or filling them with his own invention, 20th-century drama.

What is certain is that no critic seeks out bad works to review because he enjoys slashing them. Simple hedonism insures he will do no such thing. Any pleasure he might take in writing a slash (which is devilish hard work) is more than canceled by the dreariness, to a sensitive person, of having to read or sit through a bad work of art. An equally simple psychological mechanism prevents a critic from being inspired by envy. In art it's impossible not to be on the side of what you take to be the angels. To think a work good is to invest some of your own self-love in it. None of us is envious of Shakespeare, though if the received opinion about critics' and artists' envious nature were correct, he would be our first target. We have all appropriated him; secretly each of us thinks of him as "my Shakespeare."

The only envy to which a true critic (one who is above the level of a gossip column) is susceptible is that generous envy on behalf of others which constitutes a sense of justice. Critics *are* inspired by Coleridge's principle: "Praises of the unworthy are felt by ardent minds as robberies of the deserving." And a critic who was not an ardent mind would quickly desert the critical profession for politics or religion, where the opportunities are so much greater for wielding power, influencing opinion without tiresomely having to submit your case to reason, and making money by taking bribes.

Morally and politically the world is, very slowly, and largely in spite of the politicians and prophets, moving toward egalitarianism and an, in this case, unsentimental gentleness. It's slowly realizing that it mustn't penalize people for real or supposed shortcomings they can't help. Against this stream, art obstinately stands out as the one justifiably aristocratic system, which is reduced to nonsense the instant it abandons the aristocratic principle. I, whose moral and political opinions have moved so much faster toward egalitarianism than the world's that readers of The New York Times would probably consider me a dangerous anarchist, yet find myself, insofar as I am an artist and critic, insisting with aristocratic insolence that I daresay Mr. X can't help writing vile prose but, since he could help writing *tout court*, I am going to blast him for doing so.

Since art is a voluntary activity, the artist fairly puts himself up to be judged by its unrelenting standards, according to which good intentions go for nothing, accidental disabilities mitigate nothing and only results count. It is a system cruel, capricious and even more unfair than social aristocracy, since talent is not distributed with even the consistency of hereditary social privilege.

The truth the public has not yet understood about criticism is that the critic is as serious about art as John the Baptist was about Heaven but carries the extra responsibility, which John the Baptist never undertook, of knowing he may be wrong. That responsibility obliges him to be a democratic aristocrat; he won't relent in his insistence on the best, but he knows that your guess about what *is* best is as good as his. As a matter of fact, he takes art more seriously than morals and politics, which he thinks should be settled as decently and democratically as possible in order that the world may get on with the serious business of art. He believes the human imagination to be what most beautifully distinguishes our species from the beasts, and thinks that only by exercising it to the creation and appreciation of works of art shall we justify the emergence of the protoplasm from the slime.

LEON EDEL
To a Young Critic

Although Leon Edel's bibliography includes many volumes of varied literary essays and literary criticism, it is most concerned with Henry James. He has edited James's essays, his plays, his tales. Overshadowing all is the Edel biography of Henry James that has won both a Pulitzer Prize and a National Book Award.

YOU ASK about critics. You enjoy seeing your name in print; you like the authority of the word "critic." This is understandable. I suspect that being a critic is appealing to young men. Critics preside at the feast of books; they form taste; they "package" ideas; they tell their audiences what to think; they become oracles. Having found this congenial role, the steps to power are logical—adviser to publishers, aide to book clubs, giver of prizes, counselor to foundations. And what a chance, from the outset, to put your elders in their place!

I might offer you, since you ask, a few sobering thoughts about criticism—at least of the popular nonacademic kind. I think of the critic (who is a cut above the mere reviewer) as having something in common with the actor. Actors require someone else's lines to complete themselves. The literary critic requires someone else's text. Art, the poet says, holds the mirror up to nature; criticism tries to hold the mirror up to art. Let me further say that I speak only of those for whom criticism is a "specialty." Van Wyck Brooks said of Edmund Wilson that he was "a critic who could be called, almost uniquely, a writer," in other words a critic who was also a poet, a playwright, a novelist, and who wrote his criticism within a frame of creativity. We could mention others: Auden, or Eliot, or Tate. These are the complete men. But critics who do nothing but criticize are (as Proust observes) incomplete men.

The work of an actor is mimetic, and is creative in that sense. The critic is creative only to the extent that he essentially re-creates. To this end he must be reasonably well read, possess literary taste, have a grasp of the nature of feeling. No criticism of any value was written all head and no heart. The critic should also have some sense of beauty. This may seem irrelevant now for the cult of the unbeautiful rages, and literature is filled with blood, guts, drugs and semen. He should also respond to verbal beauty and to style. No one save the political writer seems to speak of "style" these days.

A critic needs to be logical; he must inspire a feeling of "sweet reasonableness." He must relate to his text as if it were a person, not a machine. Bad books are written every day, but it is no crime to have written a bad book. A failure is sometimes more interesting than a success. I am trying to suggest that it takes a certain amount of civilization to set a good critic in motion.

A young critic should try to understand that he is a strange being. The young should want to be poets, playwrights, story-tellers. What a strange thing to want to criticize rather than to create! This suggests a kind of passive belligerence. Many young critics are simply angry young men. They presume they know more, are more gifted and more capable of insight, than those who do the writing. It seldom occurs to them that they may, in the process of their criticism, scale a great imagination down to their own limited boundaries. A young critic might give thought to the irrational impulses that make him want to rush into criticizing before he has lived a little of the life of art. This would be a first step toward understanding the dangers of conceit, arrogance, condescension.

Repeat the word "humility" a dozen times a day. Keep a pencil handy to strike out pontifical words. Tell yourself that writers, painters, playwrights may sometimes be hurt by critics, but they always go their own way; they create as they must; they are singularly indifferent to the counsel of criticism. Critics do not usually instruct a talent, and certainly not a genius. Their task is to instruct the public. The public seeks the critic as guide, friend, educator, illuminator, appreciator, especially in an age when literature has become increasingly complex and requires on occasion a certain amount of "explication."

One does not begin criticism full-fledged; it's a long and arduous discipline. It must cultivate brevity, not self-indulgent prolixity; and it must recognize that "explication" is in reality the kitchen-work that precedes the critical act. The great danger in our time is that criticism will engulf literature. A critic might cultivate a wholesome fear of the endless creation of books about books. Gresham's Law could become a literary as well as an economic law. The explicators may drive out the works they explicate.

In our society, criticism has a valid social function. It provides standards for measurement and evaluation. It offers an individual viewpoint which can be only as good as the critic himself. When the critical act is carried out with imagination and skill, it can enlarge our vision. When we have half a dozen good critics to consult, we see more than we can see alone. It's a common joke that "the critics can't even agree" —as if they were a jury, and only one of two verdicts were possible. Rejoice when the critics disagree. That is when they are perhaps most useful.

Criticism, when it functions properly, can help us to recognize the second-rate and the shoddy; it makes us aware of the beauty to be found sometimes in minor as in major works—something our society, in its constant competitive search for the best book, the best play, the best of everything, overlooks. It can designate the usable for our time, and the ephemeral, and perhaps, by this, try to suggest the durable.

Its function, you see, is always subordinate to letters. Criticism rarely becomes "literature" itself; it does so only when it is written by the "complete" men—the Drydens and Coleridges, Dr. Johnsons and Hazlitts, Arnolds and Eliots. You can round out the list yourself; and remember (as Van Wyck Brooks pointed out), no country has ever erected a statue to anyone for being simply a critic.

From Alexander Pope's "An Essay on Criticism"

'T is hard to say if greater want of skill
Appear in writing or in judging ill;
But of the two less dangerous is th' offence
To tire our patience than mislead our sense:
Some few in that, but numbers err in this;
Ten censure wrong for one who writes amiss;
A fool might once himself alone expose;
Now one in verse makes many more in prose.
'T is with our judgments, as our watches, none
Go just alike, yet each believes his own.
In Poets as true Genius is but rare,
True Taste as seldom is the Critic's share;

Both must alike from Heav'n derive their light.
These born to judge, as well as those to write.
Let such teach others who themselves excel,
And censure freely who have written well;
Authors are partial to their wit, 't is true,
But are not Critics to their judgment too?
Yet if we look more closely, we shall find
Most have the seeds of judgment in their mind:
Nature affords at least a glimm'ring light;
The lines, tho' touch't but faintly, are drawn right:

Some are bewilder'd in the maze of schools,
And some made coxcombs Nature meant but fools:
In search of wit these lose their common sense,
And then turn critics in their own defence:
Each burns alike, who can or cannot write,
Or with a rival's or an eunuch's spite,
All fools have still an itching to deride,
And fain would be upon the laughing side.
If Maevius scribble in Apollo's spite,
There are who judge still worse than he can write.
Some have at first for Wits, then Poets pass'd;
Turn'd Critics next, and prov'd plain Fools at last.
Some neither can for Wits nor Critics pass,
As heavy mules are neither horse nor ass.
Those half-learn'd witlings, numerous in our isle,
As half-form'd insects on the banks of Nile;
Unfinish'd things, one knows not what to call,
Their generation's so equivocal;
To tell them would a hundred tongues require,
Or one vain Wit's, that might a hundred tire.

WALTER ALLEN
Writers and Editors

Walter Allen describes himself as "author, literary journalist and broad-caster." He is also a teacher who has visited for a term or two on American campuses from Vassar to the University of Washington. He has written a history of the English novel, a study, "The Modern Novel in

Britain and the United States," and has been literary editor of the New
Statesman.

I T IS more than a century since Miss Jennett Humphreys, a young
would-be novelist, had her interview with George Meredith in his
capacity as editor (in Britain, reader) at the publishing house of Chapman & Hall.

"He was studiously polite to me," she wrote, "and I have a memory
of a man dressed with great care—leading even to lavender-colored
gloves—his hair of chestnut color and lying in curls, or waves, round
a handsome face. What he said was patiently said, my faults being
pointed out, and his judgment over what I had done several times
repeated—'It will not go to the public.' I asked him if I might know
to whom I was indebted, and he said 'Excuse me'—which, of course,
I was bound to do."

That was 1864. In the hundred years that have passed, publishing,
one would have said, has changed almost out of recognition; among
other things, it has become big business. But has the editor's function
changed so much—or, for that matter, his position in the eyes of those
outside writing and publishing? It is true the editor is no longer likely
to wear gloves, lavender-colored or otherwise, in the office, and certainly he will not insist on anonymity. But isn't something approaching
anonymity still part of his being—at least to the extent that, of all
workers in the process of the production of a book, from its being written to its being read by the purchaser, he is, if not the forgotten man
entirely, the one whose function receives least recognition?

As to the function, one can go back to Meredith. Four years after
he had so politely and anonymously turned down Miss Humphreys'
manuscript, he interviewed, in a back room at the publisher's, at his
own request and equally anonymously (as "the gentleman who read
your manuscript"), a young man who was to be a greater poet and
novelist than himself—Thomas Hardy. The account of that interview,
given in Florence Hardy's "The Early Life of Thomas Hardy," runs as
follows:

"Meredith had the manuscript in his hand, and began lecturing
Hardy upon it in a sonorous voice. No record was kept by the latter
of their conversation, but the gist of it he remembered very well. It
was that the firm was willing to publish the novel as agreed, but that
he, the speaker, strongly advised its author not to 'nail his colors to

the mast' so definitely in a first book, if he wished to do anything practical in literature; for if he printed so pronounced a thing he would be attacked on all sides by the conventional reviewers, and his future injured. . . . The upshot of this interview was that Hardy took away the MS. with him to decide on a course.

"Meredith had added that Hardy could rewrite the story, softening it down considerably; or what would be much better, put it away altogether for the present, and attempt a novel with a purely artistic purpose, giving it a more complicated 'plot' than was attempted with 'The Poor Man and the Lady.' "

It was in fact the last of "The Poor Man and the Lady," but the point is, here is Meredith advising Hardy not to publish a novel that Chapman & Hall had already accepted and were unlikely to lose money on since the author was to guarantee £20 against loss. In England the editor is sometimes called the literary adviser, but whatever he is called, he has in practice a double function. He advises his employer the publisher; but he may also, on occasion, as Meredith did with Hardy, advise the author. He may indeed—and if he is one of the great editors, a Maxwell Perkins or an Edward Garnett, he certainly will —behave in such a way as to make it plain that he believes his duty towards authors, to literature itself, is as much binding on him as his duty to his employer.

And there is something else. Before Meredith saw it, "The Poor Man and the Lady" had been read both by Alexander Macmillan, the publisher, and his reader, John Morley. They had introduced Hardy to Chapman & Hall; and Hardy's comment here is of the greatest interest, since it spotlights the real significance of the editor as soon as we begin to think of him in terms of literary history, of his influence on writing.

"Thus it happened that a first and probably very crude manuscript by an unknown young man, who had no connections with the press, or with literary circles, was read by a most experienced publisher, and by two authors among the most eminent in letters of their time. . . . Except the writer himself, these three seem to have been the only ones whose eyes ever scanned the MS."

That last sentence deserves italics, not because Macmillan, Morley and Meredith were the only men to read Hardy's first novel but because they were the first to read it, and did so professionally, hence objectively. It establishes the central fact in the editor's relation to the author, to the young unknown author especially, that the editor is likely to be the first man from the outside world, the first disinterested person, to read the author's book. He reads it as an expert and he reads it "cold." "All right, show me" is his attitude. And he's not only the first reader, he is also the toughest the book is ever likely to have until, if it is good enough, the scholars get to work on it years later.

It is from this, from the fact that he has the power to kill, as Meredith may be said to have killed "The Poor Man and the Lady," that his immense influence for good or evil derives. It is sometimes said that editors today, particularly in the United States, have too much power, too much say in the way a book is written. I think there is something in this. I remember asking a novelist whose books I had read for a London publisher why, every now and then, in each novel he wrote he indulged in patches of what seemed to me gratuitous vulgarity. He replied that it was what his New York editor said he should do. And I do get the impression that many American authors take for granted what I would regard as a degree of interference on the part of their editors in the actual writing of a book; indeed, few English authors would put up with it.

Where books are written merely as commodity articles this obviously does not matter much; and one knows that a great many books are, in effect, joint productions of author and publisher. Perhaps, in honesty, they should be labeled as collaborations; why shouldn't the publisher or his editor claim credit for his creative talents?

In any event, the nature of the relation between the good editor —sympathetic, understanding and yet essentially critical—and the good writer, especially when he is a younger man still uncertain of the direction of his talents or their scope, is such as to make the editor's influence incalculable. Where specific authors are concerned, of course we do know a fair amount about the editor as shaper and director of talent; after all, the editorial careers of Garnett and Perkins and their relations with Conrad and Lawrence, Wolfe, Fitzgerald and Hemingway, are pretty well documented.

But it seems to me we ought to know much more. A scholar studying a writer naturally turns to the first reviews of his subject's early books to see how they were received; and good critics rightly gather together in book form their occasional reviews. There are few things more fascinating than to experience, through a critic's reprinted papers, the thrill of recognition he felt years earlier when first meeting the work of a writer now accepted as significant. One thinks, for instance, of Edmund Wilson's review, reprinted in "The Shores of Light," of Hemingway's "Three Stories and Ten Poems." But it would be even more fascinating to read the editors' reports on the early books of the significant writers of our century, to see what qualities in their work most struck those first readers, to see to what extent they foresaw what was to come.

This is not a plea for the publication by editors of collected volumes of their reports. If it were, one would have to insist that they included their mistakes in judgment, the reports that turned the masterpieces down (and how interesting those reports would be). All the same, I would like to think that someone, somewhere, is making an anthology of editors' reports on a number of the best novels of our time. It would have much more than a curiosity value.

ELEANOR CLARK
The Great Divide

For "The Oysters of Lacmariaquer," an essay in history of the famous oyster beds on the Breton coast, Eleanor Clark (Mrs. Robert Penn Warren) won a National Book Award in 1965. She is also the author of a novel, "The Bitter Box," and a collection of essays, "Rome and a Villa."

MOST of us have a strong tendency, most often frustrated, to try to do, or wish we could decently do, what we are told; and what we literary and other "humanist" characters are most often being told to do nowadays is to get together with the world of science. Understand it; make it understand us; something like that. It sounds fine, and what I want to jot down for posterity is not any objection—heavens no!— but merely some personal difficulties in the matter, as exemplified in this very sentence. I am embarrassed already.

That word "heavens" slipped out before I could stop it; it is just engrained in my "culture." (I am scared of all these words suddenly.) But what does it mean? What shape in space? What distance in light-years? In an effort to take up my share of the great challenge I recently visited the Kitt Peak National Observatory in Arizona, and I tremble to think what anybody there would make of such irresponsibility. Honestly, look at this problem at any little single point like that and you're in trouble right away. It's only on the propaganda level that it all sounds so simple.

I know of a foundation or a branch of one that has to do with relating art and churches, and where the girl at the switchboard answers all phone calls with a seraphic "Art and Worship!" I'll bet there's one somewhere by now answering in the same beautiful tones, "Science and Humanities!" You'd think we would be all set, and I suppose there do exist a few supermen as well as a number of freaks who really manage to think both ways, whether at the same time or on alternate days I don't know. There is also a rapidly growing race of middlemen who trot back and forth between the two camps with briefcases full of samples and communiqués. The expositor, the commentator, the nonoriginal thinker has never had so splendid a role.

For the mass of us drones of the creative life, the heavenly concord ends where it starts, at the switchboard, if there is one. Beyond that the words are all awry, the frequencies mismatched. We and the "disciplines" (science) are glumly huddled at opposite walls, or more politely, exchanging data on the skiing conditions or platitudes on the plight of education—great levelers, those two subjects. I use the word "disciplines" not because I like it or even think it particularly appropriate in that sentence, but because of a grudge I have to confess.

We self-employed humanist types (hereinafter to be referred to as S.E.H.'s; with all the grand verbiage now current in these areas, such words as poet, painter, novelist have come to sound old-fashioned and trivial)—anyway, we, as I was saying, used to think discipline was something you had to have a lot of to be any good at your business, but it would have been indecent to mention it, still less flaunt it. Still, now that the world has been snitched from us altogether I feel deprived and peevish, especially as a discipline in science these days, as I understand it, is apt to melt into some other from one day to the next, whereas in our usage the meaning was plain and the habit, barring alcoholism or other such misfortune, usually permanent.

But back to communication and the Great Divide—and I must insist that I am speaking purely as an S.E.H., with no reference to education or anything else outside my business—if a top-flight physicist and a true poet have ever, in the period covered by Nobel Prizes, had a really illuminating conversation I will forfeit my ski boots, one to each. Not that a writer or other S.E.H. can't have a scientist friend. I have had one myself for years—a biochemist, at least originally; I suppose he must be a geomathematician or astroneurologist too by now. We are skiing companions.

Aside from that, the relation is based on such common factors as financial probity, similar world view (mournful) and drinking habits (reasonable) etc.; also mutual respect, because we are both intellectual snobs and have heard well of one another's work from reputable third parties. We certainly couldn't judge for ourselves, though we establish contact with one another's "field" to this extent: He asks me what I think of John O'Hara, and I ask him what I should think of, say, milk. If we have been intercommunicating some higher sense of order all these years, or doing anything else the seminars are now calling for, it must have been by osmosis, since neither of us would be caught dead talking like that.

It might be that behind this reticence there lies a mutual awareness of the possibility of doing each other great damage, though I should imagine the risk was more on my side. Whatever the likeness in our procedures, and Wordsworth to the contrary notwithstanding, my friend's world is and must be anti-poetry. Of course an occasional image from it can strike a spark over where I live; science has undone the rearing horse in my line of work; obviously we have to keep our senses open to whatever is happening. I once visited, with this same friend, a lab full of sick canaries that he had been methodically (how else?) inoculating, and found the experience quite fruitful. I mean it set my imagination off. But if I had tried to follow my friend's basic thinking on the canary problem I would have lost a very good and gruesome thing.

When it comes to *content* on the professional side, he frankly states that nothing is as boring to him as trying to explain his work to a layman, and I suspect that what he means is not so much boring as degrading, by association with the horrid spectacle that present tendencies in the news world are making more and more common. That is of second-raters, in any line of work, building up public reputation or personal self-esteem, or both, by impressing the ignorant, or rather the pseudo-informed. (Practically everybody knows a little about practically everything now.) My friend is above that. He would rather have no reputation than that kind. Consequently I haven't the faintest idea what goes on in his lab.

Of course literature is not so obviously inaccessible, and free fireside chats about it are easy enough to come by, but not from its best practitioners—except in very special circumstances and then not about their own work. That could be only among intimates, and rare at that. The *pudeur* (delicacy, restraint: we have no true equivalent) in the two cases is identical, and in both is as essential to the work as legs to running or water to tea. Without that area of privacy, or secrecy if you will, the creative imagination quickly dries up. The scientist is then a mere technician, however brainy, and the S.E.H. a mere commentator on art, or more pitifully a worker-over of somebody else's big idea.

It seems that to try to understand each other in true Science-and-Humanities fashion, not through our own natural human rapport, my friend and I would have to start blabbing and prying just where it is least healthy, and the only certain result would be the rupture of an old and valuable friendship. True, that is a small sacrifice to make for country and mankind, but what I wish I could see is just what the contribution would stack up to.

If I go around saying "O.K. Science, here I come," and "Listen to me, you scientists, and I'll give you the real lowdown on what we're doing over here," is it really going to improve my next novel or stop nuclear war? Suppose a few scientists do, with heroic effort, find time to read a few extra novels or poems a year, since when has this vague beast called Humanities stopped any public disaster, viz.: pre-Nazi Germany? What you need for this is political sense, in scientists and everybody else, and by and large the S.E.H.'s aren't going to help much about that.

As for the supposed guilt of so many scientists, for all the terrible things they are now smart enough to do, of course we have to sympathize with anybody who is worried and unhappy, but the direct alleviation of suffering has never been the function of the arts either. Maybe a priest or a psychiatrist could help. I scarcely see how an occasional tussle of semantics could, although they are now as fashionable, or even how an original mind could stand the tedium of many such dialogues, whatever their public value. So it must be for our benefit, somehow to be siphoned over to the public through our works, that we're supposed to get tuned in on science.

Well, I'm all for anybody who wants to do me a good turn, but now I come to the painful part of this confession. I've tried. Kitt Peak wasn't half of it, and I don't mean just on the ski slopes either. Incidentally, I should have mentioned that my skiing scientist friend is of

European origin and grew up in the kind of natural respect for and acquaintance with nonscientific culture that many American-born scientists seem not to have had around them very closely in childhood. But now that people have to start specializing at the age of 9 or 10, perhaps that general humanist base is becoming more rare in Europe too.

I was recently driving with a group including a much younger European scientist—going skiing, of course—and at a certain beautiful turn of the road, at which I am used to people saying "Oh what a lovely view!" or something to that effect, he asked sternly, "What made the hills?" Shaken out of daydream I said, "Why, God," smiling, and have been feeling like an intellectual toad ever since. "Something glacial, I suppose," I quickly amended, but the damage had been done. No rapport there, the young man considers me an idiot.

He's not the only one who does, in his bailiwick, and I'm not the only one in mine they think it of. I have, I had, a literary friend, a woman of some repute for her unique genre in prose, which reviewers used to compare to both Mallarmé and Mark Twain. At any rate it did involve a high order of imaginative creation, outside of both fiction and criticism, and I admired it very much myself.

Suddenly in middle life, not long ago, the poor lady got bitten by the science bug, and moving in her feelings from inadequacy to guilt, she decided, quite mistakenly, that she had been "basking in the mystery of it all" and leaving out one of the most crucial facets of any subject. I say mistakenly, because she had never been in the least sentimental and there was nothing to be gained by her floundering around among mathematical formulae. That is what happened.

The subject that had struck her fancy that year had to do with the sea, and happening to be in Paris, she got hold of a scientific volume on waves, in the supposedly popular French pamphlet series with the overall title *"Que sais-je?"* She showed it to me later. *Que sais-je?* indeed. It was formula after formula, with scarcely a sentence she could read, though she had actually taken a couple of math courses in college. It all seemed to her more bitter, too, when she reflected that the author of that little book could have gotten some sort of experience from "the melancholy, long, withdrawing roar" or "the mermaids singing each to each," whereas for her his work, even so popularized, was a total blank.

To tell only the end of this sad affair, for months she haunted the

oceanographic labs and zoology, paleontology and other such departments of some of our great universities. The professors were very kind,
but since they were not aware of her kinship with Mallarmé or anybody else, and furthermore most of them had only a nominal acquaintance with Arnold or Eliot either, they had no way of grasping the
nature of her purpose. Oddly enough, several of them were rather
accomplished musicians, but that is a common peculiarity of scientists and rarely carries over into anything else. They all assumed
that she was doing another "vulgarization," which as a matter of
fact was true enough in their terms but insulting and inaccurate in
hers.

In my opinion she shouldn't have minded; she should have gotten
what she could from them and gone on about her business. But she was
too proud to be a beggar and too honest to be a thief, and the falsity
and condescension of those interviews finished her off. At last report
she had moved into a sea-shell museum in the basement of a certain
oceanographic building, presided over by a gentle guardian with vast
knowledge of shells but no academic degrees. There she wanders,
happy at last and loony as a hoot-owl, her imagination feeding on
drawer upon drawer of fossil mollusks and rare conches, from which
she expects some day to create the long-awaited epithalamium of
Science and Humanities.

I have told her story in order to by-pass my own, which involved
physics, a subject I used to get A in at school. This was really too
horrible to relate; it was only the thought of my children that got
me out in time. From one conversation in that line, it is true, I have
retained a marvelous image, usable by my humanist mind as the sick
canaries were, but that took place years before.

I sat at dinner once with Victor Hess, winner of the Nobel Prize
in physics for his work long ago in the discovery of cosmic rays. To
test his theories he had taken long flights over Europe alone in a bal-
loon, several of them at night, and although that had been early in
the century, when he spoke of those flights his face still glowed with
the old elation. "It was so beautiful up there," he said. "So peaceful!"
Many times since I have felt myself drifting up there with him in his
adventure, his dangerous joy, and have thought, "Oh but I know this,
I understand!"—imagining that science and I were on speaking terms
after all. Insane illusion. He was a very old man, from another world,
another time, and at that moment he had been speaking as a poet,
as scientists still sometimes might in his era, 50 years ago.

Nevertheless, I swear I will persist, at least in the biological sciences, though I should end up with that other lady among the sea-shells as a result. With physics, I'm afraid the rupture is definite. But I will never again refer to, for instance, moss, without finding out when it appeared on earth, where it stands in the scale of life and so on. That is the least a writer can do for his Golden Age. It will be hard sometimes, but I'm sure there will be that new golden voice at the switchboard, and I put my faith in that. Any time I am in despair, unwanted, useless, the Mesozoic gone adrift and the sky frivolous with intimations of immortality, I will be able to dial that number and be restored by the angelic syllables, "Science and Humanities!" Just so I don't get the answering service, and hear instead the sepulchral query, "*Que sais-je?*"

I. BERNARD COHEN
Science and the Nonscientist

I. Bernard Cohen is Professor of the History of Science at Harvard.

ANY LIST of major problems facing our American society must give high priority to the interactions of scientists and nonscientists. On the most practical level, the nonscientist citizen—be he ordinary taxpayer, Congressman or Senator, or Government official—reasonably expects to have some voice in determining the allocation of the annual expenditure by the Federal Government of some $17 billion for scientific research and development. The scientist, however, understandably holds that nonscientists can have no valid basis for evaluating scientific activities.

The scientist—aware of the commanding effect of his research on our national security, health and economic development—may well believe that he should have a major part in the decision-making process at the top level of national policy. Yet the counter-argument can also be advanced that national and international policy require political experience and special insights that are more characteristic of nonscientists than scientists, and that tend to derive from the market place and the conference table rather than from the laboratory. In

questions of policy, are not men of political acumen correct in arguing
that scientists tend to be disqualified from judgments outside the realm
of science because their scientific careers have given them, as has
been said, continuous exposure only to "problems that have permitted
of a possible rational solution"? Such are the questions we, as citizens
in the modern world, must increasingly face.

No one who looks at the events of the past 30 years, however, would
long maintain that the scientist has not taken his proper and con-
siderable position in the affairs of the nation. This has probably been
less a matter of choice than a result of the pressure of events, as the
power of science (so mightily displayed as the fecund force in transforming military technology) has become increasingly manifest.

The split down the middle of society between those who "know
science" and those who don't has provided a continuing thread of de-
bate in our time over the scientific education of the nonscientist.
James B. Conant, while still president of Harvard, devised a special
course that would give students of the humanities and social sciences
what he called a "feel for science," that quality of understanding
science which every scientist supposedly has, even when assessing
a topic on which his factual comprehension is small, and which the
nonscientist does not have.

Conant's attempted solution of the classic problem was part of the
shift in educational focus from "liberal education" to "general education." And along with the need for nonscience students to "understand
science," he placed a new emphasis on the necessity for our future
scientists to be acquainted with aspects of literature, history, philosophy, music and the fine arts. Thus they would become better able to
comprehend the values of our Western civilization and they would
become more potent forces for clarifying the goals of our society.
Furthermore, some study of history, economics, government and
sociology would help equip the potential scientist for a possible future
role as policy maker.

Training the scientist for public life was a new problem; the scientific education of the layman was an old one. The presentation of
science to nonscientists had occupied many of the best scientific minds
from the very beginnings of modern science as we know it, when
founders of the scientific movement in the 17th century felt the need
of enlightening their fellow men concerning the exciting discoveries
they were making.

It had not always been so. Thus Copernicus in 1543 had written his great treatise on "The Revolutions of Celestial Spheres," setting forth the doctrine of a sun-centered universe in which the earth moves, in austere Latin and—further to prevent its being generally read—he admonished the would-be reader that "mathematics is only for mathematicians." The title page contained yet another warning, the phrase supposedly to have been found on the entrance to Plato's Academy, "Let no one ignorant of geometry enter here!"

Yet in 1610, when Galileo described the challenging discoveries he had made with the new telescope, he did so in a way calculated to catch popular as well as scientific fancy. The news spread rapidly throughout Europe, with the effect that English poets—e.g., Donne and Milton—as well as Italian painters showed in their works an awareness of the new view of the world. Galileo, furthermore, wrote his "Dialogue on the Two Great World Systems" in the vernacular, Italian, and in the style of an informal dialogue, for all to read. This accessibility was undoubtedly one of the reasons why the work came so dramatically into conflict with the Inquisition. And Johannes Kepler, Galileo's contemporary, wrote an "Epitome of Copernican Astronomy" in the easily readable form of questions and answers.

What had happened between the time of Copernicus and that of Galileo and Kepler was a change in the concept of science itself. The men who were forging the new science of the 17th century were so conscious of the great advances they were making that they became active propagandists, demanding a place for their own version of scientific inquiry and a rejection of ancient and medieval learning.

The great age of Newton saw the rise of high quality books especially intended for the scientific education of the layman. One of the most famous was "The Plurality of Worlds," by Bernard Fontenelle, who described the initiation of a countess into the mysteries of the Copernical universe and the Galilean discoveries. Fontenelle was a Cartesian, but there soon appeared a Newtonian rival in the person of Francesco Algarotti, who wrote "Newtonianism for the Ladies" in the style of Fontenelle. More serious and on a higher level were Voltaire's "Introduction to the Philosophy of Mr. Newton," a splendid presentation of the whole corpus of Newtonian science for nonscientists, and Henry Pemberton's "View of Sir Isaac Newton's Philosophy," which carried a degree of authority deriving from the author's having worked as Newton's assistant in preparing the final edition of Newton's "Principia."

Yet no such book on science has ever had so wide and so continued an appeal as "Letters to a German Princess," by the great 18th-century mathematician, Leonhard Euler. This was so extraordinary a production in style, wit and mastery of subject that it was printed 35 times in nine different languages (with a succession of corrective notes to bring it up to date) from the time of its first publication in 1768 until its ultimate printing in 1858, 90 years later.

The success of these books derived in large measure from their express conviction that every educated man or woman should know not merely the latest facts, theories and discoveries of science, but also the nature and methods of science itself: both the structure and mechanics of the universe and our mode of acquiring knowledge of the external world. The philosophy of the Enlightenment embraced the revolutionary new discoveries of progressive science and opposed them to traditional ancient and medieval philosophy and classical art.

The scientific men of the 19th century expressed the same concern for the scientific education of the nonscientist as their 17th-century and 18th-century forebears. At once, the names come to mind of such men as Michael Faraday, Sir William Herschel, John Tyndall, Thomas Henry Huxley, who spoke for the scientific community (of which they were distinguished members) to the greater world of nonscientists. An important change, however, marked the 19th century: the rise to prominence of geology and the new biology. The old harmony between science and theology tended to disappear. Questions of the "Origin of Species" and the age of the earth caused anxieties and hostilities in men who found that science seemed to contradict the literal interpretation of Scripture. No longer was it the case that each major advance of science would appear automatically to bolster up "true religion."

Yet another change that occurred as the 20th century approached was a shift from an education based on private reading and attendance at public lectures to the more formal programs of mass enrollment in colleges and universities. Increased specialization produced a rapid diminution of contact between students of different disciplines, the greatest break occurring between those who pursued scientific careers and those who did not. We thus inherit a legacy of a cleavage which today has found dramatic emphasis in C. P. Snow's slogan of "The Two Cultures."

A writer of science books now faces two major problems that did not worry his counterparts in previous ages. First, so great is the degree of specialization within the sciences and so rapid are the advances on every scientific frontier that an account of new discoveries is sure to number among its readers not only nonscientists but even scientists in other fields. Today all scientists are generally reduced to the status of laymen with respect to any branch of scientific endeavor that does not border on their own narrow specialty. Thus a journal like Scientific American, though conceived for the dissemination of science to the nonscientist, is a "must" for the well-informed practicing scientist. Second, with the fate of society dependent on the advances of science and the uses to which these advances may be put, scientific exposition has a responsibility that by far transcends any mere urge to disseminate information about the "wonders" of the latest discoveries.

These new necessities are no doubt chiefly responsible for the generally high level of so much current writing on science for the non-specialist, be he layman in the common usage of that word or scientist. Many of the best such books and articles are written by scientists themselves, who have thereby returned to the tradition of Galileo, Kepler, Euler and those eminent scientists of the 19th century who were such distinguished masters of expository prose.

Many of today's science books are based on a historical presentation, well calculated to give the reader a true sense of the evolving nature of science, the changing role of science as a society-molding force, and the humane dimension of the scientific creative process. These books should certainly go a long way toward effecting a reunion of the sciences and the humanities that would be of consummate benefit to the human spirit. A combination of more scientific humanists and more humanistic scientists might even stem the ravages of blind technology.

II
The
Writer's
Occupation

GEORGE P. ELLIOTT
Writers on Campus

In "Writers on Campus" George P. Elliott introduces himself as one of them. He tells that he teaches, but he doesn't reveal that he is a distinguished author of short stories, a novelist, an essayist. His most recent (1968) collection of short stories is "An Hour of Last Things."

A FEW YEARS ago, another bloody Britisher came along telling the American Writer what a pity it was, really, that he didn't have a B.B.C. where he could earn an honest livelihood instead of having to sell his soul to some college or other. About college teaching I know quite a lot since I've done it since 1947. About the B.B.C. I don't know much, though I do know that Henry Reed, one of the best poets that ever worked for it, came over to the University of Washington in 1963 and liked college teaching enough to stay here for years on one campus or another. About the American Writer I don't know a damned thing, and neither do you.

The Writer ought to have lots of experience of real life.

The Writer should be allowed to express himself however he wants.

It's bad for The Writer to expose himself to much bad (i.e., student) writing.

It's dangerous for The Writer to talk about literature and writing in a formal way. . . .

Why don't people quit stuffing us into a category and lecturing the category on what's good for it? The American Writer—that's commissar talk. What we want is to have people read what we write, but then leave us alone so each of us can lead whatever life he wants to.

Some writers are lawyers, some are journalists, some doctors, some professors, some clergymen, some mothers of three, some scufflers and moochers; some are patronized, some have rich wives. Long live diversity!

Myself, like a large number of living writers who are American, I choose to teach college English. It's probably not ideal. But not much of anything about me is ideal—not my disposition, my teeth, the time I wake up, my house, or my liver. I teach because, of the ways of earning a living open to me, it is the one I like and do best. Doing as well as you can with what has been given you—that's what it's all about, isn't it?

There is little definable connection between the way a writer lives and the quality of his writing. There are such connections sometimes, to be sure, but they are so subtle, personal and hard to extricate from other strands of influence that few valid generalizations can be made from them. Norman Mailer, Louis Auchincloss, and Edward Albee do not teach, but the central characters of "An American Dream," "The Rector of Justin," and "Who's Afraid of Virginia Woolf?" are teachers. R. V. Cassill teaches; the central character of "The President" is a college president and of "Pretty Leslie" a doctor's wife. Saul Bellow is continuing to teach, though he no longer needs to in order to earn a living; Herzog is a college teacher, Henderson isn't. So? Generalize from these facts. Go ahead, try.

Here are some more facts. W. H. Auden taught around for a few years, but as soon as he was earning a living doing other things he quit teaching. Wallace Stevens never taught, and John Steinbeck has not taught yet (so far as I know). Nelson Algren and Robert Duncan have this much in common: for several years, off and on, they used to warn college students to beware of the dead hand of Academia, but in more recent years they have both put in stints teaching college English, Duncan at San Francisco State and Algren at the Iowa Writers Workshop. Now where are you?

An analogy. A fair amount of decadent writing nowadays is by homosexuals, and one hears a good deal of muttering about the sinister Influence of the Homosexual in American Literature Today. Proust was surely one of the finest writers of the century, and he was a homosexual whose subject was decadence: what matters is that his great novel itself is not decadent. Being a homosexual does not make a writer frivolous like Ronald Firbank, supremely intelligent like Proust, or turgidly lyrical like Hart Crane. One of the profoundly moral books of the age is "The Thief's Journal," in which Genet lays bare the immorality of his life as thief and homosexual prostitute, whereas John Rechy's "City of Night," which has lots of homosexual prostitutes in it, is dismally inept. So?

It is true that a teacher has to do an horrendous amount of talking; a writer who (like Evan Connell) does not like to talk a lot should not teach (as Connell does not). It is also true that neither drama nor fiction contains many scenes in which a teacher is presented at his essential task, teaching. For the purpose of realistic drama and fiction, what goes on in a classroom, at a seminar table, or during a private conference is tenuous, the relationship of teacher and student delicate and shifty.

The poets have done a good deal better with these subjects: Josephine Miles in "Preliminary to Classroom Lecture" ("My quiet kin, must I affront you/With a telling tongue?"), Theodore Roethke in "Elegy to Jane—My Student, Thrown by a Horse" ("Over this damp grave I speak the words of my love:/I, with no rights in this matter,/Neither father nor lover"), W. D. Snodgrass in "April Inventory" ("The sleek, expensive girls I teach/Younger and pinker every year,/Bloom gradually out of reach"). It is true, moreover, that the academic life is both abnormally conscious and quite deficient in flagrancies—bloodshed, blackmail, strikes, seizure of power at gun-point, and self-immolation as a gasoline torch. That is to say, as a subject for realistic writing, academic life has its limitations.

So does every other kind of life or occupation. But a writer is not bound by the limits of his professional experience. Imagination?

The important question is: Are these limitations seriously damaging or can a writer work within them? Is academic life real? My strong hunch is that the life is little or no handicap to a poet (if he finds it personally congenial), a serious though not insurmountable handicap to a dramatist (because the most intense life of Academia is so inward), and not too much of one to a writer of fiction (it's not half as constrained, for example, as the life led by Jane Austen or Emily Brontë). Teachers, students and administrators love, betray, flower, bully, aid, connive, pervert, glorify, itch, beget, adorn themselves and play Scrabble just like real people, and the forms within which they behave are clearer than most social forms these days.

As for power—American universities haven't been ivory towers for a generation. The power struggles over who gets to be (or has to be) chairman of the department are apt to be comical: all those ideals and polysyllables marshaled and sacrificed for *that*? But business and government have come to be so intricately involved with Academia that there is a great deal of large-scale power—the genuine article—to be fought for and used. The tension in Academia between high intellectual devotion to truth and grand temptations to money and power is not very theatrical, perhaps, but it is large enough for a big novel; moreover, it gets at something significant in American society now. The answer is: Academic life is real if you are.

The chief generic disadvantage to teaching is that when you are working you are tempted to work as hard as you can, to give all you've got to knock yourself out. Students *listen*: when you see their eyes drop because you've been goofing off, you despise yourself. But, for a writer with a suitable disposition, the profession has two advantages greater than all disadvantages combined: Time and Conversation.

A substantial amount of the process of writing occurs while the writer is gazing out the window, scratching, driving around, drinking coffee, gardening, making lists, pacing the house, napping, and staring at the ceiling, all of which takes lots of quiet time. No other job most writers are qualified for gives them anything like as many days and part-days to write in as college teaching. The pay is not great, though not as bad as professors make out—they like to talk poor. Professorial status is worth something in the world at large, and the private gratification of being adored by the young is substantial if dangerous. But the main thing is Time.

And Conversation. Writers, after all, are word people, and most of them are trying to understand something of the world and themselves. Illiterates and criminals use words more colorfully than academics, and most pedants long ago let it slip their minds that beautiful truth was what they were after. All the same, in the normal course of American life, a college campus is where you are likeliest to find satisfying conversation—to say nothing of musical performances, political ferment, sports, drama, and dance. It wasn't for need of money that Faulkner lived in residence at the University of Virginia toward the end of his life, and I doubt that it was just for money that Frost served as "poetic radiator" at Amherst and Dartmouth all those years.

M. L. ROSENTHAL
Poets of Academe

M. L. Rosenthal, professor of English at New York University, is another of George Elliott's writers on campus. He is a very active one. He has served as poetry editor of The Nation and of The Reporter. He is the author, among other books, of a history, "Modern Poets." His own verse has been collected under the title of "Blue Boy on Skates."

AT A wild symposium some time ago in New York's Poetry Center, a young Beat writer looked at the sensitive, mobile features of one of our most sophisticatedly experimentalist poets and shouted that he could not possibly be a poet—he just did not *look* like one. It was hard to tell just what in the older man had produced this outburst. His good manners? his cleanliness? his *glasses*? Surely not his poems, which would be the only dependable indication of whether he looks like a poet or not. My guess is that it was the fact that he was a professor that offended his accuser, who took the opportunity later on to suggest that the entire professoriat had latched on to a kind of sinecure, a life-long mass-grant with plenty of money, no duties and no inspiration.

Now I am a professor myself, with many years of teaching behind me, and so my reaction (irritated amusement) is both natural and suspect. To me it seems obvious, though, that some people, having once found their own studies tedious and gray, do not understand the satisfactions or agonies of the academic experience. They do not realize that this is but one form, but a real and vital form for all that, which mature experience can take. They think it inimical to the creative spirit, although many poets are teachers and their poetry does not seem diminished thereby. I have just, in fact, finished preparing an anthology of American and British poetry since the last war. It contains work by 105 poets of every group and tendency, among them Beat, Black Mountain, Sixties, and confessional poets in this country, and "Movement" and "Group" poets and their opponents in Britain. In review-

ing the available information about these people, I find that at least
41 of them are full-time professional teachers, mostly at universities,
and that at least 23 more are occasional or former teachers.

Whether this situation is good or bad for poets and poetry has
almost become one of those set debating topics. To my mind, the sta-
tistics are more significant sociologically than artistically. What they
show is that schools are to some extent a source of livelihood for poets,
most of whom are after all suited for teaching through their love of
language, their interest in ideas, and their humane sympathies. In
another sense, the topic, as an *issue*, is irrelevant because the situation,
like the poetry itself, is an expression of our moment in time, and
because the individual poets concerned are so different from one another. I am sure that the motives of Robert Lowell in teaching are
quite different from those of Donald Davie, who is a scholar and
professor in the most complete meanings of those words. Mr. Lowell
communicates well as a teacher, I understand, and has had a marked
influence on the development of some younger poets whom he has
taught; and I would suppose that his teaching satisfies important needs
of his prodigious psychic energies, which present themselves so explosively in his poems.

Mr. Davie, at the University of Essex in England, writes with a certain cool, "scholarly" intellectuality and rigorous self-control. It would
be tricky, however, to relate these qualities directly to his academic
career. Probably they were deeply imbedded in his nature long before
he decided to become a professor. They are inseparable—by a familiar
paradox of art—from the most intense feeling in his work. Another
tricky instance is that of the English poet Charles Tomlinson, who
teaches at the University of Bristol. His poems reveal a sophisticated
study of French and American models. But the knowledge is a *poet's*
knowledge, acquired through a quite unacademic struggle to free himself of the comfortable laxness that has rotted so much current British
poetry, by academic and non-academic authors alike.

More obviously, the gnarled and diffident and half anti-intellectual
writing of the American poet-professor Robert Creeley or the rhetorical, satyr-posing, bourgeois-shocking writing of the Canadian Irving
Layton will demonstrate at once how far apart a poet's adult vocation
(by which he earns his bread, I mean) and the springs of his art must
needs be.

The universities are hardly hotbeds of poets. For all the talk of encouraging creative people, there is precious little actually done, especially as the problem is a bit elusive in an institutional setting. To reach the higher professorial ranks (in the United States at least), the doctorate is still almost indispensable, and only a tiny number of poets have undertaken the necessary discipline:

> Poems are made by fools like me,
> But not while studying for the Ph.D.

Nevertheless, a certain number of colleges do make allowance for the poet's special abilities. Some of them, such as Iowa and Oregon, have highly developed special programs for writers. Some, like Dartmouth here or Leeds in England, have "resident poets." Some, like New York University, employ professional writers to teach composition. Some, like Bennington, choose their faculties as much as possible from the actively creative community. And there are all sorts of "exceptional cases" tucked away everywhere.

The real danger of this situation, I think, is not that some people will find themselves growing artistically timid, or dulled in sensibility, because of their academic experience. The danger, rather, is that the true poet—whose need to write is too fierce and idiosyncratic to be tamed all that easily—will turn his attention too exclusively to his work of teaching. The tasks of teaching assert themselves powerfully because they are unavoidably regular in their scheduling and because they are so *interesting*. They make for an intense, arduous life full of compelling deadlines and challenges and of significant personal relationships. There are temperaments that can manage this life fairly readily and combine it with that of the artist without too much violence to themselves and there are those that cannot do so.

Of course, *academic* is a dirty word in poetic circles. It *ought* to be, if it is used to disparage work that is tamely formal or pedantic, or that is a slavish exemplar of some established orthodoxy. Just a few days ago, a Scottish "Concretist" poet both amazed me and made me wince on my country's behalf by using the word in just this sense. He preferred American to British academic poetry, he said, because it was better constructed. As if, at this level, the question at all mattered! My own tastes are such that I have always, perhaps unjustly, been more interested in the poetry that storms and dreams past known boundaries than in the poetry that seeks to perfect itself within them.

Nevertheless, anyone who does not know how to love the rich values of the latter kind of writing, and who does not remain alert to the deceptive originality and discoveries it may well embody, will not be able to understand the truly new either.

Behind the more blatant dislike of such work by people whose idea of poetry is purely external—to whom any hollerer or hipster looks more "poetic" than a man quietly writing—lies the subtler contemporary tendency to discredit the whole creative meaning of the humanistic tradition. The grove outside Athens where Plato taught has the associations of this tradition, and of the pleasures of sweetly philosophical musings and reverie as well as of learning. It was called Academe.

JOHN KNOWLES
The Writer-in-Residence

In "The Writer-in-Residence" John Knowles has written a small chapter of autobiography without mention of the writer-in-residence as a writer-at-large. He has been an editor, is the author of short stories and "Double Vision," an account of travels in Europe and the Mediterranean world. His first novel, the much-praised study of prep-school life, "A Separate Peace," was given the William Faulkner Foundation award in 1960.

JUST as Socrates became a foot soldier in Athens, writers these days sometimes teach. To make the transition easier the universities have created a special sinecure outside the regular faculty progression and called it "writer-in-residence." I don't believe anyone is really sure what that is; certainly when I arrived in Chapel Hill to function as the first writer-in-residence at the University of North Carolina for two terms I didn't know, and they didn't know either. I was to pervade the university with a literary flavor, it seemed. But it is not easy to pervade 10,000 students, especially if they are not particularly interested in being pervaded. In addition I was to conduct one class in the writing of short stories. Although I had never taught anything before except the Australian Crawl, I did not foresee any special problem in teaching. After all I had spent nine months of every year in some class or other from the age of 6 to the age of 22, and I felt that a sense of how to teach must have sunk into me and be waiting.

A class in fiction writing, however, turned out to be not like any other class. It did, of course, have certain characteristics common to all classes, first and foremost of these being the impenetrable stupidity and boredom which apparently register on the faces of all students, even a class as well-disposed as this one, as they gaze with looks of marked aversion and hopelessness up at a teacher. I must have looked at my own beleaguered teachers just that way for all those years. It never occurred to me as a student that the expression on my face had anything to do with anything, and it never occurred to any of my students now. Students seem to feel that being in class is like being at the movies; the figure they're staring at is only a shadow, not a real human being looking back at them at all.

Steeling myself against this battery of youthful torpor I went ahead with the class and learned a second awful truth: the teacher must supply the gasoline for a class, which does not, as I had assumed, run somehow by itself. If the teacher runs dry the most unbelievable silence will then ensue. I had to learn to present a sovereign attitude of confidence at all times as to what would happen next or else these 12 young people would begin to doubt my existence, the class's, and even their own. Yet the essence of conducting a class in fiction is not to conduct it, but to give it to the students.

This course became much more like group therapy than a class in any academic subject. In class a student would read his story aloud, the other students would comment in turn, I would give my reaction only after having had all of theirs, and finally the author, who had not been allowed to say a word beyond reading the story, could make any statement about the story or our comments he wanted to make. Everything that could be done by the students was done by the students: for example, reading their own stories aloud instead of having them read by me. It was often an ordeal for them to do this, and that's why I made them do it. Any ordeal surmounted strengthened their sense of themselves and anything that strengthened their sense of themselves made them better qualified for achievement in the writing of fiction.

As the term wore on and they developed more confidence in themselves and each other and me, they drew more and more on what they really felt and often hid. They were almost totally uninterested in the state of the world; the atomic bomb might never had been invented; there was no Communism and not even any politics. There was only one social issue, race, on which they tended to think like integrationists but sometimes still feel a little like segregationists.

For the most part what they wrote about was strictly personal: the incomprehension between parents and children, a feeling of alienation from home and home town, straightforward sexuality, the tensions of being accepted or not accepted by the group. There was a lot of violence in their work, there was quite a bit of dissipation. There was no hypocrisy and no genteel evasion and no circumlocution. They read Faulkner and Fitzgerald and Hemingway and Salinger and Camus, and they called a spade a spade.

Despite the look of stupidity and boredom on their faces, they did not miss anything, especially any personal detail about me, my socks once happening very slightly not to match, or a trace of regional accent deeply buried in my speech, or any shadow of a predilection I had for anything. Week after week they sat there, slowly and methodically and tranquilly taking me apart.

Yet it was outside the classroom that I had to discover what a writer-in-residence was. I avoided faculty gatherings, feeling I was not supposed to pervade the faculty, and feeling also that they regarded me, teaching that year at the college level and holder of no academic degree higher than Bachelor of Arts, the way a surgeon would regard a butcher. For my part I thought of them as usually intelligent, sometimes interesting, and even occasionally gifted people who did not require, did not want, much variety or change in their lives.

I was also surprised to discover that the starving, slaving teacher sacrificing all for learning is very definitely a thing of the past. An affluent air of unhurried ease pervaded the faculty; above the instructor level a great many of them seemed very well paid, sometimes extremely well paid, and rather underworked, and this is true of all important college and university faculties in the United States now. The faculty and I passed each other leaving a wide margin for clearance, and I spent my time with the students.

They gradually evolved to suit themselves what my role was to be. My first inkling of this occurred in a beer cellar where a three-piece band was blaring rock-'n'-roll music in the foreground and a member of the Freshman Class, his black hair brushed forward to the eyebrows of a wide, weird, clownish, strong, unlikely face, eyed me excitedly and then came across to me and without any preliminaries shouted above the music, "Where is the significant?"

After a moment I roared back that the significant was within ourselves.

This pleased him tremendously; everything I said pleased him tremendously.

"Where is it within me?" he then asked.

"Well, what do you love?"

"My motorcycle."

That stopped me cold for a minute, but then I counterattacked, telling him that for most of humanity most of the time the significant had been the little plot of cultivated ground that supported their lives generation after generation and that he was enormously privileged even to be in a position to ask such a question. That pleased him a lot. But for the most part the students did not ask me large or even small questions. They did not want me to say anything in particular; they just wanted me to be.

One night the varsity football team invited me to a party. The last thing they were interested in was any literary discussion with me.

"Phyllis," someone would say to his girl, "get up and dance with the writer-in-residence."

"Look. The writer-in-residence wears green corduroy pants."

"I didn't know writer-in-residences could dance."

"How old do you think the writer-in-residence is?"

"I don't think he's in too bad shape, for a writer-in-residence."

That night I realized who I was in Chapel Hill. I was the intellectual mascot, the academic equivalent of the ram trotted up and down the sidelines by the cheer leaders at football games, to be brought out on certain occasions as a symbol of the university's connection with active writing.

However, I could also be used as research material: 10 of the university psychiatrists asked me to discuss my work with them. We met after dinner with their wives to analyze my novel "A Separate Peace." I agreed with some of their comments, disagreed with others, and very much admired their dedication to the most crucial field of science in existence. There were, however, oversimplifications I felt Freud himself would never have tolerated.

"Do you have an older brother?" one psychiatrist asked.

"Yes."

"A-ha!" he cried triumphantly, walking away, everything about my novel explained.

Worse, they seemed to assume that any writer would benefit as a writer by being psychoanalyzed, while I feared that after an analysis a writer might no longer have the emotional vision that impelled him to write in the first place, to want to write, to have to write. Curiously enough several of their wives sidled up to me and murmured that for them my novel was a good book about what it seemed to be about, hinting that I should not take too seriously what their husbands were saying. Perhaps this behavior was motivated by penis envy or identification with the aggressor, but I just took it as an honest expression of what they really thought. Not everything can be different from what it seems, I hope. Nor is literature an extension of a symptom or a ramification of psychiatry; psychiatry is among other things, a promising new growth on the great ancient trunk of literature.

They told me about the "exquisite sensitivity" of many of their schizophrenic patients, and I thought, good God, it's the exquisitely sensitive people who are locked up these days, and all the crude louts are free. I asked them what the principal psychological problem among students was and they answered immediately: sexual identity.

So the shimmering, motionless fall and the brisk little winter and long sensual spring went by in North Carolina. I'm not sure I was pervasive enough, or that I provided what they hoped for from me. But writers are selfish people at heart, selfish in the claims of their work. Since they left me great amounts of time for it, and since by definition a Southerner who is also enlightened is the most charming American there is, I was happy there and grateful.

BRIAN GLANVILLE
What Else
Should Writers Do?

Novelist, playwright, sportswriter, Brian Glanville finds the time and energy to quit his typewriter and play a good game of football (soccer).

His love of the sport is reflected in his novel of a football player, "The Rise of Gerry Logan." Some of his other novels: "Roman Marriage," "Second Home," "Artist Type."

WILLIAM FAULKNER was once asked what occupation he thought a writer should follow. Faulkner said it didn't matter much; if a writer were any good, nothing he did would do him any harm. If he weren't, then nothing he did would do him any good. The best job he could think of was playing the piano in a brothel, because the hours were easy, the company was interesting, and there was plenty of opportunity for interesting conversation.

In its way, this still seems to me one of the most sensibly ironic answers I have heard to a question which bedevils modern writers. It is, of course, a symptom of our artistic insecurity, our morbid self-awareness, that we should ask it at all.

The contemporary writer is forever questioning the validity of what he does, what he is, in relation to what he writes. Earlier generations were more robust. Charles Dickens certainly did not catechize himself when he was editing the Daily News; nor, I am sure, did Anthony Trollope, when he sat at his desk in the post office. Melville was never happy working in the Customs, but the reasons were inherent in the job itself, rather than in its presumed effect on his writing. They all would have been greatly surprised by the opening paragraph of Cyril Connolly's "The Unquiet Grave," with its assertion that "writers will not acknowledge that it is their present way of life which prevents them from ever creating anything different or better."

This self-consciousness has interacted with the contemporary difficulties of earning a living to make a writer's occupation one of his chief anxieties. Is he, in that work, selling out to the glittering world? Is he cutting himself off from wide experience? Is he depriving himself of time? Is he condemning himself to a way of thought that blocks creativity? There are very few who would be as sanguine about it all as Faulkner, and besides, didn't Faulkner have an enviable best of both worlds; a Southern gentleman-farmer who could from time to time drift over to Hollywood to make some money?

The trouble is, as Stephen Spender explained two decades ago in a germinal essay, "Prescriptions for a Modern Masterpiece," that it's no longer sufficient for a writer to do nothing but write, even should his income allow it. "Two prerequisites for artists in words," he wrote, "have today become irreconcilable. These are, firstly, leisure in which to perfect one's craft, and, secondly, the fullest possible participation in the experience of life of one's time." There is the further difficulty that such participation may in itself be harmful.

The truth is that the writer today tends to be an almost schizophrenic figure. Detached, even alienated, by definition, he must by sheer necessity of survival have one foot outside whatever profession or job he takes up. The job itself must always be secondary, even though the importance of its financial rewards may be primary. He is, in the most exact sense of the word, an amateur at his day-to-day work, a professional at his writing.

In "The Unquiet Grave," Cyril Connolly warns us of the dangers of "journalism, broadcasting, propaganda and writing for films." From these we may safely eliminate propaganda—he was writing during World War II—and firmly add teaching. Its very omission from the list shows us the speed with which it has become perhaps the most common danger of all.

This seems especially true in America, where almost every notable writer one can think of—with a handful of defiant, financially successful exceptions, such as Mailer—has succumbed at one time or another to the lure of the campus. Quite apart from the tendency of such writers to produce ingrowing fiction about university life, with its thin, limited material, its tediously over-conscious ways, there is the great problem of isolation. Not isolation in the individual sense, but isolation from the world at large, in a community where everybody, so to speak, takes in everybody else's washing, where self-awareness turns in upon itself until it eats itself alive.

I have read these campus novels *ad nauseam;* the saddest thing about them is that so many of them are written by highly gifted authors, whose talents, if put to work on richer material, would come to immeasurably richer fruition. Can there be any fair comparison of Philip Roth's "Letting Go" with his dazzling short novel, "Goodbye, Columbus," or a short story like his "Defender of the Faith"? Was Mary McCarthy's splendid technical armory, so brilliantly deployed in "The Company She Keeps," properly engaged in "The Groves of Academe" for all its style and graces?

For the writer-academician must live among academics, thoroughly estimable and necessary people whose task, however, is to criticize, teach, evaluate; to live, perhaps, at second hand. There are self-conscious people—among them, both writers and academicians—and people too busy living to be self-conscious. That there is a dichotomy between the writer and the livers is axiomatic, but this need not prevent his living among them; indeed, the consequent tension can be most productive.

Then there is the danger of journalism. Cyril Connolly himself, in his "Enemies of Promise," was minatory: "Journalism is loose, intimate, simple and striking; literature formal and compact . . . what is intended to be read once can seldom be read more than once; a journalist has to accept the fact that his work, by its very todayness, is excluded from any share in tomorrow. . . . A writer who takes up journalism abandons the slow tempo of literature for a faster one and the change will do him harm." The flippancy of journalism will become a habit, the pleasure of being paid and, still more, praised on the spot will grow indispensable.

There is much sense in such warnings, yet I think one can, without being *parti pris*, say that they are not the whole truth. Here again, I turn to Stephen Spender: "A certain tendency to promote personal attitudes and habits into a whole view of life contributes more to the ephemeral nature of much modern literature than does the combination of journalism with serious writing. (Ever since there have been newspapers, writers have earned money from journalism, and if there had been broadcasting in Elizabethan times, it is fairly self-evident that most of the Elizabethans would have written B.B.C. Elizabethan propaganda.)"

Journalism, even from the editorial chair, seems to have done no harm to Dickens. Ring Lardner, much closer to our own times—and very much closer, in experience, to myself—seems to have been quite untouched by the many years he traveled the country with the Chicago White Sox. Indeed, without those travels, he would surely have been unable to write those splendid, innovating, demotic stories. "You Know Me, Al" and the rest could have come only from a writer deeply familiar with the idiom and mores of his world. And if some object that Lardner's baseball stories were a little loose in structure, a little sentimental, let them be confronted with his short, surreal, defiantly personal plays.

Journalism, too, has this about it: that it can solve the modern writer's problem of isolation, exclusion, by bringing him into both its own special world and the world to which he may be assigned, whether it be politics, sport, society or even crime. There is nothing sadder and more symptomatic of our literary age than the writer who goes "gathering material," the lady novelist who has just been down to the docks, the senior novelist who, creativity dimmed, is forever flying off to remote, exotic places in the hope he will be titillated. When I published my novel, "A Second Home," a novel about an actress, a well meaning ass of a reviewer said that no living novelist worked harder on his milieux. God knows I have never worked on a milieu in my life; the theater is a world I know because I've been around it; professional soccer is a world I know still better.

There is the matter, too, of what kind of newspaper or magazine one writes for. If he is fortunate enough to write, as I do, for a paper like The Sunday Times (London), or The Observer, serious news- papers which encourage their staff to express themselves as freely and as elegantly as possible, all may be well. If he's writing in the popu- lar, mass-circulation papers, his space is likely to be rigorously con- stricted, while he'll be forced to write in an idiom both highly stylized and deeply vulgar, an inorganic parody of what is assumed to be an American tabloid style.

But there are more insidious perils, to be sure. There are magazine styles, particularly in the United States, which come somewhere in between popular cliché and genuinely creative, individual writing. Certain magazines, of course, rewrite material to suit a "house" style, but the pressure to conform need not be as direct as that. It may simply be that a writer, wanting or needing the large check that he knows a particular magazine will pay him, unconsciously goes along with their demands and expectations.

Creative writing, of course, comes from a deeper level than jour- nalism, one on which the imagination is engaged, trying to assimilate and to transmute its material, whereas journalism is concerned only to record. There are times when journalism can achieve notable depth, but there is no such animal as a nonfiction novel; it is a simple contradiction in terms. Either it must by lying journalism, or impure fiction.

Because it comes from a shallower level, and when it concerns football or other subjects I enjoy, I personally find journalism enor- mously therapeutic. As for the presumed stylistic dangers, these, too, are surely influenced by the level of engagement. To me, journalism is

on the whole easy, its problems mechanical ones—deadlines, availability. Creative writing is painful and difficult.

The cinema has also long been represented as one of the great
threats to the creative writer—understandably enough, since it has
sucked so many of them irretrievably into its maw. Things aren't, with
the decline of Hollywood, perhaps as bad as they were. Writers are
no longer looked upon as quite such (necessary) evils, mere worker
bees of the process, outshone and outranked by its stars, its directors,
its producers, even its cameramen. The centripetal process, away from
Hollywood, has given the writer much more say and much more
freedom. But if he's no longer a despised figure, he has still at least two
major anxieties to confront.

First, the process of writing a film is very hard on him in sheer
time and wear on the nerves. Alone in his room, his is the final word.
In the studio, the star, the director, the producer all have their four-
pence worth to add. He may write and rewrite until he's driven almost
berserk; and to specifications which probably have nothing to do with
esthetic criteria.

Then, there is the problem of wealth. Connolly has told us about
that, too. The writer raises his income, hence his standard of living,
then has to work to maintain it. I remember, many years ago, when I
was supposed to call on a producer next morning, getting home to find
a copy of a writer's magazine, with an article on Hollywood. There
had been a meeting of the local writers' chapter, at which someone
had cried, in pain and outrage, "Do you realize there are people right
here in Hollywood who are only earning $500 a week?" Five hundred
a week! I don't suppose at that time I was earning $500 a month. I
lay awake much of the night, wrestling with the hideous prospect of
corruption.

As things turned out, I need not have bothered. When I told the
producer, a small, toad-like man, what I thought of the script I was
meant to rewrite, he replied pityingly, "Mr. Glanville, you say there's
a lot of clichés in this script. If we threw out everything in this office
because it had clichés in it, we'd go out of business." Pause. Very low.
"We don't want to go out of business."

Now, on the verge of turning two of my novels into screen-plays,
I think and hope I am sufficiently armored. Yet it seems a mistake to
me to believe that film-writing can help the writer. Why should it,
when its conventions are essentially visual and, in film at its best, al-

most anti-literary? Certainly it need not do harm, but one can scarcely say more than that.

Television has many of the same dangers as cinema and journalism; I have worked in it a good deal, and find it has depressingly little to offer the writer. If one makes documentaries, one is involved, again, though far more stringently than in journalism, with the question of truth; for in television, even the recording of fact is menaced and vitiated by technical necessity. Original television plays are as ephemeral as any journalism, a hybrid compromise between the theater and the cinema.

One cannot end without talking of the woman writer, who to some degree stands outside the conflict. Some of them have complained that their exclusion from masculine life is a grave handicap. It may be argued, too, that the life of the family is no less "real," indeed a great deal more "basic," than the life of the office or the factory. Yet we know how these novelists of the hearth, the personal relationship, the indulged private sensibility, can come to seem limited and arid.

Let me quote Spender again: "At the back of every modern novel, there is an objection which becomes more and more pressing: 'Why do the characters in this novel have time to pay so much attention to their sensibilities and their feelings? The more time they have for such experiences, the less, in effect, can the reader take them quite seriously.' "

The emancipation of women seems to have done surprisingly little to bring them, and their developed sensibility, into the larger arena; or rather, when they do enter it, they seldom seem to be creative writers. Housewifery, then, is as much a "job," as much an occupational danger to the writer (though with its own special compensations, to be sure) as journalism, teaching and the rest.

The writer's choice becomes yearly more difficult. He may avoid the grosser sell-out of advertising, with its large earnings, its tricky self-justification, only to fall into literary journalism, with its endless drudgery of reviewing, its emphasis on the analytic faculty. He may escape the treadmill of popular journalism for the more subtle corruption of higher-middlebrow magazine writing. He may hack his way out of the Groves of Academe, only to flounder in the warm, well-paid morass of the cinema. One can simply hope that the writer of true originality and genius will continue not only to rise above his immediate circumstances, but to turn them to his creative advantage.

JOHN BOWEN
Out of Experience

An English critic, novelist and short-story writer, John Bowen is also a playwright. He was represented on Broadway in the fall of 1967 with "After the Rain."

I KNEW a young man once who wanted to write a novel, and the first time he kissed a girl, he said to her anxiously, "Now tell me in your own words exactly how that felt." Later he gave up literature altogether in favor of experience. It was (he said) more interesting in itself, and a great deal easier to do.

I knew another man, more dedicated than that, so his story is more sad. He was another who had decided that experience is the raw material of literature, and he reasoned that the more extreme the experience, the more intense the novel. He was not an actor; he could not fall in love to order. He could not bring himself to murder an old woman in a pawnshop, and he doubted the value of LSD as a key to the life of the spirit. However, he knew that novels with an outdoor setting were held to be popular, so he thought that a good way to prepare himself to write a book that would be both a commercial success and a work of literature was to become a fisherman in the Gulf of Mexico.

My friend was not physically strong, and spoke little Spanish. He was not suited to the life of a fisherman. He suffered—well, he had intended to suffer, though perhaps not quite so much. He became a butt. His acne grew worse. He fell over frequently, and became in every way bruised. After nine months, he took what he had saved of his pay and went to live on a tower, in a forest in Oregon, to watch for fires and write his novel.

There he discovered that he couldn't write it. It was not merely that he lacked the craft. Certainly he *had* neglected the craft of literature in favor of "real life," but that could have been remedied by rewriting. The trouble, the insoluble problem he faced there, alone in the forest looking out for fires, was that nothing would come. So much inconvenience, so much time given up, so much anticipation, and nothing to show for it; he was like a bridegroom who finds himself impotent on the wedding night.

Yet though matters may have turned out badly for the bridegroom, we cannot think him wrong in wishing to be married. Nor was my acquaintance wrong, I think, in his belief that novels are written out of experience. Not out of experience alone—imagination and empathy come into it. We must allow that a novelist is a person living among people; he is agent and patient, actor and reactor, fed by what happens to him, by his senses and his intelligence. He is, if you like, two persons, one of whom experiences, and one of whom observes and shapes the experience—like the narrator of Giorgio Bassani's "The Garden of the Finzi-Continis," who "longed for the present to become the past at once so that I could love it and gaze fully at it at any time."

Perhaps the novelist is also less than a person, inasmuch as he cannot respond fully to any moment until it is already over, but the moment is necessary for the response; the experience is the raw material from which he must make the shape. Though novels are not "real life" and have their own reality, yet experience is the basis of that reality.

Alain Robbe-Grillet once described some seagulls in one of his novels. He went to Brittany to check his description by observation, and was forced to the decision that, since the seagulls he observed were not much like the seagulls he had described, his seagulls were more real than real seagulls. Yet Robbe-Grillet had the *idea* of seagulls before he wrote. There was experience of some sort, some childish memory perhaps, if only of an afternoon in the cinema when the seagulls shrieked above the Quai des Brumes. At some time, Robbe-Grillet had laid himself open to experience, made his investment in it as we all must do, and at last, in those more-real-than-real seagulls, the investment had matured.

I know, of course, that this doctrine of experience may be exploited in the interests of selfish behavior. A novelist, as I've said, is also a person. He has personal failings. On the one hand, he may use his art as a consolation. At a time of emotional disorder and suffering, he may murmur: "But I shall use this. It will all make a book." In detaching himself from the experience, he forgets that he is not alone in it: there is someone else involved, as disordered as he, as much a person as he, whom he no longer personally considers because he has begun to turn him or her into a work of art, which has no feelings, and does not suffer.

Worse, he may enter, may deliberately enter an experience in the hope of using it—an experience involving people far more vulnerable than those who fish in the Gulf of Mexico. "I need to fall in love," he may tell himself. "My art requires it. I am too comfortable here. I shall dry up. I must leave my wife." He has special advantages in this way, because there are people for whom the idea of "creative writing" is itself so attractive that they will find even the most bat-eared, red-nosed, lecherous old creature endearing, if only he has written a novel or so. Our novelist may calm his conscience by saying: "Clearly, what I undertake for my own pleasure may cause pain to others. Yet out of this may come a work of art"—and the horrifying aspect of this statement is that, while it is morally despicable, it may also be true. Out of such selfish behavior, a work of art may indeed come. Bad men have written good books.

It may come, but then again it may not. You betray a trust, reject love, deceive a friend, destroy the social and sexual self-confidence of some immature person, and then, alone on your high tower among inflammable forests, you find it was all for nothing; no book is coming from it. There is a maxim of Lord Leverhulme, much quoted by advertising men, that he knew well enough that half the money he spent on advertising his soaps and detergents was wasted, and he would be happy if he knew which half.

It is the same with experience. The novelist does not know what he is going to be able to use, or how, or where. He may spend quite a lot of money and time in traveling round the world or keeping a mistress, and the investment may never pay a dividend, but merely depreciate, dribbling away into the forgotten as the years go by. And then some quite small piece of stock, some little five-shilling flier—a foolish quarrel in a sunny square; a freckled girl, glimpsed for a moment sitting astride a wall—will appreciate hugely into what begins a book or makes the image for it.

We know that in dreams problems which obsess us may be symbolically solved. A work of literature may be a kind of dream. I don't think I am alone in having found, in writing a book or a play, that, however I may have planned the broad outline, the actual writing of it was like following a hidden trail, that often I may have wanted to go in different directions but could not, because the story itself had its own necessity, and writing it was a process of discovering that necessity. More than that, I have discovered when the thing was done that, just as in a dream, the work was the symbolic statement of an obsession, so that sometimes I have known more about my own nature than I knew when I began it.

Experience provides the raw material, then, for those symbolic statements. If a writer knew enough about his own nature, perhaps he might be able to invest wisely in experience, choosing only those experiences that seemed likely to epitomize his own moral and spiritual problems. But if he knew that much about his own nature, he would not need to follow the hidden trail and write the book. It is easier, I think, and better to accept Pooh's recipe for writing and let things come; never to go fishing in the Gulf of Mexico except for money or pleasure, never to undertake any experience except for its own sake. In that case, we shall not be investing at all, but paying in time, money, and effort for something that it costs time, money and effort to buy. Any other use we may be able to make of it can only be profit.

JAMES MacGREGOR BURNS
Politicians as Authors

James MacGregor Burns once ran for Congress as a Democrat in a rock-ribbed Republican district of Massachusetts (he was defeated). He was a delegate to the Democratic Convention of 1952. He has written of politics and politicians in "Roosevelt: The Lion and the Fox" and "John Kennedy: A Political Profile." In addition to such credentials for his essay, "Politicians as Authors," he is James Phinney Baxter Professor of History and Public Affairs at Williams College.

RECENTLY a good many politicians have been ignoring the Old Testament hope of their rivals "that mine adversary had written a book," and Richelieu's warning, "Give me six lines written by the most honest man, I will find something there to hang him."

Perhaps the old taboo still holds. In 1966 Congressman Charles L. Weltner of Georgia brought out a book (with the unimpeachable title "Southerner") in which he looked candidly and critically at Southern politics; later, he quit his race for re-election when his fellow Democrats nominated a segregationist for Governor. Senator Paul H. Douglas published a distinguished book on our foreign economic policy, but this evidently won him few votes in the '66 elections. Congressman Jim Wright of Texas ran into a different problem. He had hardly published a study of the coming water famine when the heavens seemed to open, at least in these parts, though he will doubtless be right in the long run.

By and large we have been hard on our politician-authors. John Calhoun's defense of the South and minority power did not endear him to Northerners. Theodore Roosevelt assailed pacifists and other such "cowardly" types, before he began to run for office and had to worry about the anti-war vote. As a professor, Woodrow Wilson was even more imprudent. In his history of the American people, he condemned immigrants, inflationists, labor agitators and radicals generally. Later, after he had entered the political crucible, he felt the heat of the immigrant and labor reaction—even to the extent of offering to remove the offending references from the next edition.

Writing serious (or, at least, controversial) books seems safer for the British politician. The young Disraeli satirized Whigs and Tories, Anglicans and Papists, in his trilogy, "Coningsby," "Sybil," "Tancred," without any damage to his glittering career in politics. Winston Churchill denounced appeasers in both major parties throughout the 1930's—and became Prime Minister in the 1940's. In recent years Laborite Charles A. R. Crosland has taken on the Establishment in "The Future of Socialism" and "The Conservative Enemy." Today, he is writing not in a garret or a cell, but in his Cabinet office in Whitehall.

The American politician-writer faces a special problem today. Everyone expects him to produce a poor book; if he writes a good one, it is assumed to be ghost-written. John F. Kennedy wrote "Profiles in Courage" while recovering from surgery on his back. The book was literate—and hence, to some critics, clearly could not have come from a politician's pen. Kennedy had to go to some pains to demonstrate that it was his book; he finally asked Senator—and professional writer—Richard Neuberger to look at his notes and manuscript to certify their authorship. Some persons forgot that Kennedy, while hardly out of his teens, had already written an incisive and sophisticated study of British foreign policy before the war.

Faced with such risks, American politicians have often played it safe. The most prudent course is not to publish at all, whatever the urge. Franklin D. Roosevelt, while convalescing after his polio attack, started two big writing projects—a history of the United States and an analysis of the practical workings of American government. In each case he wrote a few pages, and then dropped the project for good. No wonder he got elected President four times; nobody accused him of maligning the immigrants, the Mormons, or the Irish. Few 20th-century politicians have stopped to write books (except for collections of speeches and the like) on their road to the White House.

The next safest course is to write books only after all the votes are in. A man can't retire from the Presidency these days, or even from the Cabinet, without ending up in the toils of the publishers. Hoover, Truman and Eisenhower have produced weighty memoirs; historians mourn the absence of the personal histories F. D. R. and Kennedy would have produced. Lesser politicos have also played it safe. In 1966, Edward Costikyan brought out "Behind Closed Doors," a sprightly and illuminating portrait of New York City politics, but only after he quit as reform leader of Tammany Hall. In my state, Jim Curley came out with his "I'd Do It Again," a nice mingling of fact and fiction, only after his last hurrah in Boston politics.

Yet if a politician feels the yen to produce a book in mid-career—and many do—he can usually find some issue that will attract far more support than it endangers. William Jennings Bryan wrote books on his travels and on Christ, Herbert Hoover on individualism (an excellent book by the way), Al Smith on his earlier political career.

In recent years Senate Democrats have been especially prolific and more daring. Senator Joseph Clark has taken a strong position in behalf of Congressional reform. Claiborne Pell has urged revolutionary changes in urban transport. Robert Kennedy set forth broad outlines of policy in "To Seek a Better World." Earlier Republican Senators Jacob Javits and Hugh Scott wrote on political and party matters. The way things are going, a Senator won't feel comfortable in the cloakroom until he has a book attached to his name.

I suppose this is a good thing; there is so much suspicion between the supposedly practical politicians and the supposedly ivory-tower intellectuals that it may help affairs if the former enter the bookish world of the latter. In that world the politician must marshal his thoughts at some length, surrender some of his Congressional immunity, run the gauntlet of the reviewers, and face the academic critics who, months after the book appears, will be picking it to pieces in the academic journals.

Thus politicians' books can serve as a small bridge between the two communities. (Whether or not academics should in turn try to enter the politician's world is another question.) In this generation more than in any previous one, I think, politicians and professors are not only talking to each other but listening to each other—and this may help improve the arts of government as well as the self-esteem of the intellectuals.

And yet I have my doubts. The more the politicians enter the world of serious books, I fear, the greater the risk of deranging the traditional and necessary balance between intellectual and practitioner.

The serious book world puts a premium on challenge, criticism, innovation, protest; the effective political world on prudence, gradualism, continuity, incremental improvement. The political world follows standards set in the competitive and popularly sensitive political arena. The bookish world finds its standards in the classical tradition, human values and in dissent itself. Over the long run, progress turns in large part on the tension between the two worlds. The intellectual serves as the cutting edge of ideology, criticism, experimentation. Innovative politicians pick up fresh ideas from the academic community, and these ideas then are captured successively by reform groups, third parties, influential elements within the major parties.

Ultimately the fresh idea becomes the property of both parties, adorns the Establishment and passes out of the arena of conflict. During this whole process politicians attack intellectuals as hopelessly impractical, Utopian, visionary. Intellectuals denounce the "pols"—with even more asperity and intolerance—as opportunists, muddlers, careerists. Sometimes the conflict becomes unseemly, as when a Massachusetts politician cites Harvard University as the "Kremlin on the Charles." But this is the price we pay for the tense and productive equilibrium between the two types.

Has not this balance been upset in recent years? The rhetoric of John Kennedy and of Lyndon Johnson seems to have been lifted right out of the pages of the radical weeklies. Their actions may fall short of their words, but even so, the programs advanced by the Kennedy-Johnson Administrations have outstripped the programs of the liberal intellectuals. Senator Clark in his criticism of Congress, Edward Brooke in his criticism of the G.O.P., Senator Pell in his transportation proposals have gone further than many of the academic writers in these fields.

We've had the strange spectacle of Americans for Democratic Action rejecting a major constitutional change—four-year terms for Representatives—advocated by President Johnson and other politicians. The subsidies given the arts and humanities—and now even the social sciences—would have been unimaginable a decade or so ago. The derangement of the relations of politician and intellectual helps explain, I think, both the querulousness of the bitter personal attacks on the President by some intellectuals, and the tendency of some radicals to abandon the fight within the traditional political arena—a fight they were helping to win—and to turn to separatist movements such as black power. Government seems to have absorbed, morselized and suffocated traditional dissent. The Presidency in particular, as I have contended in "Presidential Government," has become so all-embracing as to draw even dissenting intellectuals into its vortex.

The imbalance cannot go too far, for each side is ultimately controlled by its constituencies—the politician by the voters and the intellectual book writers by the reviewers, scholars, critics and academic disciplinarians who cast their own ballots in articles, reviews and cocktail parties. But for a time, at least, the pace of modern government, under the inspiration of men like Roosevelt, Adlai Stevenson and Kennedy, has outstripped that of the intellectuals. The Thorstein Veblens, Charles Beards, John Deweys and Frank Lloyd Wrights rarely, if ever, held elected or even appointed posts. Yet they set the intellectual—and ultimately the political—perimeters within which we protest and preach and legislate and vote today. The politician who writes a book in these times is usually moving to the drumbeat of some intellectual who wrote a generation or so before.

Yes, politicians should write books. They should also read them, challenge them, cherish them, and protect them from the book censors and book burners. But we should not in the long run confuse the roles of the dedicated vote seeker and of the serious book writer. The former must be part of this world, managing it, patching it up here and there, defending it. The latter must stand back from the world, see it whole, dream of re-making it. The intellectuals need not act like men of action as long as they can think like men of thought.

HOWARD ZINN
Historian as Citizen

The lesson of personal engagement was taught Howard Zinn during his years as chairman of the history department at Spelman College in Atlanta, Georgia, and he built upon that lesson in his book "The Southern Mystique." The same theme underlies his essay "Historian as Citizen." He is now Professor of Government at Boston University.

WHEN some historians march with Negroes in the South, and others demonstrate against Presidential foreign policy, one is led to wonder if we are witnessing a slow change in role for the historian. Traditionally, he is a passive observer, one who looks for sequential patterns in the past as a guide to the future, or else describes historical events as unique and disorderly—but without participating himself in attempts to change the pattern or tidy the disorder.

In a world hungry for solutions, we ought to welcome the emergence of the historian—if this is really what we are seeing—as an activist-scholar, who thrusts himself and his works into the crazy mechanism of history, on behalf of values in which he deeply believes. This makes of him more than a scholar; it makes him a citizen in the ancient Athenian sense of the word.

The historian is one man among men, and how free is any man to change the world in which he lives? The world's great thinkers have been quite aware of the paradox of man as both created and creative, and acted accordingly. But thinking has become professionalized and "disciplined" in modern times, with a crushing effect on the propensity to act.

For historians, there is an additional trap: The more we work on the data of the past, the weightier the past seems. Events that have already taken place develop the look of having been *necessary*; indeed they were, but only at the instant they occurred, when further interference was impossible. This necessariness of the past tends to infect our thinking about the future, weighing down our disposition to act.

Man is wounded by his history, and we then assume he must be transfixed by it.

History can work another way, however. If the present seems an irrevocable fact of nature, the past is most usable as a way of suggesting possibilities we would never otherwise consider; it can both warn and inspire. By probing the past we can counter myths which affect the way we act today. We can see that it is possible for an entire nation to be brainwashed; for an "advanced, educated" people to commit genocide; for a "progressive, democratic" nation to maintain slavery; for apparently powerless subordinates to defeat their rulers; for economic planning to be unaccompanied by restrictions on freedom; for oppressed to turn into oppressors; for "socialism" to be tyrannical; for a whole people to be led to war like sheep; for men to make incredible sacrifices on behalf of a cause.

Yet the historical experience of mankind does have limits; while it suggests some of the things that are possible, it has not at all exhausted the possibilities. Bounded in our imaginations, tyrannized by the past, we do not realize there is a universe of tricks still to be played. The past, in other words, suggests what can be, not what must be.

This is not at all to say that we are completely free at any moment in time. There is a remorselessly factual world which assails us at every turn, every decision. But because this world is *here* it exerts a disproportionate influence on our actions. The only way to compensate for this is to behave *as if* we are freer than we think. We can never—because the present is harsh and the future is shadow—weigh accurately how free we are, what our possibilities are at any moment. With such uncertainty, and recognizing the tendency toward overestimating the present, there is good reason for acting on the supposition of freedom.

Erik Erikson speaks in "Insight and Responsibility" about psychologists surprised by the strength of people, which seems to come, he says, from "unexpected encounters . . . and from opportunities beyond our theoretical anticipations."

Acting *as if* is a way of resolving the paradox of determinism and freedom, a way of overcoming the tension between past and future. It is risky to act as if we are free, but (unless one is content with things as they are) it is just as risky to act as if we are bound, and there is even less chance of reward. The leaps that man has made in social evolution came from those who acted as *if*; the four Negro youngsters in Greensboro who in 1960 walked into Woolworth's acted as if they would be served; Garrison and Phillips, against all apparent common sense, acted as if they would arouse a cold nation against slavery; England in 1940 acted as if it could repel a German invasion; Castro and his tiny group in the hills behaved as if they could take over Cuba.

Nietzsche in "The Use and Abuse of History" attacked the bullying nature of history and the sterility of academic historiography. His opening words were quoted from Goethe: "I hate everything that merely instructs me without increasing or directly quickening my activity." He called the formal detached-from-life history of his time "a costly and superfluous luxury of the understanding" while people "are still in want of the necessaries of life."

Later in this same essay, Nietzsche calls for man to free himself from the past. "People think nothing but this troublesome reality of ours is possible." And at another point he speaks of the "historically educated fanatic of the world-process" who "has nothing to do but to live on as he has lived, love what he has loved, hate what he has hated, and read the newspapers he has always read. The only sin is for him to live otherwise than he has lived."

This is the Existentialist call for Freedom, for Action, for the exercise of Responsibility by man. Too often these days the Existentialists are accused of a blind refusal to recognize the limits set by the world around them. Sartre, trying to reconcile Existentialism and Marxism, is attempting the impossible, critics have said. But Sartre does not fail to see the armies, the prisons, the blind judges, the deaf rulers, the passive masses. He talks the language of total Freedom because he knows that acting *as if* we are free is the only way to break the bind.

To see our responsibility to present and future, is a radically different approach to history, for the traditional concern of academic history, from the start of investigation to the finish, is with the past, with only a few words muttered from time to time to indicate that all this digging in the archives "will help to understand the present." This encirclement of the historian by the past has an ironic effect in the making of moral judgments.

The usual division among historians is between those who declare, as Herbert Butterfield does in "History and Human Relations," that the historian must avoid moral judgments, and those, like Geoffrey Barraclough in "History in a Changing World," who deplore the loss of moral absolutes in a wave of "historicism" and "relativism." What is ironic is the fact that when historians do make moral judgments they are *about the past,* and in a way that may actually weaken moral responsibility in the present.

Moral indignation over Nazism illustrates the point. When such judgment becomes focused on an individual, it buries itself with that person and sticks to no one else. It follows that Germans who obeyed orders during the war may now weep at a showing of "The Diary of Anne Frank," blaming the whole thing on Adolf Hitler. (How often these days in Germany does one hear "if not for Adolf Hitler . . ."?) It is this *ad hominem* assignment of responsibility, this searching the wrong place for blame with a kind of moral stigmatism, which Hannah Arendt tried to call attention to in her dissection of the Eichmann case.

But is it any better to widen responsibility from the individual to the group? Suppose we blame "the Nazis." Now that the Nazi party is disbanded, now that anti-Semitism is once again diffuse, now that militarism is the property of the "democratic" Government of West Germany as well as the "socialist" Government of East Germany, doesn't that kind of specific attribution of blame merely deflect attention from the problems of today? If we widen it so as to include Germans and Germany, what effect does this have except to infinitesimally decrease the sale of Volkswagens, and to permit every other nation in the world but Germany to commit mayhem in a softer glow?

What we normally do then, in making moral judgments, is assign responsibility to a group which in some specific historic instance was guilty, instead of selecting the elements of wrong, out of time and place (except for dramatic effect), so that they can be applicable to everyone including ourselves. (Is this not why Brecht, Kafka, Orwell are so powerful?)

It is racism, nationalism, militarism (among other elements) which we find reprehensible in Nazism. To put it that way is alarming, because those elements are discoverable not just in the past, but now, and not just in Germany, but in all the great powers, including the United States.

I am suggesting that blame in history be based on the future and not the past. It is an old and useless game among historians to decide whether Caesar was good or bad, Napoleon progressive or reactionary, Roosevelt a reformer or a revolutionist. True, certain of these questions are pertinent to present concerns; for instance, was Socrates right in submitting to Athens? But in a recounting of past crimes, the proper question to ask is not "Who was guilty then?" unless it leads directly to: "What is our responsibility now?"

Erikson, in a section of his "Insight and Responsibility" entitled "Psychological Reality and Historical Actuality," speaks of Freud's concern because his patient Dora had confronted her family with some of their misdeeds. "Freud considered this forced confrontation an act of revenge not compatible with the kind of insight which he had tried to convey to the patient. If she now knew that those events had caused her to fall ill, it was her responsibility to gain health, not revenge, from her insight." What makes this story even more interesting is that there is a suggestion that Freud may himself have been guilty of the same thing, by being annoyed with what his patient had done, and discontinuing her treatment.

It is this irony in moral judgment which explains why we are surprised when someone like George Kennan opposes a "moralistic" approach to other countries. This approach, he says—correctly—looks backward rather than forward. It leads to fixed enmities and fixed friendships, both based on past conditions; it prohibits a flexibility in the future.

In politics, the practice is common to all sides. When the Soviet Union defines imperialism as a characteristic of capitalist nations, it is limiting the ability of its people to criticize undue influence exerted over another country by a socialist nation. When it defines corruption as a manifestation of "bourgeois" culture, it makes it more difficult to deal with such a phenomenon in its own society. When the United States defines the Soviet sphere as "totalitarian" and the West as "free," it becomes difficult for Americans to see totalitarian elements in our society, and liberal elements in Soviet society. Moralizing in this way, we can condemn the Russians in Hungary and absolve ourselves in Vietnam.

To *define* an evil in terms of a specific group when such an evil is not peculiar to that group but possible anywhere is to remove responsibility from ourselves. It is what we have always done in criminal law, which is based on revenge for past acts, rather than a desire to make constructive social changes. (Capital punishment notably, but also all imprisonment, illustrates this.) It is often said that the French are always prepared for the previous war. In the modern world, we are always ready to identify those responsible for the previous act of evil.

Both history and art should instruct us. The crucial thing is to reveal the relationship between evil and ourselves. This makes it enormously useful to show (as Herbert Butterfield suggests) how Hitler could emerge out of a boy playing in the field. Or to show (as in "Lord of the Flies") how innocent children can become monsters, or (as in Bergman's film "The Virgin Spring") how a loving father can become a vengeful murderer or (as in "Who's Afraid of Virginia Woolf?") how an "ordinary" man and wife can becomes vultures.

But to survey the atrocities in world history and to conclude (as the defense lawyer did in the film "Judgment at Nuremberg") that "we are all guilty" leads us nowhere when it neglects to identify the elements of failure so that we can recognize them in the future. On the other hand, to end by punishing the specific persons who were indeed guilty is to leave us all free to act, unnoticed, in the same way. For when our day of judgment comes, it will be, like all the others, one disaster late.

If a work like "The Deputy" succeeds in having people ask, not Why did the Pope remain silent? but, Why do people everywhere, at all times, and *now*, remain silent? then the play itself has broken the silence of the stage. And those of us who are deputies of that Muse, History, now need to break ours.

III
The
Writing
Experience

ANTHONY BURGESS
The Seventeenth Novel

A seventeenth novel might seem like something of an achievement to most men, but in the Anthony Burgess catalogue it is just one more entry, an entry surrounded not only by other novels but by critical works as well ("Re Joyce," "A Shorter Finnegans Wake"). Burgess has a way with words and "language-learning," he says, is one of his recreations. He is also a composer and a pianist.

THIS English summer (1966) has been cloudy, cold, thundery, and it has matched the clinical bulletins about the British economic situation. The other night, after a painful session at the dentist's, I had a painful session watching Harold Wilson on television. We have been over-spending; we must retrench; we must restore confidence in sterling. One of my few motives for trying to earn more money must be the increase in the price of Scotch. I can think of no other motive. Foreign holidays are, thanks to currency restrictions, out, and I have no strong desire to holiday in Britain; the more I earn, the closer I approach that precipice that tumbles me into paying 19 shillings out of every pound in surtax. Two years ago the Labor Government promised us hard times; it seems to have been faithful to that promise.

It is now midnight. This morning I climbed to my study to push on with a comic novel I am trying to write. It is a great wonder to the laity that comedians are able to go on with their routines while suffering bereavement, an abscess or an economic recession. It is also a great wonder to me. Writing a comic novel can be approached with the same weariness and pain as writing a tragedy, and the weariness and pain will, with a professional, never show.

Yet there is something showing in my work that I am far from happy about, and perhaps it is only the general ambience of depression that makes me willing to speak of it. I mean evidence of dissatisfaction with the forms and tropes and vocabulary and rhythms that orthodox English provides. I am now working on my 17th novel, and I doubt if I can go on much longer in the same modes—straight narrative, naturalistic dialogue, bits of interior monologue, atmospheric *récit*. I feel, as every writer must feel on his 17th novel, that I am in danger of repeating myself.

The hero of this novel is a middle-aged poet who is working as a bartender in an American-owned London hotel. The sixth line of the first chapter describes him washing glasses. I have written: "He burnished an indelible veronica of lipstick." What I mean is that he polished a red smear that, like the imprint of Christ's bleeding face on the towel of St. Veronica (preserved to this day in Rome), seemed to be set there in perpetuity. There is no intention of facetious blasphemy: it is necessary to establish certain religious undertones as soon as possible, since these are relevant to the character and preoccupations of my poet.

Setting down the image, I was well enough pleased. It seemed sufficiently apt and original. And then came the doubt: Had I used it before? I searched through my published books—a very wearisome job— and found that I hadn't, but with no real sensation of relief. I had not used it before but, I thought, I might use it again.

The more fiction one writes, the more one sees a certain pattern of locales and situations. In my books, people drink in bars or pubs, and these are becoming more alike; worse, the drinkers are always behaving in the same way; worse still, I am more and more tempted to draw on the same kind of language for describing pub, people and behavior. Two men will fight, and the fights are becoming more like each other. Faced with the need to describe a city street, I can find nothing to say about it that I have not previously, and more freshly, said.

I have created so many characters, major and minor, that I am in danger of completing the roster and having to go back to the beginning again. There is a limited number of ways in which a woman can be pretty and a man ugly, and an even more limited number of modes for the conveying of these qualities. One's readers may not notice, since they have mostly, thank heavens, rather poor memories, but one notices oneself and one does not like to cheat. A book may bore its reader, but it ought not to bore its author. One's 17th attempt at an orthodox piece of fiction ought to carry the same tremulous glamor as one's first.

It is because of this fear of self-repetition and, more than that, this dissatisfaction with the limitations of ordinary language that I begin to look with a sort of wistfulness at the fictional experimentalists. And I have become convinced that none of these undertakes a new approach to fiction to bring new enlightenment to his readers or to carve, with Flaubertian martyr's courage, new paths for other writers. The writer experiments because he is bored. He is like God, who, suffering with Alberto Moravia's hero from *la noia*, has to create a new cosmos to become less *annoiato*.

Nabokov's "Pale Fire" is a little tedious to read, but it must have been very exciting to write. Some of the novels of the French *nouvelle vague* are, with their stasis, their concentration on things rather than people, more than a little tedious, but one can see that they had to be written to save their authors from the *ennui* of treading the worn path again. William Burroughs's cut-out and fold-in techniques, designed to give a "new look" to language, perhaps give this new look only to their author. But their author must be allowed to protect himself from boredom.

It is the need to make language genuinely new, rather than merely look new, that drives a James Joyce to create the pun-Eurish of a "Finnegans Wake." One can understand Joyce's position very well. In "Ulysses" he had used up the resources of orthodox language, not only in the fabrication of portmanteau-words, pastiche, mimicry and mockery, but also in the exact notation of action and speech. What could his next book be except a new limitation or a tame repetition unless he broke language up and recast it? The author is told to think of his readers, but he must also think of himself.

Ideally, a novelist should be not just a polyglot but a panglot. Let him write his first novel in English, exploiting all the resources of the language; then let him shake French by the scruff of the neck and go on to demotic Greek. One can only be truly creative if one creates not merely a subject but the medium in which that subject moves.

The most that the average novelist or poet can do is to fashion an idiom; sometimes this does not seem to go far enough. Neither Schönberg nor Picasso was content with an idiom; it had to be a new language or nothing.

I cannot create a new language, though I have found, by accident and with a shock, that, in my novel "A Clockwork Orange," I made a transitory dialect for real as well as fictional teen-agers. But I feel that I must, to counter my own weariness, do something new. The new fictional images that present themselves to me in the still summer watches, with the wind temporarily quiet, are fantastic. Will they work?

Before The Times of London changed, for the worse, its format, I dreamed of a novel in which the hero's life was presented in strict Times form, from opening advertisements to closing crossword. I am dreaming, more wakefully, of a novel presented as a mock-biography, complete with photographs and index. I have thought of telling one story in the text and a counterpoint story in footnotes. In delirium it occurred to me that I might recast one novel already half-written in the form of a small encyclopedia, so that the reader, armed with all the relevant information, might work out the plot for himself.

These things require a courage which perhaps very few professional novelists, faced with the need to earn a living, can really possess. A married woman can find this courage more easily than a married man. Sterne began "Tristram Shandy" from the fortress of a clerical living. Joyce at least had a patroness.

And yet, when one looks at some of the experimental novels that stem from Sterne or from Nathalie Sarraute, one is struck by the salutary realization that the new shapes are not really enough. Sterne had Uncle Toby and Mr. Shandy; Nabokov has Kinbote; Joyce had both Bloom and Earwicker. There are certain things that the novel cannot do without, and the greatest of these is character. Some of our young British experimentalists grumble because of lack of appreciation, but they have no real cause to grumble. They have all the Shandeian tricks off pat, but they have none of the Shandeian grotesques.

The terrible daring of "Ulysses" comes off because Bloom and Dedalus are big enough to survive their torturing. Tell a young experimentalist to try something on the lines of the lying-in hospital scene in "Ulysses," and he will produce a passable pastiche history of English literature, but he will not have the human tension of Bloom's first true meeting with Stephen. A novel should not be an evening of conjuring tricks; it should be a genuine play.

What I have said is obvious enough. The fact remains that, at least for myself, to make novel-writing a genuine intellectual stimulus I must impose on myself certain formal stringencies. The big secret perhaps will be the rendering of these so unobtrusive that the reader will think he is reading something very orthodox. The listener to Alban Berg's opera, "Wozzeck," may not be aware that one act is in the form of a symphony and another in the form of a suite, but that does not invalidate Berg's sense of the need for such a subtle imposition. I have myself, perhaps overcautiously, followed Berg in certain novels, making one paragraph a Petrarchan sonnet set as prose, turning a whole opening section into a slavish simulacrum of Wagner's "Das Rheingold" (nobody noticed; in any case, the novel—for a quite different reason—got itself banned), identifying, in "Nothing Like the Sun," the drunken narrator with the dying subject of his narration.

The reader may draw his own conclusions, and they will probably not be favorable. One conclusion may be that I should give up writing novels, but another may be that the traditional novel-form is no longer very satisfying to the novelist.

Having said all this, I feel a little better now. The night air is warmer, and tomorrow brings the task of pushing on with my comic novel. What I have already written may cease to seem pedestrian and become fresh, incisive, original; the new sheet in the typewriter may fill itself with all sorts of daring felicities which, pleasing the reader, shall not have bored the author. In any case, one must get on with the work one thinks one does best. The fact that one can have doubts about it may be a good sign, since doubt, as we know, is an intermission of faith. Only the very bad writer is always absolutely sure of the value of what he is doing.

ALEC WAUGH
The Novelist as Hero

In "My Brother Evelyn and Other Portraits" Alec Waugh says of himself that "the things that have made my life a continuing adventure—

*sport and gallantry, soldiering and travel—have been side shows in the
last analysis. Though my achievement is so minute, I have always put
writing first. I have been most alive seated at a table in a hotel bedroom
facing a solitary day.*" He has been writing for more than fifty years:
novels, short stories, essays, books of travel, memoirs, and most recently
"My Brother Evelyn."

THE first novelist to become a friend of mine—Ralph Straus, who
was for many years the chief reviewer of novels on The London Sunday
Times—gave me this advice, "Never make a novelist the hero of a
novel."

It might seem at a first glance that no species of mankind was
better fitted for this role. The novelist is unfettered by routine. He is free
to travel. He carries his office with him. The story can shift from one
continent to another, one climate to another. The cast of characters
can be changed every chapter. The hero is admirably equipped to conduct a series of romances. H. G. Wells has said that a successful amorist
has only two requirements—"leisure and convenient premises"; and
who, on that point, could speak with more authority than H.G.? The
novelist is, moreover, subject to swift and complete changes of fortune.
He can hit the jackpot of films and book clubs and become rich overnight. He can invest his savings in a play and lose them in a week.
Most men envy the novelist his freedom, and the novelist himself,
though he might not encourage his son to follow in his footsteps,
would not exchange his lot with any man's.

Yet Straus was adamant in his warning. "The hero of a novel," he
insisted, "must be positive. He must stand for something. He must
fight for something. You will never convince the reader of the reality
of a novelist's working problems. He will seem a playboy. That is
fatal."

The trouble is that the novelist's problems are essentially undra-
matic. They are staged in his own mind. You can describe him seated
at his desk, with the pile of manuscript rising at his side, but you cannot persuade the reader that he is really working, in the way that you
can when you describe a rescue party digging out the survivors of a
landslide. The "ardors and agonies" of composition cannot be made
exciting as can the running of a race or the tracking down of an arch-
spy. His meetings with publishers, editors and agents are social occasions. There is no rival to be elbowed out of office, no managing director

to be appeased, no recalcitrant shareholder to be cajoled. It all seems very placid and harmonious.

Yet, in fact, the novelist's anxieties are constant and acute. He is presented with a three-pronged problem. He has to acquire the material for his novels. He has to attain the peace of mind in which to write them; and he has to fit into the pattern created by these two demands, the human beings with whom he is personally involved.

There are times when plots come to him so fast that he fears that his pen will never have time to "glean his teeming brain." There are others when he stares at a blank sheet of paper dolefully. He is written out. He has run dry. He must renew himself. What is the remedy? A two months' trip to the Far East will give him the material for six short stories. He should sell five of them to the "glossies." He should gross £8,000. The trip should not cost him £2,000. A profit of £6,000 will give him the leisure and peace of mind to settle down to that major novel that the pressure of the day-to-day demands of livelihood have forced him to put aside. He is investing in himself. He sets out with the high hopes.

But the trip does not take two months, it takes three. A friend in Bangkok says, "Why miss India, now that you've come so far? In point of fact, why not go right on round the world while you're about it? Pan-Am will issue a new ticket. It won't cost so much more." Nor does it, but the incidental expenses do. And he doesn't get six short-story plots but four, and only one of them makes the "glossies." So that by the time he has settled the overhead expenses that have accrued during his absence, he is exactly where he was before he started. His decks are still uncleared.

If he is to settle down to that major novel, he must ask his publisher for an advance. He gets his advance, but there is a string attached. The novel must be delivered by a certain date. He shrugs. If he really concentrates, he can get it done in nine months instead of the year that he has planned. It is simply a question of harder work. But time moves quickly. He is in the end tempted to hurry those last chapters and the novel suffers.

Or it may be that he suspects that his characters move in too narrow a groove professionally. They are all connected with the arts, with publishing, advertising, radio, the theater. His cast ought to include lawyers, politicians, men of business. How can he get to know them? How can he lengthen the radius of his interests? He remembers having had a cozy gossip in the club car of a train with a New England Senator. Why not invite that Senator to dinner? He would come if he were told that he was going to meet an important playwright. The playwright would come to meet a Senator. The plan succeeds. The invitation to the Senator rates an invitation in return. He repeats the experiment with a state Governor whom he meets through that invitation. He enlarges his acquaintance, but at a cost that mounts with geometrical progression.

Debt is one of the chief occupational hazards of the novelist, yet it is not to a vicious but a virtuous circle that he is bound. This avidity for fresh experience is the core of his vocation. It is indeed this need to encounter and respond to the multiple aspects of the world about him that makes him a storyteller rather than a historian or biographer.

The novelist has to search for new material. He also has to find the leisure and peace of mind in which to write his stories. A biography or a travel book can be written in the pursuit of a conventional routine. Its author can go to a library every morning in the same way that a stockbroker goes to his office. A novel is altogether different. A novelist has to live with his characters and his story for weeks on end. He must exclude stimulating contacts. He needs isolation, the day-to-day eventlessness of a cabin in the woods of the MacDowell colony or a small hotel bedroom—the equivalent of a monk's cell—in Nice, out of the season.

Most men get married at least once, and when they have no legal ties they tend to be emotionally entangled. As matrimonial timber the novelist is the worst bet on the market, not through a lack of moral fiber, but because the time schedule of his work is as much in conflict with the reasonable requirements of a wife as is that of an actress with a Wall Street husband's. A woman likes a man out of the house first thing after breakfast if not before. His return in the evening is her zero hour. She plans for it, cooks for it, dresses for it. For her, as for him, it is the reward and recompense for nine hours' work. That cold, that very dry martini knits up the day's ravell'd sleave. There is no such zero hour for the wife whose husband works down the hallway and demands that the house be quiet. If, on the other hand, he seeks a solitary retreat she is very lonely.

Nor does she get any consolation out of his trips east of Suez. He prefers to go alone: not because he hankers for opium dens and bagnios, but because the Orient is a man's world and he gets his material listening to men who would not be outspoken in the presence of a respectable female, and in clubs and bars where women are not allowed. How relieved I was when my daughter announced her intention of marrying a rational male who played at cricket and worked at Lloyd's!

The novelist, I repeat, is presented with a three-pronged problem. It is a problem to which I have myself found no solution. I doubt if one exists. Either the work or the home life suffers. Usually both do, through an attempt at compromise. It is an acute and constant problem, but it does not produce the dramatic situation out of which a novel can be built. My old friend gave me very sound advice.

V. S. PRITCHETT
Writing an Autobiography

Victor Pritchett's autobiography, "A Cab at the Door," ends with his leaving England as a young man to make his way in France. He's been fascinated with foreign places ever since, and in the midst of a busy life as critic, novelist and teacher, he has found time to be a world traveler and to write something about what he has seen. Three of his recent books are concerned with cities: "London Perceived," "New York Proclaimed," "Dublin: A Portrait."

ON THE face of it, to write one's autobiography is the easiest and most grateful task in the world. No search for anti-hero or hero: he is you. No search for material, it is all there: your own life. No imagination is necessary; the question of structure—one of the most difficult problems in writing—is automatically solved by sticking to chronology, year after year. The first person singular seems to be the perfect camera-eye. Unless you suffer from a neurotic block, your childhood and early youth have long ago crystallized. This is the most vivid and certain part of your life.

So you set out. You write 20 pages and suddenly you stop. Why is it you are bewildered? Why do you have the sensation of being in a rowing boat in the middle of the ocean and having lost your oars? Who is this "I," you wonder, which of my many selves is writing? And what kind of autobiography did you mean to write? What is its theme? There is nothing to do but start again.

Let us suppose you are a famous statesman or general, a great bull
fighter, opera singer, a surgeon or sportsman, or that you have been very
close to the famous, a valet of the eminent. You have made your career;
you have had adventures; you have known crowds of people. You will
have kept notes, letters and diaries all your life. The public will expect
that you reveal what you know and will hang upon your indiscretion.
You will be writing your reminiscences or a memoir; you will not in the
strict sense be writing your autobiography at all. Your truth will be a
contribution to social history or anecdotage. Or suppose you have been
the witness of a great event and put that down: the event and not yourself is the subject. You will be only a collection of enviable glimpses.
What if you are a natural diarist—say, a Pepys or an Amiel—and inevitably reveal yourself? Does that make you an autobiographer? Rarely.

The born diarists are the snails of life: they are secretive and en-
closed in their shells, and their whispering contributes either to history
or—as in Amiel's case—to a case history. The pure autobiographer is
concerned with shaping a past from the standpoint of a present that
may be totally unlike it. That is why you tore up those 20 pages and
paused to consider who your first-person singular is and what "truth"
you intend to state.

For there is no absolute truth. You will be unable to tell all or you
will be incapable of it. Or let us hope that you are, for one definition
of a bore is that he is a man who tells you everything. The writer who
has—and quotes—his diaries or preserved letters is in great danger
here: this has been the bane of Victorian autobiography and is a continuing danger in America where keeping records has been enjoined
almost as a historical obligation. The Boston memoir is the classic example.

Your difficulties with truth-telling arise from the fossilization of
memory. Perhaps hypnosis could dissolve a trauma that has become
sacred; but I cannot see what can be done about the fact that it is easier
to remember things that happened 40 years ago than those that occurred in the last 10. Our lives are really a collection of adroit generalizations which enable us to push on from the present minute. The longer
one lives, the less certain one is of who one is. So many people and
events have swarmed in that the sense of a self—Gray's "pleasing anxious being"—who lives an hour, a day at a time and not in collections
of years, is dispersed and even vulgarized. One begins to think there was
no "I" after all.

And, in fact, the "I" is a relatively new invention. To start with,

it is exclusively European in origin. Asia and Africa have no autobiographers. About seven years ago I read an excellent if severe book
called "Design and Truth in Autobiography" by Roy Pascal, who
pointed this out and added that in Europe there are no autobiographies
in the classical period.

The genre can be said to have started with St. Augustine, but centuries passed before a Cellini, a Geronimo Cardano, a Saint Theresa
appeared in the Renaissance. Unlike ourselves these writers are not
recreating a past from the standpoint of the present; Cellini casting his
statue, Saint Theresa in founding her covent, are proclaiming new
selves in a new world and are conscious of themselves in the act. They
differ from us in being very little conscious of their society as an overwhelming influence.

It is not until we reach the 18th and early 19th centuries that the
confidence a man has in his society and his belief in the pleasure and
interest of his private tastes and habits give him an avid concern with
himself in relation to it. It is the age of the great autobiographers—of
Rousseau, Gibbon, Franklin, Goethe and Casanova. Later, the stren-
uous effort towards self-realization among the new middle class, urged
on also by the idea of the Romantic movement, gives us Harriet Mar-
tineau, John Stuart Mill, John Ruskin, even Henry Adams, and still
later Wells and Beatrice Webb. Leonard Woolf's recent volumes are
written as a valediction to a civilization determined on suicide.

In our own time, Mr. Pascal says, a writer like Koestler shows the
self passing through historical calamity and asking why it was so chosen.
One offers oneself as a sample of the historical process in one's own
life time. And here, I wonder, if the present vogue of autobiography has
not something dubious about it. Doesn't calamity really make nonsense
of the distinctive individual; doesn't its stamp make us all alike?

What reason have I to believe that I have more than the common
interest? I may be only a type. Am I dramatizing myself because I am
lonely? The "I" in Cellini or Goethe, Newman and Henry James is a
pronoun of pride; isn't it a badge of wistful desperation for us, the only
thing left so that it has to "do" for everything we have lost? Fortunately
for the autobiographer the social process still goes on even if it runs
down, and the individual still asserts himself, but frantically now in the
midst of it.

I have myself written an autobiography and can speak of the practical difficulties. I was forced to reject the official sounding family

memoir. Unlike Bertrand Russell, I am not a great man or a public figure. I cannot draw on distinguished, public-spirited ancestors or famous family connections. I have visited Society, but, like most writers, only for a minute or two. That kind of life is no good to us. I have belonged to no celebrated set, and although I have met many celebrated people (for, as they say of London life, everyone knows everybody), I have not been very intimate with them. My most intimate meeting, I think, was with Georges Carpentier, the French boxer, who accidentally stepped back and trod hard on my toe on the Channel boat when I was off to France in my twenties. He walked away without saying a word.

As for my literary reminiscences or my reflections on literature in the past 45 years, they must wait. I am not fond of shop talk. But, being self-centered I could not resist writing about the unlikely background that made a writer of me. I confined myself to my prewriting years. At 21 they ended; after that, being a writer, I found myself being met by what I had already written.

After 21, unless one is a note-taker, a letter keeper or diarist—which I have rarely been—memory blurs, years and phases telescope. What about my inner life? I have not so far shown any talent for the confessional. That requires a certain temperament. In one sense all writing is a confession. But after 21, whether he is confessional or not, the autobiographer who writes intimately is in the difficulty that many people who were important to him are still alive. As a storyteller I have no consideration for people; nor should I have. But I cannot involve the living in my "truth" (though I have to admit that the discarded mistresses of great artists have not hesitated here).

The odd thing is that sitters will often tolerate a portrait done "warts and all" by a painter, but do not care for the same thing in print. They ring up their lawyers at once; and even praise offends, for one has not praised them for what they would like to be praised. From the autobiographer's point of view, people live far too long. Society asks too much of the "truthful" autobiographer when it obliges him to live on to his nineties before he can speak. By that time, as Somerset Maugham's nonagenarian revelations showed, one is apt to be vinegarish.

I can think of no vainglorious autobiography since Cellini, unless Frank Harris counts. There have been dedicated believers in imaginative lying like Ford Madox Ford. Goethe spoke of his "poetry" but also of his "truth." There have been exploiters of self-accusation like Rousseau. The three main difficulties of autobiography are one's self-pity, one's shames and one's self-justifications. It is also difficult to write exactly about chastity in a period like the present when it is regarded as ridiculous. Only the Turgenevs can write about early love; only the Pushkins can tell with a poet's brutality of how and why it ends. To feel is to tire. So much of love is love of love.

It is also hard to record one's early opinions truthfully: one has forgotten their force. Self-pity is fairly easy to deal with now for we have been toughened. As for shame, one must not wallow. The youth you are ashamed of was, among other things, an engaging fellow; if he was a prig and pompous ass most of his contemporaries were pompous asses and prigs too. It was part of the general charm. The French who have an extreme regard for the solemnities of adolescence miss this romantic Anglo-Saxon worry. The real problem is how to avoid subtle and secretive self-justification, especially when one is recording discarded emotions or beliefs. Here one's standpoint of a present totally unlike the past is liable to bully or skillfully deceive.

Roy Pascal points out that Tolstoy's "A Confession" like other confessions of religious experience, has the fault of devaluing earlier experience, so that the unity of personality is broken. The sinner and the reformed sinner are, in fact, inseparable, and it is hard to admit this. We usually cover up by one or two eloquent but hollow passages. Schweitzer makes his development too logical. Henry Adams was attached to democratic ideas for longer than he admits in the "Education." We are so anxious to show that our blatant errors did not last a long time.

This common dilemma would vanish if we saw that it is normal for many of us to hold one belief or emotion and its opposite at the same time. And here it is hard to admit that one was swayed by snobbery, self-interest or the influence of persons now despised. It is hard not to convey that only the highest considerations really weighed with one. The phlegm and coolness of a Gibbon with his "I sighed as a lover but obeyed as a son" is beyond most of us. And it is dangerous even to be too good at candor; it may be nothing but vanity which was Valéry's criticism of Gide (Again I take this from Mr. Pascal): "To spin words to one's confessor is a serious matter: it will make him forget to absolve you."

For myself I had long ago recognized that, like my story-telling mother, I was an inventive person. I was one of those, I had to see, who invents himself and had not much capacity for self-analysis or introspection except of the dreariest kind. I would be less interested in myself than the story I saw in other people: the most boring part of my autobiography described my early literary efforts. I could only be careless, so that my character, for good or ill, would become plain in what I said about others. I novelized and was, no doubt, inaccurate in this or that, but I told my truth. I never cease to be startled by the fantastic interior of most lives. I inherit a good ear and memory for what is spoken: I swear by the dialogue I have written.

My judgments are another matter. A more earnest, more detailed and documented narrative might have been more accurate. I think it would have been tedious. A tragic interpretation could have been made. Either would have been "true." I would find it impossible to continue the story of my life in the same vein. This suggests to me that where modern autobiography so often fails is that it tends to be written in the same key throughout.

EDWARD DAHLBERG
The Writer's Plight

"I prefer to be a recluse," Edward Dahlberg once said, and a loner he has been throughout much of his long life, a life filled with disagreement and controversy with many of his literary contemporaries. It has been a productive life as well. From "Bottom Dogs," a novel, in 1930, the record includes novels, essays of literary criticism, chapters of autobiography, (most recently, "Because I Was Flesh"). He is at work on a literary autobiography.

ONE of the seven deadly sins of literature is the book review, which writers require. The dilemma of the writer perhaps is irreparable. Often his sacred memorabilia may be decimated by an apprentice. Then there is the hack, and as the name implies, he saws the poet, as though he were the prophet Isaiah, into four quarters.

Often those who cannot write denounce those who can; or if someone happens to care for a collection of verse he is incapable of eulogizing it without proving that he knows far more than the author. How frequently does a criticaster fall upon—and in a scurvy English—a poet who has committed a pair of solecisms, or concern himself with the punctuation he deems improper.

It is not my intention to catalogue those who have sunk wisdom. However, there is "The Journal of Jules Renard," Englished by the poet Louise Bogan and Elizabeth Roget. It is an enchanting diary, and the language is clear and dear to the heart of any devotee of letters. Yet as Ben Jonson remarked, "There be some men are born only to suck out the poison of books." The venom of one assailant flowed copiously through his comments. A steadfast biography about Ford Madox Ford, by Frank MacShane, was clawed by an Olympian dwarf, who took up so much space quoting mixed metaphors and occasional grammatical errors, it was difficult to find out, but not impossible, that the attack was made up of the most dreary and sluttish words. Doubtless there were flaws in this very lengthy book, but what is important is that the biographer excavated a whole period of literary culture with which most people are unfamiliar. Persons who cannot make a good book do not have sufficient understanding to realize it is impossible to compose a faultless one. Men are hopelessly frail, even writers and their executioners, and their errors come from their brains, which are as weak as any other part of the body.

May nobody think I have the vapors and am in the dumps; what I allege to be the plight of the writer is asserted with Jovian serenity. I never put together a shoal of vowels and consonants for mammon or for that other whore, fame. I propose to go along as I always have done, sowing dragon's teeth when necessary, and seeding affections in the souls of my unknown readers if I can. There is no nostrum, and the best I am able to do is to describe what happens, and let those who disagree with me read somebody else's follies.

Literature is politics, and the latter apart from the former is demagogy. Whatever justice there is in a people depends upon the purity of the diction employed by its seers. What then is the position of our literati? Are we a young nation already in its dotage?

Yesterday I looked at a New York newspaper, and at least 10 of its pages were about the motion-picture rabble, radio buffoons, and criminal and ruttish television programs. I glanced at its obituary notices; prominent attention was given to the deceased president of the clothing manufacturers, and to the director of women's shoe stores. There were less than four lines about a respected poet and novelist. I scarce knew this man, but should he have written one albic page he is worth more to America than millions of moneygrubbers who do not care a whit for a great continent now glutted with abscessed cities and deviscerated garage towns.

There is no golden age of letters. In olden Thebes, statues were erected to honor wrestlers and jugglers, but there was none to commemorate Pindar and his odes. That Anaxagoras, the Athenian cosmographer, wished to starve himself to death is rueful evidence that one century is as baneful as another. However, that Pericles importuned the desponding thinker to go on living for the sake of philosophy is a piece of history. When one Greek city-state was at war with a rival, the conquerors were so delighted with their captives, who marched reciting hundreds of lines of Euripides, that they freed them.

Jonathan Swift was the most potent figure in England for about four years, and it was not uncommon for a Prime Minister to hurry to Swift's chambers to seek counsel before delivering an oration or framing a law. When the proprietor of a London bookstore informed Lord Bolingbroke that Robert Burton, who wrote the fantastical "Anatomy of Melancholy," was standing only a few meters from him, the aristocrat came over to Burton and gave him a low bow.

Trash is our god, particularly if it is the latest novelty. One celebrated noddy of our times exclaims, make it new, but I say, make it human!

An Argentinean described the North American as a torpid and materialistic Caliban. How can we produce an Ariel, and at least, in small part, become a utopia of wise readers? Greed must not be our polestar, and though I detest any species of censorship, what are we to do about those who debauch the minds of a commonwealth to acquire riches they cannot even use?

Recently a broadcasting company purchased a large publishing house. I cower as I consider what will occur. The more caitiff factory fiction that is printed, the fewer intelligent readers there will be in the land.

Does not every one owe as much to the Republic as the Colonial poet, Edward Taylor, or Thoreau, Emily Dickinson and Sherwood Anderson gave to it, willing to be paupers or anonymous in order to create the imponderabilia which is the health of the populace?

We live amidst vulgar products and none escapes the evil effects they have upon us. Handle a shoddy volume or stand eight hours rolling rubber tires down a noisome aisle, and who after that is not vacant and coarse? Let a man dote upon twelve sonnets and he will not be a drumbling fool in his amours. How much longer can the American read pulp, fusty paperbacks, and listen to the commercial lullabies, those odious canticles sung to sell cleansing powders and mouth disinfectants, before we have a generation of simians?

In spite of the remarks I make regarding the poverty of savants, let me add that the real mendicants are those who are ignorant. The point is not whether I can afford to be a writer, but can the citizens of the United States be emptied of all the thoughts we have inherited from the Nile, Babylon, the Tigris and Euphrates, and the old England that is now a corpse?

Since my callow youth I was a zealot for erudition. It was not unusual for me to eat one meal a day in order to purchase a second hand copy of Gissing's "By the Ionian Sea," Tolstoy's "What Is Art?" and Goncharov's "Oblomov." A true writer is a learned reader. One wise man will conduct you to another, and oleaginous fiction will increase your indolence. Petrarch confesses: "Augustine bade me search for Seneca 'On Superstition'; Lactantius and many others made me desire the 'Republic'; and Suetonius set me looking for the 'Roman History' of Pliny." Moreover, many will tell you they desire to be makers of poems but few are those who have enough character to resolve that they are going to study Plutarch, Tacitus and Propertius.

A very courteous young man, who lived on the same floor as I, said he had decided to be an author, but I saw he was spending his time and money reading depraved poets and prosers. One day, arguing with him over his lumpish and moldy hours, and finding my admonitions were useless, I demanded he leave straightway, and not return until he became an exuberant bibliomaniac. He gazed at me with unimaginable astonishment; unable to understand why he was not sensible enough to depart, I realized I had requested him to quit his own apartment!

Across from my wizened flat was an older man who pined to be a painter, but who never did anything but gnaw the venetian blinds and bite his own spirit. After a brief acquaintance, I insisted that he work, and he replied he could not because his walls were green. "In heaven's name," I expostulated, "paint them white." After my austere censure, he explained he wanted to write. How perverse is the heart, and who can know it?

Let us go back to those who ravish our best quatrains and *belles lettres*. Every time shoaly doggerel is praised, pensive verse is lost. How

tiresome are the canting chimes of our pedantic journals on Henry
James, Pound, Eliot, Lawrence, Gertrude Stein and Hemingway. One
might imagine there had never been such figures as Theophrastus,
Porphyry, Plotinus, Clement of Alexandria, Gavin Douglas, Samuel
Daniel, Owen Felltham or La Bruyère. Who refers to Dekker's "Plague
Pamphlets"? As one French critic said: "You can't find eight profes-
sional writers who have read Voltaire."

The cult of sameness obtains in New York, Paris, Rome and Copen-
hagen. This creed is as odious as the Marxists' St. Bartholomew's Night
when books that were not in agreement with Stalinist doctrines were
slain. Has anything changed? Nowadays all one has to do is to announce that Pound or Fitzgerald is a basilisk and his next novel is
thrown into limbo.

A San Francisco versifier sent me three epistolary genuflexions, telling me how much he admired "The Sorrows of Priapus"; he asked me
whether I would give him a copy of it, which I did. A number of
months thereafter, several thousand words, shrieking like the mandrake
that has just been plucked, appeared in Poetry magazine divulging
countless gargantuan defects of mine; my *admirer* stated I did not understand life. I met him in the Eighth Street Bookstore one day and
asked him, and without any squalid or hostile feelings, "Tell me, do you
understand life?" to which he replied: "My God, no." Since I regard
work as far more noble than what people claim is uninterrupted everyday ecstasy, I do not care to repress the temptation to cite the Comte
de Villiers de l'Isle Adam: "And as for living, let us have our servants do
that for us."

Years before the death of Sherwood Anderson, it was quite typical
both of his adherents and adversaries to tell him that he was confused.
There are many sophisms about clarity of emotion, for who has lucid
moments except at rare intervals? Only bores have very clear minds, and
how transparent they are. Bile is often mistaken for a panegyric; in
the Goncourt "Journals" there is the following observation: "The
greatest and most malignant conversational wit that Saint-Beuve possesses consists in tearing a man to pieces in the guise of defending
him."

The quandaries are unsurmountable. Myriads of trumpery wares
come off the printing presses every year, and what editor has the
strength even to glance at a title of them? However, since so few books
are worth his attention, why does pecuniary garbage receive the applause while literature remains a clandestine commodity? I do not

like to repeat the worn-out shibboleth, the freedom of the press, but is it a platitude to ask the columnists of sundry periodicals and papers, what do you propose to do with your liberty?

We deeply sympathize with a Russian whose opus is suppressed because he refuses to abide by the Communist party line, but when our own memorable thoughts are not even noticed, what do we do about that? Whether a truth is hidden from readers for ideological reasons or whether a volume that does not give off a drowsy, opiate scent of money is inhumed, are we not censoring culture in the United States?

The most obsidian hazard is the attempt to make a truthful book. What I mean by truth is words put together in a style that will delight the reader and whet his faculties. Long ago I resolved to be, like Crates, a jocose iconoclast, to see whatever my eyes compelled me to regard, without blinking the worst by calling it the best and to accept my hindrances as the fount of any perceptions I may be lucky enough to discover.

SEAN O'FAOLAIN
And Svengali Was a Reviewer

There is nothing insular about Sean O'Faolain. He knows London. He is at home in America (he has a Harvard M. A.). He loves Italy and has written about it. But Ireland, after all, is where his heart is, and it's Ireland that has been the subject of his histories and biographies and the theme of his stories. Several years ago, he published an autobiography, "Vive Moi." The critics liked it. "He is unsurpassed," one said, "as a concise explainer of modern Irish history and personalities." Said another: "In a way it tells what it is that makes an Irish writer."

THE well-known story about Noah Webster and the maidservant alleges that when Mrs. Webster caught him kissing the maid she said, "Noah! I am surprised," to which Noah, deeply pained, replied, "No, dear! I am surprised. You are astonished." It may mildly astonish the non-writer to hear me confess that I always feel equally surprised— caught embracing a muse in public—whenever I come upon a review of one of my books. For while it is true that once a writer publishes his private thoughts he invites public comment on them, it is also true that he never becomes inured to it. And if any author wants to tell me that reviews never give him the slightest jolt, I can only reply that he is either a liar or a very bad writer indeed.

I cannot believe that any real writer ever visualizes his readers when he is writing. He is far too busy straining to hear what his character is saying to him to have time to wonder what his reader will ultimately hear from them both. "You," said Yeats, in effect, to O'Casey when Sean wrote his first propagandist play, "The Silver Tassie," "have no business trying to educate your public. You should be concentrating on letting your characters educate you! It is what Shakespeare did with his characters." Sean was furious. But Willy was right.

Of course, when the writing job is done, the whole situation alters. Art becomes Trade. Our agents and publishers see to that, and every writer is sensibly grateful to them for their kind attentions. Nevertheless, even then, he does not really connect with his readers until he sees his first review. Then he realizes, with a shock, that his privacy is about to be invaded by a lot of eavesdroppers, noseyparkers, listeners-in, readers-in and voyeurs who have nothing else to do but tell him what they have the gall to think about this lovely relationship he has been having with the creatures of his imagination, or his memory, for the last two years or so.

At this point, any self-respecting writer must often wish to high heaven either that he could afford not to publish at all; or, ideally, that he could afford to publish not more than 12 copies of each of his books for his 12 best friends. Even 12 might be too many at my age. James Stephens once said to the ageing A.E., both then at the height of their fame, "I don't believe I now have more than 6 friends left in the world." A.E. sighed into his graying beard and, in his gurgling North-of-Ireland accent, replied, "I have 3."

Do I, then, never read reviews of my books? Every word of them. It is a compulsive obsession. It may also be a form of unconscious masochism, not because my reviewers are often unkind—on the contrary, over some twenty-two books and some thirty years of writing, practically all my reviews have been generous, sympathetic and favorable—but because, with about a dozen delightful exceptions in all that time, the last things most reviewers seem to want to do is to write literary criticism.

Instead of analysis and judgment, I have generally got—and most writers get—news-items, personal, i.e., self-referential, reactions, summaries of plots or other content, entertaining remarks about the life or personality of the author, more or less irrelevant topical, political, social, religious or other commentaries on the subject of the book, with a line or two thrown here and there like confetti (or napalm) at the book itself, and so on.

Consider a recent edition of The London Observer. There they all are, all over again. Compton Mackenzie is engaged in writing a monumental autobiography in eight volumes; the sixth volume gets three inches of summary, ending with confetti in the shape of the finely mixed metaphor: "His teeming yesteryears are still as clear as a bell." I find three novels by the late Marie Corelli given 21 inches of expert summary, entertainingly woven into her life-story, enlightened by one or two shining critical capsules on the lines of: "Over 500 pages of 'Lilith' for only five shillings—one cannot but call it value." (Can't one?) Anita Loos gets a top-of-the-page photograph for her autobiography, "A Girl Like I," and about 18 inches of life-story in which an occasional passing remark (about, for example, her "unamiable philistinism") or the final stinging sentence, "Her book catches the chilly zest of its age," show us what good criticism this reviewer could have written if he had wanted or had been encouraged to do so.

But the snappy headlines for the reviews are the most revealing of all. "A Maidenhead of Aunts," "A Girl Like Miss Loos," "Hedonist" (this for poor, idealistic, highminded Compton Mackenzie!), "All Passionaria Spent" (this for the famous Spanish revolutionary Dolores Ibarruria), "Corelli Rides Again." They are revealing because they are the language of the entertainment business.

Of the dozen reviews of my books that I still gratefully recall, some two still give me the rarest pleasure. In reviewing my first book of stories, away back in 1932, the novelist Charles Morgan suggested that this was another Irish romantic struggling hopefully with the despotism of reality. To a young writer it was at least a suggestive, and at best a valuable basis for conscientious self-argument. I pondered it for years. The second review gave me the wry pleasure of Wit dispensing Justice. It was by Cecil Day Lewis. In approving a novel I had written, he could not help observing (truthfully) that my style, though handsome when it stood up, had an embarrassing way of occasionally "peeling off like wall-paper." From one craftsman to another, a priceless warning! I never took it enough to heart.

I soon found out, however, that the saddest truth about all reviews is that any writer who believes in their words of praise is lost; because if he does believe in the praise, he must also logically believe in the dispraise; the end of which could only be that he would soon start behaving like a captain who sets his course by the votes of his passengers. Not so long ago, for example, I published a book of stories and tales in America and London. Were I to heed the reviewers, I should be as blown about as the sea-faring Sir Francis Chichester.

Glancing over them, I find that one reviewer holds that I am now writing exactly within the limits of my powers; a second that I am writing well below them; a third that I am writing far above them; and a fourth confesses that he does not know what I am doing at all. A fifth (American) welcomes stories by an Irish writer that are about something else than the mist that does be on the Irish bogs and the rich gabble that does be in Dublin pubs; but a sixth (Irish) declares that while it is all very well for American or English writers, like Hemingway or Graham Greene, to write about Spain, Paris, Africa or Mexico, "we expect our native short-story writers to stay in their own backyards"; or if they must venture abroad in the flesh they should at least leave their characters safely behind them.

A seventh (American) decides that while my language is musical my mind is conventional; while an eighth (in The London Times), ignoring my wretched mind, speaks of my "deep, tough but touching sensibility." A ninth (Irish) finds my title story less than credible, but a tenth (Welsh) thinks the same story "a moving comment on change, love and human fellowship, swiftly shaped out."

I must in honesty add that this same man also compared me most unfavorably with Jack London, whom he was, for reasons best known to his editor, reviewing in the same column. He decided that beside "the demonic drive of this untutored, but striving and naturally powerful writer," I stand exposed as a chap with nothing to offer but "elegance, psychological insight, deft humor, pathos and a little fantasy."

It enchants me to imagine the teetotum effect on some sensitive young writer of such contradictory reactions. "O Lord!" he might cry. "From here on, I must always try to be powerful, untutored and demonic, while at the same time carefully cultivating my deep, tough but touching sensibility. I must never again take my characters out of the Irish backyard—though, of course, if I want to be a Hemingway or a Greene, I must at all costs avoid the Irish pubs and the Irish bogs.

Furthermore I must destroy this conventional mind of mine, while swiftly shaping out moving comments on love, change and human fellowship. . . ."

I think it might be salutary for every writer to remember that between Beowulf and Byron, literature in the English language got on very nicely indeed without any reviewers at all. It had to—for the simple reason that reviewing, in our sense of the word, did not and could not exist before about 1840 or so, there being no popular press for it to exist in. After all, Trevelyan records that in 1795, on the very brink of the 19th century, the circulation of The London Times had swollen to 4,800 copies and that of the once influential Morning Post had dwindled to 750.

In such circumstances, literary reputation had to wait modestly on time and the grapevine. There were critics, but these were solid men like Johnson and Francis Jeffrey, taking anything up to 12,000 words for a "review." There were also far fewer books, of course: a main cause of the rise of the capsule review and the swift magisterial judgment of our times (Genius! Marvelous! He takes his place in the first rank!). We live in the days of instant Fame—that brief thing which Pushkin compared to a colored patch on a ragged garment, both soon to perish.

I have just been looking at the modest birth of a great novelist, the first (1811) edition of Jane Austen's "Sense and Sensibility"—three slim volumes in mottled calf, "By a Lady." Such modesty persisted to at least as late as 1871, when we observe an equally modest arrival. It is the date of Thomas Hardy's first, and also anonymous novel, "Desperate Remedies."

But by then the reviewer of fiction has also begun to show his power. The Post and the Atheneum received Hardy's novel favorably; a leaden-headed review in The Spectator snuffed it out so effectively that within days, poor, handsome, young, dreamy, bearded Tom Hardy saw his firstborn remaindered at Exeter railway-station for half-a-crown. He never forgot his agony of despair as he sat that afternoon on a country stile on his way to Bockhampton, and wished he was dead.

Still, though reviewers might then foil or delay a reputation, they could not yet invent one—they were not numerous enough; but they soon would be. Reviewers were made necessary by the growth of popular education, the new public created by the industrial revolution, the fashion for miscellanies and magazines, the popular fame of novel-

ists like Charles Lever, Wilkie Collins, Sheridan Le Fanu, Charles
Reade and, above all, Dickens. It was Dickens who did more than anything else or anybody else, by his serials and his public readings
throughout America and England, to wed publicity and publishing
into one big, flourishing, commercial business.

Certainly by the end of his century and the start of ours, publishing
had begun to learn all the tricks of commerce. I glance at Galsworthy's
"The Man of Property" (1906). By comparison with Miss Austen's
silent fanfare, it is a vulgar shriek—green cloth, the title strewn diagon-
ally across the cover in gold, no more foolish modesty about authors'
names, advertisements inside the book, and a loose slip from Messrs.
Heinemann offering all possible information about all their publications. Within a decade, jackets were blaring; books were gossip; novelists were news, and Svengali was a reviewer.

Why otherwise should a sensible man like Mr. Gladstone call on
Marie Corelli to say, "I recognize in you a great power," and stay
gossiping with her for two hours when he should have been in the
House of Commons fighting over The Deceased Wife's Sister bill?
Why otherwise should the Prince of Wales ask her to join his circle
at Bad-Homburg? Or Ella Wheeler Wilcox kneel to her when they
met? Why, but because they were all mesmerized by Svengali, as, even
still, even I can be by a line of print declaring that J. B. Shortshaft II
is America's New Genius, or that Frances Loosestrife has broken the
fame-barrier with her colossal "My Gentle Breast."

It is not the fault of reviewers or of editors. The great popular public does not want good novels; it wants kicks. It is also in large part
the fault of the writers. Ninety per cent of them do not deserve anything else but an entertaining review, and 90 per cent of them do want
instant Fame.

Am I being captious? Or worse still, stupid? Don't I want my
books to sell in vast numbers? It will break my publisher's heart—one
of the kindest of men—but I frankly do not. I should be greatly dis-
turbed if they did, though I am pleased that they always go on selling,
modestly—to date about 8,000 copies of my last book, between America and Britain. I doubt if Jane Austen ever sold as many in her lifetime. My poor publisher is always wanting me to make it a million.
But how can he? I am in the luxury trade. He is not. I am the sort of
writer whom publishers have to publish to have the brass (in every
sense) to be able to publish the stuff that they would not have the

brass to publish if they did not also publish a few rare fellows like me. I have no compaints. It is an excellent system. It is all part of Democracy, at its usual best and worst. After all, if I were in Russia, I would now be in Siberia. In Ireland they merely put me in the doghouse.

JOHN LE CARRÉ
The Undercover Man

The spy novel was not invented, of course, by John Le Carré (David John Moore Cornwell), but its popularity was given a tremendous boost by his best-selling "The Spy Who Came in from the Cold," the most successful of his several novels. He is a former member of the British foreign service. His essay is based on an address to the American Booksellers Association in 1965.

SUCCESS in writing is like success in nothing else. An actor, after all, even a musician, is a creature of the crowd. We do not fear for him when he plays to a full house, or takes his bow before jubilant admirers. His artistry may even profit from that mystical relationship to a live audience, and take wing in the momentum of response as a gull rises in the storm. The spirit of conquest is his ally; we need not fear for his corruption. But for the writer success is a multiple hazard, and deeply marks the very matter of his work.

A writer is not a creature of the crowd. He must live with it, yet remain apart from it; like a spy, he must use it, and report upon it, be one with it, yet infinitely wary. Like a spy his real work is done alone; it is thus that he describes his privacy in the idiom of the public.

Like a spy, he is dependent upon those whom he deceives. Though his mood may ultimately be one of compassion, he must be fiercely detached; he is a hunter and the crowd is his estate.

He is an illusionist. He will show you a character as a conjuror shows you an egg, and ask you to believe in the parts you cannot see. Like a spy he needs to work in secrecy; his deceits are the fabric of his life, so that without them he is nothing. Like a spy he needs to put even the smallest details of his daily life under the spell of an absolute design, so that nothing he does, alone or not, is irrelevant to his work. And certainly, like a spy, he negotiates other people's emotions and has very little relationship with the truth. He relates not what is authentic, but what is credible; like a spy he selects from a great quantity of material, in order to arrange, analyze and communicate whatever is really worthy of his use. Like a spy his survival may ultimately depend upon his simple skill as a storyteller.

Thus, like a spy, the writer moves among his fellow-men with nostalgia, envy and revulsion; it is this tenuous, painful unease which tautens his perception and forces him to communicate.

In this process he may wear many disguises, according to his mood. He will change his identity as he changes his stories, as other people change their clothes. Thus he is often taken for things he is not. He may write about the jungle with bitterness or with anger, but he is not asking anyone to cut down the trees. Those writers whose novels read like pamphlets of protest or rejection may be quite indifferent to the reforms they set in motion. You must not blame him for this. Any decent work of art will detach itself from the circumstances of its inception; an oil painting, when it leaves the artist's hand, will be seen in countless lights by countless different eyes; the very pigment lives a life of its own; no one will ever know whether the Mona Lisa was a duchess or a woman of the town.

When he weeps about the plight of others he is using their pain to illustrate his own; when he laughs, their joy; and when he is angry, their violence. Now all this: this solitude, this ambivalence, this so delicately adjusted balance, is suddenly disrupted by success; the phantoms whom once he could freely visit, and from whom he could once freely withdraw, assume earthly bodies and trample him in their enthusiasm. In a moment he has, ridiculously, become an institution —and did he not abhor all institutions?

In a moment the crowd has embraced him, and was he not afraid of the crowd, proud in his detachment and sovereign in his privacy? Once he had gleaned corn on the edge of the field; now the whole harvest is his. Once he was heard at a distance, an orator in an empty park; now they have given him the Albert Hall.

His system is hopelessly disrupted; he looks around with hostility for a reason. Here it is: he is caught in the machine.

He has heard of that great apparatus which was set up in order to drown the critics' protests and convert the public taste into the plaything of Hollywood and Madison Avenue. "The machine," he cries with relief, "the machine has got me."

Now he will play the writer to his discovery, gaining a mastery of his material until it masters him.

First, he will watch the machine, try to calculate its habits. He will observe, he supposes with detachment, the gradual distortion of his own identity. He will see, on television screens and in the press, a crude abstraction of his real self which he is invited to admire. He will hear himself talked of and quoted not in words but in numbers, like a price on the stock exchange. Is Le Carré's new book less interesting than Le Carré's new deal? All this is the fault of the machine. He will see himself in a distorted mirror, and have laid into his mouth sentences of terrible vulgarity.

If he does not talk constantly of money, other people will do it for him. He will recognize, with that corrosive eye which is the instrument of his craft, that the machine is not only concerned, as he supposed, with the dubious prestige of great sums; it knows its business better than that. It is engaged in turning the writer into an institution which will underwrite and where necessary supplement his faltering talent. It is there in fact to take the chance out of his future. He has become a property.

Next, in his alarm, he examines fellow writers who have lived longer with success than he. He finds them, with some justice, a disparate and lonely crowd.

He finds good writers who, because of the machine, appear to have idled away years in self-examination, or even worse, embraced the machine with frenetic enthusiasm, running to the public for refuge from the responsibilities and dangers of continued creation. You could call these the looking-glass writers, who dance and lightly spar with their own reflections. Others have fled in alarm to live like lonely posts in old houses, no longer finding their way back to the world. In every corner there seems to lurk a warning of what he might himself become. His worst nightmare is that tragic figure of the literary world; finding nothing in the present, afraid of the future, he plods like an old athlete round the old track, hearing in his imagination the lost echo from the arena.

Only one kind of writer seems entirely at ease: that happy charlatan whose alchemy is unchanged since the days when the pornography seller wandered from one Chinese village to another, beating his drum to summon the faithful. The machine made him, he has contentedly embraced it, and now it is converting his traditional wares into monuments of international vulgarity.

He will also discover that there are writers, dead or living, whose talent far exceeds his own, and whom the machine has so far ignored. This makes him furtive, even ashamed; perhaps after all the machine was right, and selected him because he is a vulgarian, as the pop singer is the vulgarian of music. Perhaps he is that adolescent of whom George Orwell wrote, instinctively able to appeal to the immature mind. And since the machine is there to compare, label and price writers who cannot be compared, labeled or priced, is he not a fraud anyway, who had better steal what he can before he is caught?

Before long he has convinced himself that there is no way of beating the machine, that the machine has chosen him as a cruel caprice; and scarcely has the machine had time to seduce him, then he has fallen head over heels in love with it. Others will be destroyed by failure, he will be destroyed by success.

Remember that success often catches a writer at his most morbid time: that is to say, when he has finished a book. He has been to the limit of his ability and seen what is not beyond. He has been his own critic; he has matched his intention against his performance, and seen how inadequate he is. Worse, he has not yet lost his heart to a new project; he is a chameleon in search of a color. No one can win then. Those who admire his book do so for the wrong reasons; those who condemn it hurt his vanity.

What comfort can we offer him, poor fellow, in his success?

First, perhaps, we can more accurately diagnose his illness. We can, I think, with justice point out to him that except at the very lowest level, Hollywood and Madison Avenue do not create public taste, but run after it as fast as their short legs will carry them; we can prove to him that his selection—this surely is important—was as much the work of an individual as his own writing.

His publishers exercised their judgment and having done so, enlisted the booksellers. The process of selection began with the writer, continued with the publisher and the bookseller, and finished—for good or ill—with the public, the critic and the reader. He need not, surely, be ashamed that his publisher set up an apparatus for selling his book: would he have been happier if, instead, it were left, like a Roman child, to survive or perish on the hillside?

Publishers and booksellers hold with the writer the power to beat the machine; as long as they back their private taste and judgment, the machine will be kept in its place, selling the poorest pulp to people who would probably buy nothing else.

This in turn should give him hope, and free him from the temptation to compromise; it should remind him that if success has brought him anything, it has brought him the right to experiment, to explore the edges of his talent.

But whether or not he comes to terms with the machine, whether he learns to live with it, to laugh at it, whether he runs from it or attacks it, we can be sure of one thing: He will never be quite the same.

R. K. NARAYAN
Advantages of Anonymity

R. K. Narayan, one of India's outstanding writers (he writes in English), is the author of many novels, short stories and essays. His novel, "The Guide," has been dramatized and was recently produced on Broadway. Graham Greene introduced him to the West and to Graham Greene, Narayan says, "I owe my literary career."

IN ANCIENT India the sculptor or painter added his name, if he did it at all, as an afterthought, in a curve of foliage or an ornamental bracket, and left it at that. In all that profusion of carving or fresco work, you would have to search for a signature. It seemed to matter little, as far as the quality or the endurance of his work was concerned. It bothered no one except research scholars and historians interested in labeling and classifying things.

It was the same with composers and poets. Thiagaraja, who lived over a century ago, composed a new song each day in his life, in the Telugu language of South India, and has left a vast treasure of musical compositions that form the core of what is known as the Carnatic system of Indian music. He wove his name unobtrusively amid the words at the end of a song. Other composers, his contemporaries, em-

ployed certain sobriquets to indicate their authorship. Such an identification mark was known as a *mudra* (in Sanskrit), meaning insignia
or seal.

Epic poets or dramatists sometimes mentioned their names in the
dedicatory stanzas at the beginning of a work, but always demurely and
inconspicuously. Sometimes the poet referred only to his patron.

Kamban was a Tamil poet of epic stature. He lived in the ninth
century, according to certain scholars; others infer from internal evidence and cross-references in other works that he lived in the 12th
century. He composed the "Ramayana" in the Tamil language at the
rate of 600 stanzas each day. In the dedicatory stanzas, and also here
and there in the body of the main work itself, he mentions not so much
himself as the name of his patron Sadayappa, a nobleman who supported him and encouraged him to write. If we are to gather any
biographical data, it must be from such scattered and casual references. The ancient writers were most reluctant to reveal themselves.

The provocation for a composition was not a desire to achieve
fame or material rewards but an inner satisfaction. Most compositions
arose from the impact of an esthetic moment or a mystic state. Valmiki,
the original composer of "Ramayana," in the Sanskrit language was
known as the Adi Kavi, which term could broadly be translated to
mean Poet of Poets. He is said to have composed the 24,000 stanzas
of "Ramayana" in a grand vision. There was no question of even
writing them down; he recited them, and his disciples memorized and
passed them on orally.

Sometimes I entertain the notion that it might be a good idea to
omit the author's name from the title page of his book. Then the book
would be forced to live on the strength of its contents rather than as
"another brilliant book by the same author." It might help the author
to concentrate on essentials, to make an effort to create something
that could have an absolute existence by itself, without reference to
the personality of the author. The author might feel free to write what
he likes as he likes at that particular moment, without being bound
by the image the public has created for itself of him and his work.

All reviews, criticisms and evaluations make for self-consciousness.
Personally, I should like to be able to say that I never read the reviews
of my books, but it would be unnatural not to be interested in the
immediate reactions to a new book. And I must admit that as a human
being I anxiously await the appearance of at least the reviews printed
in the first week of publication of my book, in order to judge whether

it will survive or not. After the first week I gradually lose interest, when I realize that the notices that follow are repetitions and more often than not reproductions of what the publishers themselves have said on the jacket. (I hate to use the word "blurb.")

Total blanking out of an author's name on the title page may not be practical; it might lead to confusion, particularly in our competitive civilization, where a bookbuyer is expected to pick out one book rather than another through advertisements, reviews, recommendations, and various other devices. Although the author may have no part in the promotion of his book, he should perhaps do nothing to confound it. Hence an identification becomes necessary in order to launch a book —but could it not be limited to a *mudra*, as in the ancient system, rather than a total revelation of the author's personality and personal life?

I avoid reading all analysis and evaluation of my writing. It is not because criticism depresses me. On the contrary, if I had to choose, I would rather have adverse criticism than excessive praise. The critic who flays you leaves you untouched if you are a hardened writer (ever interested in watching irritable men in action) and finishes you if you are squeamish. The greater danger, it seems to me, lies in overpraise. All those elaborate analyses of motives and values in my writing that I sometimes come across lead me into a world of letters where I feel a stranger. All such intellectualization could be extremely damaging to a writer's sense of perspective. Self-forgetfulness is essential for a writer's welfare. Obliviousness to one's public, one's purpose, and even (with apologies) to one's publishers or editors, would be salutary and keep the writer above certain temptations.

Apart from reviews, studies and theses, there is another source of embarrassment for a writer. When you enter a room and announce yourself as a writer, you will notice that most people look uneasy, as if you had said that you were a man-eater. They appear to worry lest you should turn on them for being ignorant of your writing. Once at an American college I was invited to lunch with the members of the English faculty, and they went through it as if dreading lest I should tell them, "Give me four good reasons why I should not consider you all illiterate for not being aware of the existence of my books."

They avoided all book talk until we arrived at the dessert stage, when one of the professors timidly ventured to ask, "Are any of your books available in English translation?" I replied, rigorously suppressing any trace of emphasis, "I write in English." Whereupon he looked panic-stricken and rose, saying, "I have to catch a plane for Washington." Others followed suit, explaining that they had urgent meetings to attend.

Equally devastating can be the pleasure of someone at recognizing the fact that he is in the presence of a live writer. "Ah, you're a writer! Wonderful, wonderful. You must tell me what you write, how you write. Do you dictate or type? Give me a list of your books and where I can get them. I have a son who wants to be a writer. I want you to meet him sometime. My wife, too, reads a lot and knows a lot about books." I feel that in a healthy society a writer should be able to pass unnoticed.

Someone has said, "I generally avoid meeting writers. Either the writer proves better than his books or it is the other way around. Either way one feels a jolt when meeting a writer." Those who find the book better than the writer suffer from the fact that they have built a picture of the writer from his books.

A writer creates a world of characters and situations and philosophy that have a life of their own and may have no relation to him. After writing 10 novels and a number of short stories, I find that I have created good men, bad men, idiots and saints. Once they have served their purpose, they pass clean out of my memory. I have no time to think of them again, although for months every one of those characters could have occupied my thoughts obsessively while the story was in progress. Once the last line is written and "The End" is inscribed with a happy flourish, out goes the character. But this is a situation that the reader is not likely to take into account.

A reader is attracted or repelled by a character and expects the writer to offer various explanations and interpretations of the particular character and his or her philosophy. The reader will also have the advantage, having gone through the book recently and possibly more than once. But the writer is likely to have forgotten the whole subject, especially if he has had to write a great deal else since then. When people expect him to say wise or significant things about his own book, they may find him tongue-tied and disappointing. In my view, to find the author less than the book is an excellent situation.

The really unhappy situation is for a person to scintillate in his comments, observations, repartee, and, above all, in laying down the law for good and bad writing—yet produce a poor book. This man is one who flowers in the hothouse of human associations, but shut him up in his room alone with the typewriter (since no writing is possible without isolation at some stage), and you will find that he wilts. For a year or more his friends keep hearing that he is busy composing a masterpiece to end all masterpieces, for which purpose he has retired from society. When the book comes out, however, his friends are forced to remark, "He talks so well! Why does he write like this?" No one can explain this paradox.

Anonymity has its advantages. If the book is good, the book is known. If the book is bad, the author remains unknown.

KURT VONNEGUT, Jr.
Science Fiction

As a man who writes for a living, Kurt Vonnegut, Jr., is probably entitled to give advice to the young writer, and he did just that for a couple of seasons at the University of Iowa's Writers Workshop. His own novels, in addition to "Player Piano," which he mentions in his essay, include "Cat's Cradle" and "God Bless You, Mr. Rosewater." Expect another at any moment.

Years AGO I was working in Schenectady for General Electric, completely surrounded by machines and ideas for machines, so I wrote a novel about people and machines, and machines frequently got the best of it, as machines will. (It was called "Player Piano," and it was brought out again in both hard cover and paperback.) And I learned from the reviewers that I was a science-fiction writer.

I didn't know that. I supposed that I was writing a novel about life, about things I could not avoid seeing and hearing in Schenectady, a very real town, awkwardly set in the gruesome now. I have been a sore-headed occupant of a file-drawer labeled "science-fiction" ever since, and I would like out, particularly since so many serious critics regularly mistake the drawer for a tall white fixture in a comfort station.

The way a person gets into this drawer, apparently, is to notice technology. The feeling persists that no one can simultaneously be a respectable writer and understand how a refrigerator works, just as no gentleman wears a brown suit in the city. Colleges may be to blame. English majors are encouraged, I know, to hate chemistry and physics, and to be proud because they are not dull and creepy and humorless and war-oriented like the engineers across the quad. And, because English majors can scarcely sign their own names at the end of a course of English instruction, many become serious critics. I have already said what they then do to the drawer I'm in.

But there are those who love life in this fulsome drawer, who are alarmed by the thought that they might some day be evicted, might some day be known for what they really are: plain, old, short-story writers and novelists who mention the fruits of engineering and research. They are happy in the drawer because most of the people in it love each other as members of old-fashioned families are supposed to do. They meet often, comfort and praise one another, exchange single-spaced letters of 20 pages and more, booze it up affectionately and one way or another have a million heart-throbs and laughs.

I have run with them some, and they are generous and amusing souls, but I must now make a true statement that will put them through the roof: They are joiners. They are a lodge. If they didn't enjoy having a gang of their own so much, there would be no such category as science-fiction. They love to stay up all night, arguing the question, "What is science-fiction?" One might as usefully inquire, "What are the Elks? And what is the Order of the Eastern Star?"

Well—it would be a drab world without meaningless social aggregations. There would be a lot fewer smiles, and about one-hundredth as many publications. And there is this to be said for the science-fiction publications: If somebody can write just a little bit, they will probably publish him. In the Golden Age of Magazines, which wasn't so long ago, inexcusable trash was in such great demand that it led to the invention of the electric typewriter, and incidentally financed my escape from Schenectady. Happy days! But there is now only one sort of magazine to which a maundering sophomore may apply for instant recognition as a writer. Guess what sort.

Which is not to say that the editors of science-fiction magazines and anthologies and novels are tasteless. They are not tasteless, and I will get to them by and by. The people in the field who can be charged fairly with tastelessness are 75 per cent of the writers and 95 per cent of the readers—or not so much tastelessness, really, as childishness. Mature relationships, even with machines, do not titillate the

unwashed majority. Whatever it knows about science was fully revealed in Popular Mechanics by 1933. Whatever it knows about politics and economics and history can be found in the Information Please
Almanac for 1941. Whatever it knows about the relationship between
men and women derives mainly from the clean and the pornographic
versions of "Maggie and Jiggs."

I taught for a while in a mildly unusual school for mildly unusual
high-school children, and current science fiction was catnip to the boys,
any science fiction at all. They couldn't tell one story from another,
though they were all neat, keen. What appealed to them so, I think,
aside from the novelty of comic books without pictures, was the steady
promise of futures which they, *just as they were,* could handle. In such
futures they would be high-ranking non-coms at the very least, *just as
they were,* pimples, virginity and everything.

Curiously, the American space program did not excite them. This
was not because the program was too mature for them. On the contrary,
they were charmingly aware that it was manned and financed by
tone-deaf adolescents like themselves. They were simply being realistic:
they doubted that they would ever graduate from high school, and
they knew that any creep hoping to enter the program would have to
have a B.S. degree at a minimum, and that the really good jobs went
to creeps with Ph.D.'s.

Most of them *did* graduate from high school, by the way. And
many of them now cheerfully read about futures and presents and
even pasts which nobody can handle—"1984," "Invisible Man," "Madame Bovary." They are particularly hot for Kafka. Boomers of science
fiction might reply, "Ha! Orwell and Ellison and Flaubert and Kafka
are science fiction writers, too!" They often say things like that. Some
are crazy enough to try to capture even Tolstoy. It is as though I were
to claim that everybody of note belonged fundamentally to Delta Upsi-
lon, my own lodge, incidentally, whether he knew it or not. Kafka
would have been a desperately unhappy D.U.

But listen—about the editors and anthologists and publishers who
keep the science-fiction field separate and alive: they are uniformly
brilliant and sensitive and well-informed. They are among the precious
few Americans in whose minds C. P. Snow's two cultures sweetly inter-
twine. They publish so much bad stuff because good stuff is hard to
find, and because they feel it is their duty to encourage any writer,
no matter how frightful, who has guts enough to include technology

in the human equation. Good for them. They want buxom images of the new reality.

And they get them from time to time, too. Along with the worst writing in America, outside of the education journals, they publish some of the best. They are able to get a few really excellent stories, despite low budgets and an immature readership, because to a few good writers the artificial category, the file-drawer labeled "science-fiction," will always be home. These writers are rapidly becoming old men, and deserve to be called grand. They are not without honors. The lodge gives them honors all the time. And love.

The lodge will dissolve. All lodges do, sooner or later. And more and more writers in "the mainstream," as science-fiction people call the world outside the file-drawer, will include technology in their tales, will give it at least the respect due in a narrative to a wicked step-mother. Meanwhile, if you write stories that are weak on dialogue and motivation and characterization and common sense, you could do worse than throw in a little chemistry or physics, or even witchcraft, and mail them off to the science-fiction magazines. A marketing tip: the science-fiction magazine that pays the most and seems to have the poorest judgment is Playboy. Try Playboy first.

ANDREW SINCLAIR
The Dear Departed

In the following essay Andrew Sinclair describes some of his adventures as a biographer, but like many another Englishman, his talents do not lie in one field alone. He is a novelist. He is a translator from the Greek. He has written a history of American Prohibition and an account of the emancipation of American women.

THE trouble with research is that the dead usually have families alive to defend their bones. However short or long a time ago some hero died, his kith and kin still keep vigil, ready to rain fire and lawsuits on historians who do their foul excavations in the cemeteries of the archives. Even centuries do not relax the watchfulness of the families of the great. Look at the de Sades who not long ago took legal action to prevent their ancestor from appearing on posters in Paris linked to the unholy Marat.

I remember when I was tramping across the Scots Borders on my way to England, I found the whole of the area round Hermitage Castle up in arms because of John Arden's broadcast play about the 16th century, "Armstrong's Last Goodnight." The castle guard told me that Lady Elliott was gathering the clans against Arden because the playwright had called an Elizabethan Elliott girl a whore. And he had done worse than that. He had put the most famous lines of Wee Jock Elliott, the man who had nearly saved Scotland by stabbing the catastrophic lover of Mary, Queen of Scots, into the mouth of another Border warlord, Johnny Armstrong. So an Armstrong was made to say the notorious Elliott warning, "Who dares to meddle wi' me?" Thus the Borders were hopping mad over a bit of misquotation from four centuries back, which seemed to them to be as bad as making Noah say, "Après moi le déluge," or Lady Hamilton gasp, "Kiss me, Hardy."

The descendants of American Presidents are even keener to stand by the reputation of the man who put the family name in the White House. Even if the President himself was something of a Cromwell and wanted his picture painted warts and all, his death leaves his defense in the hands of those who want to shroud him, not expose him. The Chinese may worship their ancestors, but we like to wrap ours in cotton wool. And by insisting *De mortuis nil nisi bonum*, we really mean that we want historians to state, *De mortuis nil nisi bunkum*, with footnotes.

Alas, research does lead to digging up dirt about the dead, if the evidence is buried, in the interests of historical truth. Thus, really, it is better for the families of the great departed to cremate the evidence than to persecute the gravediggers. For historians and dead men's heirs are ancient enemies. What the historian wants to reveal, a family often wants to conceal. The historians would often prefer that a great man's widow put herself on the pyre like an Indian widow rather than burn the man's papers; they sigh wistfully for the days of the old despotisms of Europe and Asia, when a new monarch put the whole of the old blood royal to death for fear of rivals, and turned his scribes loose to dig up horrors about the pretenders to the throne.

But now a man and his family have the unquestionable right to edit the evidence on his life; historians have to make do with what great men forget to eliminate about themselves.

Even the Presidential papers are the property of the President, his wife and his heirs. The outgoing President can remove the records of his Administration from the White House along with his socks. He may then edit the records to his own taste and return them to the Library of Congress or to a home-town memorial library; his family retains control over the material after his death. And woe betide the historian who tries to use Presidential papers without the proper permissions.

I wrote a political biography of one of the murkier American Presidents, Warren Gamaliel Harding. It yanked me out of my address at Ivory Tower, Cambridge, England, into a smoke-filled atmosphere in Columbus, Ohio, one that Harding's famous political fixer, Harry Daugherty, would have gone green to achieve. The story went that the Harding papers had been cremated by his widow down to the last cinder; but in fact his widow had died too soon after her husband to do much about the burning. The remaining papers rested in peace under family and home-town control for the next 40 years. Then tireless persuasion by the former Curator of Manuscripts of the State Historical Association and the approaching centenary of Harding's birth led to the Harding papers being opened to qualified researchers, *without strings.* Some 325,000 pieces of Hardingiana made a surprising appearance, and the fun began.

I was first in the field in an Ohio spring. I had done the secondary and conceptual work in advance, and I was there on the day the papers were opened. Alone and undisturbed, helped by the dedicated curator, I spent some time looking at the more important papers, which the curator picked out and had copied for me.

Columbus is bonny, doubtless, to the Columbians; but I felt rather pre-Columbian towards the civilization which had conquered there. It was still a town of little but politics and intrigue; I swear I heard in the dining room of my hotel, where Harding had once stayed and plotted, one Ohio politician saying to another, "Hell, we don't want justice, we want *control.*" Only as I worked in the archives with the curator to reproduce as much as possible in as short a time as possible did I feel that history might still be as guileless as a campus stroll under cherry blossom boughs.

I got my material and got out of town. By August, I'd written up my gleanings into the first draft of a political study called "The Available Man," which was not a biography of Harding so much as an examination of the myths of political availability which allowed a mediocre man like Harding to become President and perform adequately in office. But I had been warned. By now, I knew that there were several full-scale biographies of Harding in the works, with their authors all juggling and jockeying for position at Columbus. It was going to be as hot and intriguing when I was to return to check my footnotes against the original papers as it had been when the sweaty Chicago convention had picked the "dark horse" Harding to run in 1920.

I returned into the small room at the archives with the rivals sitting round sniping at one another, the curator punctured in the cross-fire, and an atmosphere of 100 degrees and 100 per cent humidity and no air conditioning. Mayhem was everywhere. One historian had discovered some Harding love letters, the curator had fallen on more compromising material, the family was running scared and threatening million-dollar lawsuits, and another of the historians was counseling the family how to prosecute his rivals and leave him with a clear path to first publication. Into this brouhaha, I walked with my manuscript.

Now Harding, who was no slouch in Ohio politics, had taught me how to act in that night of the long knives. First, he always protested the inadequacy of his performance and the humility of his aims in order to make his enemies underrate him. So when my rivals asked me about my work on Harding, I replied, "How can I have done much on him when I have spent so little time in the archives?" Second, I had learned from Harding always to treat competitors as friends, even if they were seeking to do me in. So I blandly kept out of the guerrilla war, saying that I knew too little to take sides in the grapple over the Harding remains. And third, I remembered Edgar Allan Poe's purloined letter, and I left the manuscript of my book in full sight on the table in the archives when I went out for lunch, on the principle that no one bothers to examine the obvious.

So I checked my sources and left Columbus unscathed, although the admirable curator was soon forced to leave for another job. I sent my manuscript on to an academician who was editing the series in which it would appear, and then I gave the work a final revision. I was careful to paraphrase all Harding material, for I needed the family's permission to quote. Thus I was clear of legal counterattack.

There is only one golden rule in research, where the families of the dead may be militant: *When in doubt, don't quote—paraphrase.* It's not actionable.

The publishers set "The Available Man" in type in two weeks, an incredible job. I corrected the proofs and left for England without a scratch. News of my break for print, however, had gotten back, and one of my rivals supplied a detective report of exactly how much time I had spent at the archives to the editor of the series, who promptly withdrew his name and support although he had already passed and praised the manuscript. The historian turned private eye had, however, failed to mention how Xerox has changed the geography of historical research, so that a researcher can take away in six days in a trunk what might take him six months to work through in an archive.

My publisher, however, a man of sterling solidity and wrath, refused to be rattled by mere expert advice. He was damned and he published, and "The Available Man," like Warren Harding, had a modest success. For it was no detailed biography; it merely used points in Harding's career as pegs on which to hang analyses of American political myths. There was nothing libelous in the book; in fact, by treating Harding as a serious politician rather than a school for scandal, it did something to restore his reputation as an astute operator who got to the White House on the merits and chance of his availability.

A truthful history can never harm its subject, however much it exposes him. Readers seem to like great men better for knowing about some of their ruses and frailties. Now I am honored by Harding's home town, not prosecuted by it. I bounce messages to Harding Memorial Dinners by satellite, while my rivals sit there, overtly friendly and inwardly fuming—and still unpublished.

Instant history, alas, suffers from the virtues and faults of speed; to the quickest belong the spoils, if he can scamper without shedding scholarship. And history is no longer perpetrated in the pure air of Academe. The archives now have their smoke-filled rooms and the historians have their conventions, where they hire and fire the party faithful, and make and break reputations with the élan of Harry Daughertys. Every trick from spying to counseling the families of the dead on how to sue is used in order to hobble rivals in the race to publication.

History, as can be seen in the Manchester case, can become an extension of politics by other means. Biographers have to tread warily now; no man is long enough dead not to have a family or rival biographers to defend his bones. It no longer puzzles me that some historians have become Presidents; if you finagle your way in the first profession, the second is a joy ride.

J. H. PLUMB
Trials of a Biographer

The 18th century is the specialty of historian J. H. Plumb, but there is nothing of that century about him unless it is the comfort of his rooms in Christ's College, Cambridge. He is one of those versatile English scholars who can write a life of Sir Robert Walpole; a history, "The Growth of Political Stability in England, 1675-1725"; edit a historical series for an American publisher; review the pornographic classic "My Secret Life"; and after hours discourse knowingly on silver and porcelain and wine.

IT WASN'T a dungeon, but it felt like one. There were no windows. The high stone walls were criss-crossed with iron gratings that supported shelves for the dispatch boxes containing the manuscripts. A heavy iron door strengthened the prison-like atmosphere. It was prudently left ajar, so that I could be watched, or possibly to let in a little warmth. None came, but conversation filtered through, distracting me from the great Duke's correspondence. Obviously money was short, for these Dukes had been extravagant as Dukes will be, and the present one was feeling the pinch. Unlike some of his immediate ancestors, he had married for love: a dangerous act for a Duke. The tired voices drooled on as I rapidly searched the correspondence for references to Sir Robert Walpole on whose biography I was working. And then suddenly a sentence hung clearly on the air: "I cannot see why the Duke needs a second footman when he dines alone."

A gross solecism, for there was no reply. And the silence and the cold became so intense that I had to wrap myself in the family standard that I found folded in a box. Outside, the famous palace flaunted its baroque chimneys against the pale blue, wintry sky. It seemed odd, against all this magnificence, that I should not only be sitting in this bleak dungeon but also paying a guinea a day for the privilege. It was consoling, however, to think that I might be saving the Duke from the ultimate sacrifice of a second footman. Still, it proved worth the cold and cost to handle the letters of Robert Harley, Robert Sunderland, Henry St. John, Sidney Godolphin, Walpole, James Stanhope and the rest, men whose characters I was beginning to know at least as individual human beings instead of names.

Although I was charged for my daily visit to the muniment room, (the only noble house in 30 years of my experience to make such a charge), it had been exceedingly difficult to gain access. Letter after letter had gone unanswered, and only when I discovered that an acquaintance of mine, who, at that time, was moving in circles attached to the Court, had personal contacts with the Duke, was I able to gain admittance. Usually when a friend effects an introduction to a noble family, one is shown the front door, this time it was the back —cold, comfortless and expensive to boot. Still, I was consoled to have contributed my mite to the second footman. And the receipts are in my muniment room.

By then, of course, I had wormed my way into so many noble households that I was almost prepared for anything from dreamlike wealth and luxury to nightmare anxieties. One could never tell just what would happen, and nothing was more deceptive than appearance. Take Earl A and Baron B. The Earl had behind him years of service to the State. I was introduced by a cousin. A charming invitation followed to stay at the house (justly famous for its architecture, furniture, pictures and park) as long as I wished. I was received with infinite courtesy.

Immensely aged, thin to the point of vanishing and stone deaf, the Earl talked slowly and incessantly about his career, and then about "The First Man" and "The Second Man," not as you might think, Adam or Cain, but the First Earl or the Second Earl. The monologue finished, I was allowed to go to my room. It seemed higher than Heaven and as cold as Hell. Heating none, the furniture exquisite. The bathroom, a perilous quarter of a mile away, was as vast as a tomb designed for an Emperor, and as cold; the bath itself a miracle of brass and Gothic fretwork. Between the bathroom and the bedroom there were chests, tables, consoles, commodes teeming with fragile bric-a-brac, set like expensive traps to catch anyone who ventured on that devious path. There was no lighting. Terrors clearly abounded. Perhaps warmed by drink and food, it might be endurable, so I thought.

I skipped a bath, put a cardigan under my dress shirt, and descended.

A tiny glass of sherry did not bode well. The butler announced dinner and led us into the most magnificent dining room in which I've ever eaten dinner. Seventeenth-century paneling and carving at their best, Van Dykes, Gainsboroughs, Reynolds, and here and there a stormy Ruysdael or an icy van der Neer—all beautifully lit. A small table, candle-lit, set with exquisite silver, the center piece a wonderfully chased Charles II porringer. The butler served a very small cheese soufflé, so small that I wondered why he did not put the dish in front of me. Then to my horror I realized that my place was set with one knife and fork. There were two bits of toast melba on the table, one each; the butler poured water from a massive silver beer jug; the dessert followed—a beautiful apple—and the Earl interrupted his endless story of how he got the Garter to express his pride in his own apples.

The night proved long and bitter as hunger and cold fought each other. I had to pile the floor rugs on my bed. I thought of trying to sleep in a hot bath; the journey seemed too perilous. Reading was impossible, for there was no bed light. It scarcely seemed worth it after all, for the contact between the First Man and Sir Robert was peripheral. The hours slowly passed to the rumbles of my stomach and the chattering of teeth.

At the first light I was up; by 7:30 A.M. I was on the way to the village, two miles distant. Early as it was, I persuaded the shop to open and sell me chocolate. When I got back, I was just in time for breakfast.

On the sideboard a row of gleaming entree dishes—everything that might tickle an English country gentleman's fancy was there: kidneys, eggs, sausages, bacon, mushrooms, kedgeree, haddock and even a kipper. And if you hated hot food, there was the largest, pinkest, most succulent ham I had ever seen this side of Virginia. The chocolate of course, had blunted my appetite, but the Earl's was in better shape. After a mountain of porridge and a large kipper, he demolished two rashers of bacon, sausages, mushrooms, scrambled eggs and paid a magnificent tribute to the splendor of his own apples. After he had finished the Garter story again, he held my eye. "The Men," he said, "always enjoyed their breakfast. The Fifth Man rarely ate anything else."

The archives contained nothing but a bombshell: a packet of letters indicating that the First Man enjoyed not only his breakfast but his boy friends. Nothing, however, to do with Sir Robert Walpole's life, so not usable, at least not until the Last Man dies (he has no heirs), but he is proving indestructible, moving with the same inevitability up his nineties as he did his eighties. Not only is he going to be the Last Man but the Oldest Man. I like to think of him still pecking away at his cheese soufflé in that vast and splendiferous dining room, or hogging his breakfast in the morning room roseate with mahogany. And all the time his tiny, bright blue eyes made it clear that the joke was on me.

Lord B. was different. First of all no one believed that he existed. One of my oldest and most aristocratic friends vaguely remembered a very old man of the name being seen in the House of Lords about 10 years before. Debrett indicated that he was still alive, just on 90, but doubt was cast (wrongly it appeared) on its accuracy. However, Queen Mary, who knew everyone, said he existed still. So my friend summoned him and his wife to lunch. They appeared, dressed like some faded figures from a Victorian album, prepared to go to Ascot.

He was in morning suit, white waistcoat; she in strangely aged lace and straw, although she was at least 50 years younger than Lord B. Like the Earl, he was stone deaf; when equipped with a splendid silver trumpet and shouted at, a little filtered through. His wife was so gentle or so genteel she did not speak. Lunch was not a success, but before they left I had an invitation to stay at their manor house in the depth of the Welsh Marches.

I went with foreboding. A manor house in the Welsh foothills in February was scarcely alluring, and as I drove through wind and fog and later driving rain, I cursed Sir Robert. He was taking me into too many odd, cold and uncomfortable circumstances. The manor house was Victorian, rambling, ivy-covered, half hidden by dripping laurels and funereal cedars. A gnomish maid opened the door, and a hound as vast as the Baskervilles' bayed at me. Foreboding turned to certainty. I followed along a stone-flagged corridor, replete with stag-heads, up a bare and crackling staircase to my room. There a fire was blazing in the grate, the warmth was as cozy as the crisp chintz, the gleaming brass and the deep lambskin rugs. I could scarcely believe this Cinderella act or the admirable bathroom *en suite*. I turned on the taps: they were real. A quick change. Downstairs I was greeted by Lord B. dressed in a dinner jacket that could have been Disraeli's, but in his hand was a glass of champagne. Joined by his handsome son, some

70 years his junior, we polished off the bottle. Dinner was breathtaking: splendid English food with wonderful French wines. The old man and his wife retired immediately; the son and daughter full of wit and intelligence kept me talking until long past midnight.

The next day was crowded. I kept mentioning the archives, but only for the subject to be quickly brushed aside. Lord B. owned a great house as well as a manor house, and he had ordered this to be opened up. We were to lunch there, and he had invited a dozen or so guests to meet me there for luncheon. The house was magnificent, yet almost unknown. The pictures belonged to a 17th-century collection and had never left the house. Luncheon was grand but disastrous. A bright, lively and seductively attractive woman on my right took all my attention. I became so animated that I turned sharply in my chair—an exquisite shield-backed Sheraton in white and gold. It disintegrated under my weight. Although assured that Partridge would soon put it right, the glamour faded. I longed to disappear and get at the archives.

Not to be. There was a famous drive through the park. There were ancestors' tombs to view, a splendid country-house tea to demolish (complete with three local schoolmistresses who had been bidden like serfs to attend), then baths and champagne and claret—and no archives. I was leaving the next morning, and by the next morning Lord B. had gone—gone to take the air on the cliffs of Dover, which he did for one week in four and to which he attributed his longevity. And who can say he was wrong, for he went on to see his son reach his majority, and on again for another five years to free the gift of his estates from the liability of tax. Then he died, just short of his century.

But the archives. They were given to me after breakfast in a small basket that the English use to gather strawberries in. Most I learned had been sent for salvage during the war; the rest burned just before I met Lord B. at lunch. There were two or three letters about parliamentary elections and a book of accounts about the building of the great house; not a word about Walpole or Lord B's ancestor who ferociously opposed him. Yet who could call this a fruitless journey?

Of course all were not so replete with human comedy or aristocratic eccentricity, but it was rare to find many manuscript owners as beautifully organized, say, as the Duke of Devonshire. His admirable and helpful librarian knew his way blindfold through the well catalogued manuscripts, which are so extensive that no one working on modern English history could come away from Chatsworth empty handed.

And kindness and consideration from owners of manuscripts were more usual than not.

The conditions varied from the odd to the magnificent. One peer was living in an overgrown rectory (his mansion had burned down) with seven daughters and two sons. The muniment room was the first landing on the staircase, and all day long small girls with large solemn eyes would peep over the banisters at the weird academic monster. Another kept his papers in chests in his drawing room, so one spent the day *en famille* with dogs and visitors and telephone calls, all very easy and warm and familial.

Most were eager to help. Most knew the myths about their family but rarely its history. I quickly learned never to question the impossible ancestoral stories. If one did, it created such gloom that one felt an oaf for the rest of the day. Most were solicitous for one's comfort, sometimes too much so—as when I was put in a bed of exceptional historical importance in which Charles II and Nell Gwyn had slept. It was harder than iron and short even for me. I suppose they did not sleep any more than I did, but then *I* wanted to.

For most of the noble houses I penetrated I was, of course, something of a curiosity, slightly intimidating by reason of my academic standing and scholarly knowledge, yet time and time again I was offered hospitality stretching over days. The traditions of a great house were still strong; and I had glimpses into ways of life—of those long-maintained aristocratic traditions with their curious mixture of arrogance, acceptance and courtesy—which were as valuable for my work as were the letters of Sir Robert himself.

Above all, was the sheer tenacity of these families, their assumption that the world would always be theirs. I remember in the forties the Marquess T., during the last years of Attlee's government, standing in the splendid marble hall built by Inigo Jones for his ancestor, and saying: "After all, we lived through the Civil War and we ought to survive this." And I expect they will. Twenty years later they are still there as perky as ever.

IV
On
Style and
Styles

FREDERIC MORTON
Vhere Iss Charlotte Street?

After Frederic Morton finally located Charlotte Street, he came to America. For a time it looked as though he might be a baker. Instead, he became a writer, publishing a first novel at 23, the year he was graduated from New York's City College. His biography, "The Rothschilds," was a best seller for many months.

To COMMIT yourself to serious writing is an act of recklessness and planned vulnerability comparable to tightrope-walking. If the idea strikes you as facile romanticism, let me add that the main peril of this highwire act is not just that you may crack your skull. It's that you'll crack your skull outside the spotlight. To plot such self-exposure —and then to be overlooked!

Now take the committed writer using a language other than his mother tongue. What is he, in his abandon, but a tightrope-walker with a wooden leg? I am saying that, naturally, because I've got such a leg. My native language is the Viennese version of German. Until the age of 14 my English vocabulary consisted of one word: the soccer term "goal," pronounced "go Al."

A cripple embarked on acrobatics is bound to evoke radical feelings. Some onlookers are filled with fixed disdain, others are moved to exorbitant generosity. To start with the nasty sort, The Saturday

Review once quoted the deliberately Teutonic speech of a minor German character in one of my novels and then, taking the tone to be typical of the whole book, flayed me for raping Shakespeare's fair tongue with such gutturals. The (London) Times Literary Supplement, on the other hand, went to the opposite extreme: "Social and emotional intrigues are Mr. Morton's forte, together with an unusual elegance of style and a delight in the unexpectedly droll that recall Mr. Nabokov. Writers like these, like Conrad, who approach English as a new language—and with a finesse—find in it a magic that native writers often miss."

Of course it's pleasant to be quarantined like that, beyond one's probable merits, on an alien Olympus. But there's an implication here, on the part of the dear Supplement, that it's actually easier for a foreigner to write accomplished English than for a native; an insinuation that the Muse, prone to exogamy, will lie down more readily with an exotic. *Unsinn!* I could say. What about the feel for slang and idiom, for the spontaneous phrase, which is the birthright of the author to the language born? What about his ancient camaraderie with words in which he's dreamed and puled since infancy?

Yes, I can rehearse that argument. I am not sure I believe in it. Deep down I'm really with the Supplement. But it was hard to account for the leaning until the other day when I came across a sentence in Jean-Paul Sartre's autobiography: "All writers have to sweat . . . one speaks in one's own language, one writes in a foreign language." I realized that just because I'm a chronic immigrant, this schizoid bind of Sartre's doesn't apply to me. My life is more consistent than that. For 27 years now, I've been speaking *and* writing a foreign language. Perspiration, uncertainty, wariness have become a tradition with me, a premise which makes easier the writer's daily bafflement before the unknown continent that is the blankness of each new page.

So I don't pity myself but the native, for whom, poor thing, the transition from the spoken to the written is much more cruel. The very words in which he laughs and curses and buys deodorants, turn into technological obstacles as soon as he sits down to work. Language, the most natural thing while in the mouth, becomes, the moment it must be coaxed from the typewriter, a Medium Of Expression, a Vehicle Of Ideas, a Repository Of Symbols; in short, a damn nuisance. But I, the alien writer, am never ambushed by alienations like that. I may not lick them any better, but they are second nature.

I think I really entered the literary game in London's Victoria Station back in 1940, a 14-year-old, new-baked refugee trembling before a giant bobby. As my family's front-ranking English specialist (thanks to a year of lessons in Vienna), I had just been dispatched to ask for directions to our hotel. I stepped forward, turned over in my mind all the possibilities of the English language, and finally said, "Please, vhere iss Charlotte Street?"

Since then I've worked on my diction, lost my accent and even won a National Book Award nomination. But the sweat has never stopped. I still hear myself saying, "Please, vhere iss Charlotte Street?" The shadow of the bobby always hovers, even when I'm buying the morning paper. I say, "Throw in the News too, will ya, Hank?" I'm being American with somewhat the same artfulness with which I'm a storyteller in my study. My wooden leg, you see, creates a tightrope every time it touches ground; and when I get to the real highwire, the difficulty is familiar, almost dear. There I just do my perennial balancing act professionally.

If English has always been constructively perilous that way, I have also found in it, from the very start, something that seemed to predispose it toward art. After German, after four years of Gymnasium Latin, after such long indenture to finely shaded rigidities, this new language had virtually no grammar and thus no pedantry. All hard things in it had to do with the eccentric exuberance of its phonetics where the same spelling or the same syllable formation produced wildly different pronunciations.

The daring that gave "butter" and "butcher" different vowel sounds enchanted me. And I was particularly impressed that a yeoman word like "the" should contain such a very fine (and for long unattainable) lisp. So the difficulties of learning English were marvelous rather than menial. I felt like a baker's apprentice who instead of scraping pots finds himself sculpting however badly, a wedding cake.

And that is why I was delighted, but not surprised, when my tutor in Vienna graduated me overnight from the English grammar's "my aunt has an umbrella" to Oscar Wilde's "The Nightingale and the Rose." Not that it came home that here was a language which, better than any other, can wring grace out of simplicity. I only felt, and have been feeling ever since, that in an English-speaking universe, my aunt's umbrella can touch off a haunted fairy tale.

But English managed a still neater trick for me when it naturalized Huckleberry Finn. Yes, you read right. I'd been given a German translation of the book when I was down with the mumps; and though I followed the story with interest, I couldn't bear the harsh Berlin accents—especially repugnant to a sick little Viennese—into which Huck's dialect had been rendered. Unfortunately the illustrations matched the tone; Huck's rags fit him like a Junker's uniform, and I suspected that if he brought his bare feet together, you would hear a click of boots.

The image stuck for a long time. Ten years later, as a senior at New York's City College, I picked up the book again. What wondrous Americanization! Huck became a lovable vagabond; the Mississippi became an American river; and all that gritty Berlinese melted into soft rustic Missourian. Every reference book insists that Mark Twain wrote it that way originally. Maybe, maybe not. I can't help believing it was the genius of the language which rescued Huck from the Teutonic.

The experience confirms my surmise that English is especially amenable to linguistic emigration. Being a hybrid of Germanic and Latin roots, it lacks the xenophobia of "purer" tongues. Often, foreign inflections will nourish rather than distort it. The foreigner, in turn, senses such hospitality. Embarked on a love affair with his hostess— this is, of course, an autobiographical confession—he may consider his previous marriage to another tongue as an enrichment instead of a complication. Or, to put it more precisely in reverse, English seems like the culmination of one's first language. When I met George Santayana in Rome in his 86th year, he spoke of the long Spanish conversation he'd had with another visitor just before me. "I forgot very little," he said. "But you know what I like best about talking Spanish? Talking English right afterwards."

I know that pleasure: clearing your palate with bread in order to fully savor a great vintage, though the wine is not yours but is served to you as a privileged guest—some special, exhilarating, serendipitous claret. Perhaps this sensation explains why there are many quite important writers who turned English over on their tongues *afterward*. What other language has developed an émigré galaxy of Conrads, Santayanas, Nabokovs?

Still, when I consider my particular wave of emigration, the German and Austrian Jews who reached America in the late thirties, I see very few confrères. That seems strange at first because my parents' generation, riding the crest of Middle European emancipation, produced Werfel, Broch, Zweig and Hofmannsthal. We, their children, are, on the one hand, beneficiaries of the heritage; on the other, we have spent a good portion of our education and life in the United States. A promising combination, and yet much more significant American literature is being written by descendants of depressed Eastern European Jewry.

I wonder if it was our very class that sterilized us. To the Jews of the steerage years the New World meant enormous promise, enormous involvement and, ultimately, often enormous disappointment. It meant a rush for an impossible Goshen, and the collision with its impossibility produced those vivid bruises—from Odets's "Golden Boy" to Mailer's "An American Dream"—which make up much of our vital literature. Immigrants of our own wave failed to make such sharp, deep contact. We did not sail toward a fairy tale with its vast potential for fulfillment or betrayal.

The New York skyline signified first and foremost simply an escape from the gas chambers. As a life-preserver it was unforgettable. As an experience it was overshadowed by the cataclysm from which we had been preserved, and by the great nostalgic ghosts of what the cataclysm had destroyed. Grateful as we were, we gained the shore, we felt the gangplank tilting down, not up. Instead of dreaming forward to the American dream, we dreamed back to the affluence and *Kultur* of our pre-American lives. America saved us but did not consume us, and therefore none of us became its poets.

It is no accident that those émigré writers who have "broken through" in the new country use the American scene mostly as a target for very European perceptions. Nabokov uses the American scene as a perfect foil for his aristocratic virtuosity. On a more journalistic level, Joseph Wechsberg purveys the sophistications and discriminations of a Continental connoisseur. I'm a good deal younger than these two—in fact I've been through such *echt* Americana as three years in a New York vocational high school—and yet I seem to work best when using a trans-Atlantic focus. My most successful book was about a great European clan; my most anthologized short story deals with my own family just before the *Anschluss*.

And yet, and yet! Where would my fine nostalgia be if I could not level it from so perfect an exile? If, above all, I could not dress it in that new language in which I've learned to long for old things? Here is the ultimate miracle my writing tongue holds for me: it lets me see in English the childhood I lived in German. It pours a wonderful strangeness over the familiar. It confuses me, and yet I sense that I can do no better than yield to the bewilderments of this double vision, to its perils, its insights, its doubts. Do you know what I mean? Do you really? Please, vhere iss Charlotte Street?

STANLEY BURNSHAW
Modern Hebrew Poets

Stanley Burnshaw, as the following essay suggests, has been a bridge between verse in foreign tongues and verse in English. "The Modern Hebrew Poem Itself" interpreted Hebrew verse. Earlier he performed the same service for verse in French, German, Italian, Spanish and Portuguese through a collection entitled "The Poem Itself." Some of his own poems have been collected in "Exiles and Late Testament" and "Caged in an Animal's Mind." Stanley Burnshaw was formerly president of the Dryden Press and a vice president of Holt, Rinehart and Winston.

WHEN I agreed, one evening some years ago, to try to do something about making the new poets of Israel "available" to English-speaking readers, I had no idea of the kinds of surprise in store for me. Worse, I was filled with doubt as well as uncertainty, having read all the verse translations from modern Hebrew that I could lay hands on. Most of them had left me unsatisfied, and yet I had been stirred often enough to have felt uneasy. True, as Frost had said, "for self-assurance there should always be a lingering unhappiness in reading translations." But mine was unhappiness aggravated by bewilderment. How could many people of excellent taste speak with such warmth of Hebrew poets whose words-in-translation had left me cold and discomfited? Was there something in me that had blocked my way to the poets? Was it only the absence of wonderfully gifted translators? Or were there some elements in the originals that simply could not survive any carrying-over by the conventional medium of verse?

I inclined to the last possibility, for a book I had just published seemed to offer keys for unlocking doors. That 1960 volume, "The Poem Itself: 45 Modern Poets in a New Presentation," made no at-

tempt to translate a modern foreign poem into verse; it began instead
with the most literal rendering possible. Freed from the demands of
meter and rime, such a prose "equivalent" could incorporate alternate meanings and even untangle syntax. Thus equipped, a reader
might begin to read and even to hear the foreign original, line by
line—but he would of course need something more, since poetry is
by nature the most condensed arrangement of words. He would have
to be given clues where there were allusions and the missing words
where the poet had used ellipses, not to mention various other aids for
unveiling the multiform riches of the poem itself.

Could such a method unlock the world of modern Hebrew verse?
A visit to Tel Aviv in January, 1961, brought an enthusiastic response
from a leading Israeli poet and translator, T. Carmi. Born in New
York and educated there and in Palestine, he was more aware than I
of the complications that would face us: he knew both languages well!
But we decided to make the attempt; and before long we were on our
way, having been joined by a third native American, Ezra Spicehand-
ler, Professor of Literature at the Hebrew Union College. Thus all
three of us could approach modern Hebrew poetry from an "English-
speaking position," while the present writer would remain typical of
the American reader for whom "The Modern Hebrew Poem Itself"
was to be made. (The book was published by Holt, Rinehart and
Winston.)

With a grasp of Hebrew too negligible to mention, I found myself at once asking questions—demanding clearer and clearer explanations in behalf of myself and my fellow-innocents. Answers were not
always available, even with the aid of dictionaries and source books
piled high in the Carmi living room. For a number of passages the
poets themselves had to be consulted, questioned, confronted; but at
least one refused to answer and five others were no longer alive. Twelve
Israelis and three Americans had written drafts on the 69 poems we
had chosen. At least two or three revisions were always required
—and not only of the discussions. I remember several days when
Carmi and I spent four or five hours on a literal translation of a
20-line lyric, in the hope—sometimes naive—that the collaborator
would agree to accept our editing.

Quite soon after I had begun to ask questions, I came to discover
one reason why all the verse translations from modern Hebrew that
I had read earlier had failed to make me respond. To put it bluntly,
often I could not know—and the translations did not tell me—*what*

the poems were talking about, for many of these poets make allusions
in a way peculiarly their own. Taking for granted a pervasive familiarity with an immense traditional literature, they refer to words,
phrases, passages—ideas, stories, attitudes—with confidence that the
originals will also resound in a reader's mind. Or so it seemed as I
gradually grew aware of the breadth of the "field" that a Hebrew
poet can "light up" with a word or a phrase: more than two thousand
years of an oral and written tradition including, along with compendia
such as the Bible, the Talmud and the Prayerbook, individual works
by poets, philosophers and sages.

To be sure, such alluding to traditional contexts is not unique to
modern Hebrew poetry. In European literature it goes back at least
to Dante. In English it appears as early as Chaucer and as late as
Eliot, with his quotations from five languages in the last lines of "The
Waste Land." Hebrew poets, however, usually restrict their allusions
to works of their own tradition, whereas others range at will, ignoring the frontiers of nation and culture. Thus, though no longer
self-excluded from Western secularism, the modern Hebrew poet continues in intimate relationship with his own heritage, evoking passages from an ancient and still venerated sacred literature which—
regardless of his private attitude toward religion—he feels to be inseparable from his own and his group's survival.

Often a modern Hebrew poem will light up the field with a reference to a passage in the Bible but with a sharp reversal of meaning.
Note, for example, line 8 of Amir Gilboa's "Isaac." In the back of
the reader's mind is the familiar story of Abraham's sacrifice of Isaac
—"And Abraham stretched forth his hand, and took the knife to
slay his son" (Genesis xxii:10)—but the Abraham of Amir Gilboa's
poem cries out "It is I who am being slaughtered." Less immediate for
English-speaking readers is the Biblical quotation in Chaim Bialik's
"On the Slaughter," a poem of wild mourning in the wake of a po-
grom. Here the context transforms the life affirming statement "Live
in thy blood!" (Ezekiel xvi:6) into a hideous imprecation against the
murderers. Sometimes a poet's Biblical echoing will amount to no more
than a suggestive phrase: Yocheved Bat-Miriam's association of the
dimensions of the Holy Ark—"A cubit and half is my height"—with
the "plot of earth reserved for [her] last rest."

Occasionally a powerful poem will be all but meaningless without its source. Haim Gury's "Odises," for example, in which the protagonist is a fusion of Homer's hero and a legendary Hebrew sage,

Honi, who fell asleep for 70 years and upon waking found himself a
stranger among his own people. A poet such as Gilboa may summon
an ancient line from the Talmud—"The face of Moses is like the face
of the sun and the face of Joshua like the face of the moon"—in a
weirdly modern atmospheric poem about a Joshua who is both the
Biblical conqueror and the speaker's brother. To say that such verse
makes secular use of sacred referents may be tempting but it does not
always apply and it leaves out of account complexities of mood and
manner.

"What do modern Hebrew poets write about?" I am often asked.
The question is impossible to answer even for one who has tried to
read all the poems of an extraordinarily productive movement, as I
have not; and yet something can be said on the basis of my own ex-
plorations. My best answer would be, "They write about themselves," if I could specify the variety of individual selves and their
collective difference from their predecessors, whose work had been
predominantly sacred. Born and reared in the tradition-centered *shtetl*
(small Jewish town), the pioneering poets of the 1890's were suddenly
plunged into the stormy secular world of pre-Revolutionary Russia.
While accepting a modern view of man intellectually, they remained
bound emotionally to their strictly Jewish experience. Thus we find
in the lyrics of the greatest of these poets, Bialik (whose public verse
was hailed as prophetic statement), a constant struggle between Judaism and Western secularism, the old and the new, faith and doubt,
inhibition and abandon, the "house" and the outside world. By contrast, his younger contemporary, Saul Tchernichovsky, sought to trans-
fuse Western literature into Hebrew poetry—he made translations
from 15 different literatures. Fascinated by the pagan world, he not
only inveighed against the repressiveness of Jewish tradition but ex-
tolled pre-Biblical Canaanite cults. In "Before the Statue of Apollo,"
the Jewish people are depicted as rebels against a Nietzschean god
of life.

As this pioneering period (1880-1924) drew to a close, the center
of Hebrew poetry shifted to Palestine, where younger East-European-
bred poets were having their first encounter with the earth of the
promised homeland. Typical of the range of response is the work of
Abraham Shlonsky, for whom the building of the new country and
the tilling of its soil are acts of worship, but who can also write of the
loss of faith, the shadows hovering over Europe, the boredom of life
in a modern city.

No such alternation of mood is found in Uri Zvi Greenberg, whose ultra-nationalist verse proclaims a quasi-mysticism of blood, race and Jewish destiny. Or in Yonatan Ratosh, avowed enemy of Judaism and Zionism, whose poems, when they pray, invoke not Yahweh but the Canaanite deities Baal and Asherot. Nathan Alterman, on the other extreme, as troubadour and creator of Israel's new urban myth, has almost limitless range, from the romantic ballad of love and death to political satire. Least ideological of all is Lea Goldberg, one of whose main themes is her Lithuanian childhood. At times her verse conveys the paradoxical sense of foreignness that the semitropical terrain of the homeland aroused in artists newly arrived from Northern Europe. As the writer David Shimoni once lamented, the snows obscure the deserts.

Quite new attitudes emerge in the poetry written since 1948, the year of Israel's independence, as the idealism of the war period—when "people spoke in the first person plural"—gave way to the primacy of the individual. For example, irony and existential ennui mark the work of Yehuda Amihai, for whom the intensities of the experienced moment, rather than eternal values, hold meaning. Another influential poet, Amir Gilboa, identifies himself with Biblical characters in such ways as to transform them into living contemporaries—but to say this gives no hint of the range of his "subjects." Nor would it be possible even to suggest those of other writers—such as Carmi, Nathan Sach, Gury, Dan Pagis—by referring to poems of aspiration, bitterness, fury, faith, or poems on the relationship between a man and a woman, the individual and the public world, the meaning of the Nazi holocaust. For once ideology has given way to subjectivity; there is no limit to the poets' themes.

But can they create a living literature out of a dead language? The question is commonly asked, even by writers who perhaps ought to know better. For contrary to widespread impression, Hebrew has never been dead as classical Greek is dead, nor has it been mainly sacramental as has Latin in recent centuries. Even in the darkest period of its people's history, Hebrew was used for literary prose and verse, communal records, personal and business correspondence and the like. But it has not been continuously alive as English and French have been alive, and its widespread literary use did not begin until the secularist-modern movement ("Enlightenment") of European Jewry had gained momentum a century ago. As a vehicle in everyday living, Hebrew is one of the youngest languages in the world. Moreover, alongside modern English and French, for example, its vocabulary appears limited; and this limited vocabulary has been in service for centuries in writings with which well-educated readers of Hebrew are, to put it mildly, extremely familiar.

No wonder such readers of modern verse will hear all kinds of echoes from earlier contexts—or that some Hebrew critics, with the passion of lexicographers, pay more attention to the etymology than to the poetry. Nevertheless, this linguistic "situation" has unique consequences, involving many things, from the mintings of new words to the echoings of the old that are inescapable. Even one who comes to the poems as ill-equipped as I am soon stops being surprised to find multiple reverberations in a single sound. In certain ways, then, the nature of their language would seem both to help and hinder modern Hebrew poets—and yet they may have only begun to show us what remarkable things can be made of this mixed blessing.

Most of the poets writing in Israel today seem as much at home with Western Modernism as with Hebrew Classicism—which they somehow merge into one. "Isaac," for example, is both a Biblical poem and a surrealist experience in which the poet also has been witness, participant and speaker. "Spring in the World" finally unsays all that it appears to have been saying. In fact, the more one explores, the more one is likely to come upon fresh ways in which the poets blend elements of an ancient religious tradition with the most avant garde of secular approaches.

Isaac

Early in the morning the sun took a walk in the forest
Together with me and with Father
And my right hand in his left.

Like lightning a knife flamed between the trees.
And I fear so the terror of my eyes facing blood on the leaves.

Father, Father hurry and save Isaac
And no one will be missing at lunchtime.

It is I who am being slaughtered, my son,
And my blood is already on the leaves.
And Father's voice was stifled.
And his face pale.

And I wanted to cry out, writhing not to believe
And tearing open the eyes.
And I woke up.

And bloodless was the right hand.

          —Amir Gilboa (literal translation by Arieh Sachs).

Spring in the World

The flowers are big, as if
[It were] possible to live inside them,
[There are] transparent clouds in the blue,
As if the heart had been comforted (pitied).

Butterflies [are] bursting out, as if
They had never seen the light.
My body [is] with your body, as if
[There were] no boundary between blood and blood.

Flames of birds, as if
The sky had been completed at last,
Buds of laughter, as if
[There were] spring in the world.
          —Tuvya Rubner (literal translation by Dan Pagis).

          Both selections from "The Hebrew Poem Itself."

ALAN PRYCE-JONES*
Difficult or Impossible

I T IS not so very long since I took a freighter trip to Europe in order
to make myself read "Ulysses" from cover to cover. I knew that it demanded 10 days of plain living and a deck chair, a total absence of distraction, and an overriding sense of purpose: otherwise I should, as
often before, drop the book after 50 pages.

* (Another essay by Mr. Pryce-Jones appears on page 22)

Between New York and Liverpool, then, I did what I had set out to—and did it, moreover, with very great delight. Given the right time, space and opportunity, given an incentive—later I was to teach a university course on, among other writers, Joyce—the difficulties of "Ulysses" fall away. What remains is a masterpiece.

Also a worry. Like others who read a great deal, I have put certain books aside in the conviction that I shall never get through them. Sometimes my own mental sloth is at fault. I may, for instance, start on Spinoza's "Ethics"; but very soon exhaustion will set in. I suppose I cannot care enough about either ethics or Spinoza to face a long sequence of propositions, proofs and corollaries. But usually it is not so much sloth as inability to understand that repels me. Yet, if by taking some extra trouble, I can find real delight in "Ulysses," may I not be missing a comparable pleasure through neglecting, say, the "Cantos" of Ezra Pound? Or, anyway, the stiffer parts of Browning's "Sordello"?

This is a comparatively new problem for readers to face. It is only in the last 50 years or so that serious writers have taken to writing without any necessary urge to communicate with an audience.

Of course there have always been difficult writers, and in every language. Tacitus is a difficult writer; so are Dante, John Donne, Gerard Manley Hopkins, Stefan George, and a legion more. But their difficulties are not insoluble. Difficult writers of smaller scope, such as Hart Crane or Dylan Thomas, may slip into incoherence at times, but they compensate for moments of inattention by greater moments of splendor.

Lately, however, things have changed. The reader has become, not a necessary complement to the writer but a more or less friendly witness to the birth-pangs of the writer's ego. Things will not be made easy for him. When Cyril Connolly designed his "The Unquiet Grave," he dismembered a journal and put the pieces together again according to consistent changes of mood, after the fashion of symphonic movements. Not so William Burroughs 20 years later. He simply dismembers his book and does not put it together again.

Or take poetry. We know poetic logic and prose logic to be different things. Docketed as statements, some of the most famous lines in all poetry amount to very little. "Now lies the Earth all Danaë to the stars." Or, "Man comes and tills the fields and lies beneath,/And after many a summer dies the swan." A purely prosaic mind might point out that in the first, the connections between Earth and Danaë, raped by Zeus in the guise of a shower of gold, is tenuous, even if the stars are numerous and of the right color. And in the second, that Tennyson's pretty image of death-in-life is no better than rococo. Why drag in the swan, unless as a decoration? Why state what is not true: that Man is likely to be a pastoral being buried on the scene of his labor?

Declarative logic has nothing to do with the case, we retort. We may not go as far as Housman, who said that he knew himself to be in the presence of poetry when he felt a physical shudder of pleasure, yet each of us knows when he is in touch with poetry even if he cannot exactly define the nature of poetic substance.

But what happens when the poet goes far beyond Tennyson in flight from prose? In these lines, for instance:

> Honor, or color, point
> they called it, between the middle chief
> and the heart, point
> And if the nasturtium
> is my shield
> and my song
> a cantus firmus

This section of a contemporary poem is complete, I might add.

The crux here, I think, is that Tennyson is visibly writing "poetry." Our minds are therefore prepared for the reception of sensations and sequences remote from the plain stuff of prose. By contrast, a writer like Charles Olson—from whose "Maximus" poems my quotation comes—is trying to create a poetic effect by using the language of prose in a manner utterly remote from prose-writing. The impact on the reader's mind is much like that on his palate were he to bite into what is obviously a peach and find that it tastes of hamburger.

There is, I know, a kind of reader who is responsive to the impenetrable. I also suspect that he is not so very unlike the kind of reader who allowed himself, 70 years ago, to swing along to the cantering anapests of Swinburne for the sake of an occasional bright illumination. Much of the time, Swinburne offers no more than a beautifully orchestrated chaos of sound. But from time to time the chaos clears. You cannot exactly swing along to the music of the contemporary avant-garde, among whom anapests are to seek; but the ratio of chaos and illumination is about the same.

The sufferer will be that pedantic reader, like myself, who dislikes chaos. It is not that we mind difficulty. We do not even mind auto-

matic writing, such as the surrealists used to practice. We do not
mind having to wrestle with words before pleasure can be extracted
from them, nor do we mind, occasionally, taking a trip into the subconscious of a writer we trust.

But we are wary. In a lifetime crowded with books, and with
reading time limited by the claims of living and dying, we do not
want to waste hours on bad avant-garde any more than on bad Swinburne. Only: How do we know the bad avant-garde from the good?
Charles Olson (the poet quoted above) for one, has documented his
own aims and techniques very fully. With his help, we can see what
he is trying to achieve, and we can widen our sympathies to include
what, at first sight, may look incomprehensible. But much of what
comes our way we are expected to take on trust. Great slabs of prose
and verse are laid before us without any indication that the writer had
much in mind except a great slab.

Even the conscientious writers of an older school may let us down.
Scholarly readers, who have wrestled for days with "The Waste Land,"
in the light of Eliot's notes, have to face the fact that to some extent
they have been spoofed. Besides pen in hand, Eliot often sat with
tongue in cheek, so that after nearly 50 years we have to start all over
again and decide how much of "The Waste Land," like Max Beer-
bohm's vision of Matthew Arnold, is "not wholly serious." So where do
we stand with "Naked Lunch," with the novels of Michel Butor and
Alain Robbe-Grillet, with the laxer pages of Jack Kerouac and the
denser annotations of Gregory Corso?

The answer must be: Develop a literary Geiger counter, if you can.
Catch the warning tick which betrays the dangerous presence of talent and, more explosively, of genius. The tick was very much easier to
catch when there were rules of taste, technique, feeling, which could
either be obeyed or broken. Tick. "Maud." Try again. Total silence.
Ah, well, "Enoch Arden." Tick. "Middlemarch." Total silence.
"Adam Bede." In those days the counter worked well enough. But
now, with so much junk about, much of it exalted by nervous critics,
much of it glittering with doubtful color, it takes a supersensitive
electrode to respond.

In order to obtain a very few works of genius, we have to wade
through these junk-yards as patiently as possible. It is no use complaining that much of modern writing is slack, or unmeaning, or arrogantly
futile. Such trivialities now take the place of Victorian fluency, just as

four-letter words replace the oversweetness of sentimental fiction a
century ago. The run-of-the-mill swings this way and that, between
excess of sugar and excess of acid. What matters is to keep the senses
fresh enough to recognize the approach of a masterpiece. Which
means, in practice, that good literature is in its usual state of near-
eclipse, with the codicil that talent is rather rarer than usual, and the
daily bread of writing rather less well baked.

ROBERT GORHAM DAVIS
What's in a Name?

*Robert Gorham Davis, professor of English at Columbia, writes as
easily of the eighteenth century as he does of the contemporary in literature. He has been a frequent contributor to The Times Book
Review.*

IN DECIDING on names for his characters, an author has an unfair
advantage over other parents. He knows so much better how his child
will turn out. When Saul Bellow named Augie March, he had already
conceived a hero restlessly on the move, marching ahead, with august
ideas of himself. Henry James saw in Adam Verver of "The Golden
Bowl" a self-made American, sprung from the soil, full of verve and
zest for life. In choosing names like "Murdstone," "Scrooge" and
"Gradgrind," Dickens was being even more obvious.

When parents baptize a flesh-and-blood child, they can only hope
that his qualities will match his name. Choices like "Ernest" or
"Prudence" tell more about the parents than the child. Ernest turns
out to be frivolous; Prudence lets money run through her fingers like
water.

Except as they show national origin, real family names are equally
irrelevant. Originally they did tell how a man looked or where he lived
or what he did. Time broke the connection. The Hills moved to the
valley. The Fletchers stopped making arrows. The Stewarts (sty-
wards) no longer tended the king's pigs. They became kings themselves.

In fiction it is different. The author can match the name to his knowledge of the character. Names can be epithets also, can describe and categorize. When we miss their meaning, part of the author's intention is lost.

This poses a problem for translators. If New Yorkers named Schneider and White travel to Paris, they do not enter themselves on the hotel register as "Coupeur" and "Blanc." When English historians write about the emperor Frederick Barbarossa, he does not turn into Frederick Redbeard. But when La Barbe-Bleue, the wife-killer, crosses the Channel, he is addressed, of course, as Blue-Beard.

In fairy tales, the memorable names that are really epithets change with the language and remain transparent. Snow White is Schneewittchen in German and Blanche-Neige in French. Cendrillon in France, with her "petite pantoufle de vair" becomes Cinderella in England, her slipper now turning into glass because "vair" (squirrel fur) was taken to be "verre" (glass). For the Grimm brothers, she is Aschenbrödel, "Ash Maid," as one of their translators calls her. But "Ash Maid," compared to "Cinderella," loses the flavor, especially delicious to children, of something which is at once epithet and name. Like Odysseus in the cave of Polyphemus, children relish jokes about "Mr. Nobody."

On higher literary levels the problem is more complex. Ben Jonson called his great comedy of greed "Volpone, or the Fox." His English character is Sir Politic Would-Be, but the other meaningful names, since they have to sound Italian, stay untranslated. They include "Mosca" (the fly), "Voltore" (the vulture), "Corbaccio" (the crow) and "Corvino" (the raven). To identify the creatures hovering around the presumably dying fox, the non-Italian-speaking reader depends on footnotes. These can never equal the effect of hearing a familiar word in his own tongue.

The names in Shakespeare's "A Midsummer Night's Dream" are as charming as the play itself. In foreign-language versions the fairy names "Peaseblossom" and "Mustardseed" are always translated. Sometimes the names "Quince," "Bottom," "Flute," stay English, with their humor pretty well lost. Sometimes equivalents are found. Starveling becomes "Meurt-de-Faim" in French, "Schlucker" in German. In one Italian version Quince, Snug and Bottom because of their trades become Wedge ("Il Cuneo"), Auger ("Il Trapano") and Shuttle ("La Spola").

Where characters are strongly individualized or identified with a

national culture, translation is impossible. "Raskolnikov" simply cannot be turned into "Schismatic," "Dr. Faustus" into "Dr. Fortunate,"
"Sancho Panza" into "Sancho Belly," or "Lysistrata" into "Miss De-
mobilizer" (literally "the undoer of the army"). And so readers miss
the pointed meanings. The hero of "The Fall," by Albert Camus, is
Jean-Baptiste Clamence. John the Baptist, in the famous words of
Isaiah, was "the voice of one crying in the wilderness." How many
readers had the Latin of the Vulgate (*vox clamantis in deserto*) clearly
enough in mind to recognize the Biblical allusiveness of "Clamence"?

There is no way of rendering in another language Odysseus' play on
the connotations of pain and woe that his name could suggest in Greek.
To avoid such loss, Shelley called his version of "Oedipus Rex," "Swellfoot the Tyrant," but this is possible only in comedy. "Swellfoot"
sounds neither dignified nor Greek, yet this is exactly what "Oedipus"
means, and is a direct reference to his being exposed as an infant with
tightly bound feet.

In Book Eight of the "Odyssey," the Phaeacians, a seafaring folk,
entertain Odysseus at games. In the Butcher and Lang translation we
are told that among the noble youths are "Acroneus, and Ocyalus,
and Elatreus, and Nauteus, and Prymneus and Anchialus, and Eret-
meus, and Ponteus, and Proreus, Thoon and Anabesineus, and Amphi-
alus, son of Polyneus, son of Tekton." Resounding Greek names
though these are the list seems a bit excessive, since we never meet
their bearers again. But in the translation by William Rouse, we see
why Homer included them and why they amused him: "Topship and
Quicksea and Paddler, Seaman and Poopman, Beacher and Oarsman,
Deepsea and Lookout, Goahead and Upaboard; there was Seagirt, the
son of Manyclipper Shipwrightson." Homer was inventing flavorful
names suitable for sailors, and the whole effect is lost if we do not see
their meaning.

This is true not only of names of characters, but of naming generally. Children love plant names that describe figuratively: "snow-
drop," "snapdragon," "jack-in-the-pulpit," "lady's slipper." They bear
the same magic as "Snow White" or "Cinderella," the same magic
that the Greeks found in names like "Calypso" (the hider), "Cyclops"
(round-eyed), "Aphrodite" (foamborn), "Demeter" (barley-mother).
The lady's slipper belongs to the genus Cypripedium, a term that
sounds as melodiously meaningless as did at first the names of the
Phaeacian youths. Actually it is as explicit as they were. It means, in

fact, lady's slipper. "Pedium" is the Latin version of a Greek word for sandal, and "Cypri-" refers to Aphrodite, known as the fair Cyprian because she chose Paphos in Cyprus as her dwelling place after emerging from the sea.

In their etymologies, dictionaries of course tell us what metaphors or descriptive terms lie buried in familiar names: pachyderm ("thick-skin"), rhinoceros ("nosehorn"), hippopotamus ("riverhorse"), geranium ("crane"), delphinium ("dolphin"), chrysanthemum ("gold-flower"). But here, as with the names of characters, our being told the meaning by a reference book is not the same as hearing the name declare its own meaning in the language of everyday speech.

When the New Testament in English mentions "Golgotha," it explains it is the "place of a skull" or simply calls it "The Skull." The name "Calvary" does not make us see a skull in the same way, even after we are told that "calvaria" is the Latin for skull (from "calvus," bald). Hearing the word "lobster," after learning that it comes from the Anglo-Saxon "loppe," spider, does not give us the same sense of spiderness that we get from the term "spider monkey." Even though we recognize its Greek components, "dracocephalum" is very different from "dragonhead." Americans driving behind a truck in Germany take a pleasure in the word "Sprengstoff" that they do not get from "explosive."

The vividness caused by a name's proclaiming its own appropriateness works for all words, not just for proper names. There are hundreds of thousands of words in the dictionary because new ones are constantly being made out of old ones. We compound them, add prefixes and suffixes, use them in transferred, figurative senses. When we can see how a word describes the thing or idea it names, linguists call it "transparent"; when we cannot, it is "opaque." A rose by any other name would smell as sweet, but the London Underground could not just as well be called "the skyscraper," and ping-pong could not just as well be named "football." These are transparent terms with an evident appropriateness to what they name. "Newspaper" is a more transparent term than "journal" and "movies" than "cinema," even though "kinema" means movement in Greek.

We have taken much of our English vocabulary, especially our intellectual vocabulary, from Latin, Greek and French, where the process of making words by compounding, by affixing, and by metaphorical transfers, had already occurred. Words that were transparent in the original became opaque in English, especially as users became more ignorant of Latin, Greek and French. The formal written vocabulary in England in the 18th and early 19th centuries was highly Latinical, but all the schoolboys were set to writing Latin and even classical Greek as if they were living languages. "Mouse" for a black eye is transparent for us; the word "muscle" is opaque. For those schoolboys "muscle" (Latin "musculus," little mouse) was perfectly transparent. It is the little mouse that runs under the skin when you flex your biceps. Dr. Johnson was only partly joking when in his famous dictionary he defined "network" as "anything reticulated or decussated, at equal distances, with interstices between the intersections."

ERIC PARTRIDGE
Degraded Language

When Eric Partridge came up for his oral examination at Oxford, he was reprimanded for a slang term in the preface to his thesis and for two colloquialisms in the body of the work. He watched his language thereafter, made a career of it, and urged others to watch theirs ("Usage and Abusage," "The World of Words"). He also made himself famous as an expert in slang and colloquialisms as the compiler of "A Dictionary of Slang and Unconventional English" and its many editions.

P ARTLY because of the moral and intellectual disruptions caused by the war of 1939-1945, and partly because of that general lowering of the standards of civilization which has, during and ever since the war of 1914-1918, distressed all those for whom civilization consists far less in scientific and technological advances (although they too are important) than in the spiritual and moral well-being, and the intellectual healthiness and sanity, of the human race, there has arisen an every-man-for-himself, allied with a do-it-yourself, cult that affects life at all levels.

These two cults obviously form two aspects of what may perhaps be called the cult of self-sufficiency. As they are visible in, so do they affect both the practicalities of life—the everyday business of living—and its intangibles and imponderables or, differently phrased, its embellishments and enhancements, its values and spiritualities, which do so much to mitigate the fundamental, yet not insuperable, tragedy of the human condition. The tragedy is not insuperable, for, in the last resort, man can be defeated only by man: death, as such, connotes not defeat but an ending; and death in war, like death by torture in the cold war, brings mere obliteration, not defeat.

The enhancements and the consolations are, in the spiritual and moral spheres, afforded by religion and philosophy and, in the intellectual and esthetic and emotional, by music, art, literature and drama, all four of which, moreover, manifestly possess moral and spiritual values. To these embellishments and solaces we must, with grave reservations, add cinema and radio and television. But literature, music, the arts and the rest all exhibit deterioration, fortunately neither irreparable nor necessarily permanent nor, much less, inevitable; a deterioration caused by that undermining which is well named the leveling process.

The danger lies in the fact that it is not a leveling upwards, a raising of standards, but a leveling downwards, a lowering of standards. Thinking persons, however, will sooner or later realize that the envious ones, those for whom "anything goes," have yet to learn, as life will probably force them to learn, that ultimately "nothing will go" for them. The don't-cares lack a driving ambition, let alone a compulsive aspiration; they also lack integrity of any kind whatsoever—for instance, they regard intellectual integrity as a chimera, moral integrity as a drug; and so they are obliged to content themselves with mediocrity. That the obligation is enforced by their own blindness and laziness seems never to occur to them. Nor does it occur to them that their entire attitude reflects the state of mind and the kind of mind in which, and only in which, such an attitude can exist at all: an attitude of crass conceit and artless arrogance.

For the lazy, the lethargic, the envious, Bedlam is as musical as Bach or Beethoven or Brahms; an indolent insolent daub is foisted on us as an example of genius. A level of dull, uninspired, almost painless monotony, and the I.Q. of a cretin, are by them ranked as superior to high intelligence, profound thought and deep feeling, and a controlled, hence effectual, imagination. By them, idle fancies, naïve and childish when not nasty and brutish, are equated to the imagination they neither possess nor understand.

In language—with which I am here concerned—the clumsy, prolix, often ambiguous, almost incoherent speech of an illiterate or, at least, of a meagerly educated person is for them as good as—indeed, it is preferable to—the speech of someone adequately educated and at least moderately cultured. No one can prevent them from thinking in this stupid and short-sighted way. Not to think in this way would lead to unease and discomfort. Yet they do not thus defectively think from a noble spirit of independence nor even from a rugged assertion of individuality. They are encouraged by many who should know better, and incited by many who know much better.

The results are, from every point of view, utterly deplorable, as much for themselves as for others. For these, the far too easily satisfied—for these, the envious ones—suppleness and subtlety become impossible and therefore suspect; delicate distinctions become difficult and therefore disagreeable; variety becomes an unwanted elegance, and elegance a dirty word. The ease and simplicity they fondly suppose they are achieving elude them; nor do they understand why. Eloquence becomes even more reprehensible than elegance, perhaps because, unless they return to the past they scorn and spurn, they almost never encounter it in their own sort of speaking and writing. In the matter of elementary communication, they are, despite their adamant belief and assertions to the contrary, doing their utmost to destroy communicability and to render communication itself nugatory because they not only fail in clarity of phrasing, and in perspicuity of sentence, but also prevent the very possibility of achieving clarity and perspicuity. Clarity and perspicuity have followed those other qualities into obloquy: they, too, are suspect, hotly though the levelers would deny it.

But the underlying, irresistible reason for—the originating cause of —all those qualities becoming suspect is that the levelers ("No one shall be our superiors, but we ourselves are superior") hate, because they fear, superiority of mind and spirit; they envy it, therefore they pretend to despise it; they do their best to prevent its emergence and exercise; they would, if they could, outlaw it. Why, if *they* lack it, should others have it? "All animals are equal, but some animals are more equal than others." The fact that they cannot prevent its emergence nor stifle its existence, escapes them, as it has always escaped their predecessors and their similars. They avert their eyes, these dullard Pharisees, from the fact that ambiguity, most dangerous of faults, and tedium, most deadly of defects, and a drab parochialism, bleakest of myopias, inevitably accompany, for they issue from, such an attitude, such a state of mind, such a *non*-state of spirit.

Little wonder that mediocrity and monotony flourish in speech and writing, whence exhilaration and enchantment, sweet reasonableness, beauty would all, if the levelers had their envious way, be banished. Nor am I thinking only, or even mainly, of literature and oratory: I am thinking of all communication whatsoever by the written or the spoken word. The vehicle of all speaking and writing, as of all thinking, is language, the readiest and most accessible of all the means of communication. (Signs and symbols themselves imply language.) Damage that vehicle and you damage the most important means by which progress, whether spiritual or moral or intellectual, moves to its ends. You don't need language to enable you to invent something or to make a truly scientific (as distinct from a mathematical) discovery; you do need it in order to describe and explain, to publicize and promote, that invention, and to profit by that discovery.

Slow down that vehicle and you slow down communication, thinking, progress, civilization, the very life, perhaps the bare existence, of mankind. This is precisely what is being done by the slow-minded, the dull-spirited, the sluggish-hearted, along with those more dangerous animals, the indifferent, the callous, the misanthropic; by all those whose sensibilities have been blunted and whose humanity has become indurated and desiccated; all those by whom pity and mercy are held to be a weakness, kindness a waste of time, sensitivity a luxury none can afford, intelligence a blind alley and a dead-end (but doctrinaire intellectuality a virtue), morality "strictly for the birds" and spirituality a myth.

Anyone believing in the worth and value of the human race, in its immense potentialities, in "man's unconquerable spirit," finds it difficult to condone, impossible to approve and unthinkable to abet the most insidious and the surest means of destroying civilization. To degrade language is to degrade civilization. To persist in the degradation of language would finally so damage it that it would be dangerous to use it, except for the most primitive statements and questions and orders. As language grew more and more meager and inept and hazardous, so would civilization very quickly become like a crippled and bewildered animal, less equal than the others.

The envious ones miss an all-important facet of grammatical rules and recommendations, a point that, being paramount, should also be obvious. The rules were not evolved as an instrument of torture, nor yet to clog the advance of learning and thinking, much less to make things difficult for the dull. They arose from sheer necessity. First of all, to ensure and maintain intelligibility; then, one step higher, clarity; after that, adequacy and suitability to the sociological, not merely the social, situation or context; then, ease and elegance of effect and economy of effort; finally beauty and eloquence, or, at the least, charm. Anyone would, on hearing or reading the proletarian pundits, be excused for thinking that they regarded good English, at whatever level, as an accursed status symbol. These defenders either of clumsy, verbose, solecistic English or of a meager vocabulary, appear to feel affronted by anyone who possesses an accurate and various vocabulary, a clear expressiveness, some slight appreciation of economy or power or beauty. To them, the language of the taxi-driver, the hauler, the porter has the same value as that of the practiced speaker or writer.

To them, "I ain't never ever done no 'arm to nobody nowhere" is as clear and effective as "I've never harmed anybody," or, more emphatically, "Never have I harmed anybody." "I don't know as how yer Ma would like it if yer ol' man mucked up the 'all with 'is dirty clodhoppers! D'yer think as she would?" is, in their opinion, as neat and economical as "I don't think your Mother would like it if your father dirtied the hall with his heavy boots, or do you think she *would?*" To them, Landor's

> I strove with none, for none was worth my strife;
> Nature I loved, and next to Nature, Art;
> I warmed both hands before the fire of life;
> It sinks; and I am ready to depart

might just as well—or rather, even better—be expressed in some such prose as this:

"I never fought with nobody, for nobody was worth it. I loved Nature best of all, and after it, I loved Art. I made the most of life while I could do so, and now that I'm past having any fun, I'm ready to clear out."

How, one may fairly ask, do the simplicitarians propose to write adequately—conveying the wonder and the beauty, the power, the distinction and the delight, the mystery and the glory—about a supreme poem or novel, a great painting, a lovely, deeply moving piece of music? How engage in an acute metaphysical or a delicately ethical or a mundanely intricate argument or discussion, if the vocabulary and the style are limited to the circumscriptions of bare communication and to the inadequacies of literacy and the fatuities of half-baked minds?

Good—that is, clear, effective, entirely adequate—speaking and writing will ease and smooth the passage of general thought and the conveyance of a particular thought or impression in statement or question or command. Bad speaking and writing do just the opposite and, worse, set up doubt and ambiguity.

Why are the envious ones so desperately eager to cut off their noses to spite their faces? Why do they imagine impositions and injustices that lack validity and do not, in the fact, exist at all outside their fevered imaginations? Is it because they sense their own shortcomings and—"their nature, right or wrong"—they cannot bear to see them exposed? Or is it because they lack the generosity of spirit to recognize that there are men and women with minds much superior to their own, and that good speaking and good writing spring from that superiority?

RONALD GROSS
Found Poetry

There are at least two sides to Ronald Gross. One is his deep concern for education, shown in part by the books he has written ("The Revolution in the Schools," "The Teacher and the Taught"). The other is his enthusiasm for experimental poetry. He is the author of "Pop Poems" (found poetry) and has recently published a collection of concrete poems, "Handful of Concrete."

THE *objet trouvé*, that rogue of 20th-century art, is now crashing literature under the name "Found Poetry." On the B.B.C.'s Third program, John Daniel has been reading poems he found in the London telephone directory, his insurance policy, a cookbook, "Das Kapital," and his grandfather's World War I diary. Daniel, a college lecturer in English, is seeking to publish the diary *in toto* as a found poem. WBAI-FM in New York City broadcast a reading of labels—

The Canister Papers—with no foreknowledge of Daniel's program. William Burroughs has cut up copies of the Paris edition of The Herald Tribune, scrambled the pieces together, and thrown them at the reader's eyes and ears.

New York poets John Giorno, Jackson Mac Low and Tuli Kupferberg make poems out of newspaper items. Norman Mailer claims that some of the most interesting writing in America appears on men's-room walls. Even so staid a literary personage as Graham Greene plucked a poem out of a Pan American Airways guide book and submitted it to the found-poem competition in the New Statesman.

The impulse comes, of course, from the painters and sculptors, who since Marcel Duchamp and Kurt Schwitters have been dragging all manner of things into the galleries and "anointing" them as art. The line is fairly direct from Duchamp's bottle rack and urinal to Warhol's Brillo boxes, Jasper Johns's American flags, and Jim Dine's bathroom. Artists in other fields, like John Cage in music, have contributed their findings. The makers of "happenings" insist that the best performances take place outside of theaters, with the dramatist simply announcing that what is happening *is* drama. An Off-Off-Broadway theater has extended the idea to a production where, for 50 cents, you can watch people who have moved in and are simply living on the stage.

There are some illustrious precedents in literature itself for the use of found material. John Dos Passos' newsreels in "U.S.A." come to mind at once, and more recently William Carlos Williams' incorporation of historical documents, personal letters and such in his masterwork "Paterson." Up till now, though, writers have not used and savored found material for itself but rather subordinated it in a work composed mostly of original material.

Now writers seem suddenly to have discovered that, in the words of avant-garde publisher Jonathan Williams, "poetry is where you find it."

The range of effects in Found Poetry is wide, from sportive to bitingly satiric, and sometimes quite poignant. Evocations of familiar styles are frequent, as in the lovely John Betjeman which Lionel Burman found in the London classifieds and submitted to the New Statesman contest:

> The Headmistress
> Of a successful independent
> Girls' preparatory
> School

Now retiring
After a long career
Of creative teaching
And cooperative achievement
Seeks to leave
Her grateful governors
With a capable
And imaginative
Successor.

For the same contest, Bernard Phillips carved out of the Warren Report this shockingly objective elegiac verse:

J F K

The body
is that
of a muscular
well-developed
and well-nourished
adult
Caucasian male
measuring seventy-two
and a half
inches
and weighing approximately
one hundred
and seventy
pounds.

The rules for Found Poetry vary. Classically (in a manner of speaking), a Found Poem keeps the words just as they originally appeared, merely rearranging them into lines to bring out their poetic quality. The source may be almost anything, so long as the original intent was not poetry. This stricture rules out most advertising copy, whose extreme effects are usually intentional.

When I began to find poems, however, it soon became clear that, as Duchamp himself had suggested, "ready-mades" need not be pure, but could be "assisted," "rectified" and "modified" (like his mustachioed "Mona Lisa"). So with found poems. The most telling effect is produced through manipulation of the raw materials. The devices of the contemporary pop artists suggested the techniques necessary, including change of focus, texture, proportion, the blow-up and repetition.

As I worked with labels, tax forms, commercials, contracts, pin-up captions, obituaries and the like, I soon found myself rediscovering all the traditional verse forms in found materials: ode, sonnet, epigram, haiku, free verse. Such finds made me realize that these forms are not mere artifices, but shapes that language naturally takes when carrying powerful thoughts or feelings. The result—which I call pop poems—are true Found Poems, nonetheless: the material is all "given," nothing added, nothing taken away. The poetic techniques that have been applied merely emphasize certain nuances inherent in the material itself.

Two of my favorites indicate how different techniques may bring out the import of commonplace material.

Yield

Yield.
No Parking.
Unlawful to Pass.
Wait for Green Light.
Yield.
Stop.
Narrow Bridge.
Merging Traffic Ahead.
Yield.

Yield.

Yield.

The source for this imagist fragment is obvious. The second is based on an Associated Press bulletin printed in The Denver Post:

Miss Farrow Just Smiled

Singer Frank Sinatra
honeymooned, somewhere,
with his third wife,
Mia Farrow, today
after a Las Vegas
wedding performed
between plane flights.

Exactly where they went
hasn't been determined.

After the ceremony
the couple walked out
on the apartment's patio
and Sinatra beamed:
"How are you, baby?"

Miss Farrow just smiled.

After the ceremony
the couple walked out
on the apartment's patio
and Sinatra beamed:
"How are you, baby?"

Exactly where they went
hasn't been determined.

Singer Frank Sinatra
honeymooned, somewhere,
with his third wife,
Mia Farrow, today
after a Las Vegas
wedding performed
between plane flights.

Exactly where they went
hasn't been determined.

After the ceremony
the couple walked out
on the apartment's patio
and Sinatra beamed:
"How are you, baby?"

Miss Farrow just smiled.

Found Poetry is great fun, of course, and gives laymen the vicarious pleasures of creating poetry. For poets, the composition of Found Poems provides an intriguing exercise in observing ordinary language and in using a limited repertoire of technical devices to transmute dross into literature. And just as pop, op, and "minimal" art offer a respite from the subjectivity of abstract expressionism in painting, Found Poetry offers some relief from the private symbolism of contemporary verse.

Found Poems have a distinctive fascination of their own, I think,

deriving perhaps from that ambivalence art critic Françoise Choay
discerned in Duchamp's *objets trouvés:*

"On one hand, the industrial product is denounced in all its anonymity, its banality, its essential poverty which deprives it of human
and poetic qualities. On the other hand, it still remains an object which
a simple decision on the part of the spectator can extract from its context to give it mystery and opacity."

Found Poetry is also one—and maybe a self-preserving—reaction
to the Niagara of words that surround us. A cataract of linguistic be-
musement, cajolery, anesthesia, provocation, titillation, sensuality,
harangue, sentimentality, brutalization booms through every minute
of our lives. Yet—like tourists standing on the ledge just behind the
cascade—we remain safely dry as the torrent hurtles down inches from
our eyes. Our senses are sated and numbed; we hardly see the potential
for destructiveness, or the elusive charm and sometime beauty of our
semantic environment.

By snapping this language into sharp focus, we can perhaps better
understand and therefore better withstand the barrage. Found Poetry
turns the continuous verbal undertone of mass culture up full-volume
for a moment, offering a chance to see and hear it with a shock of
recognition.

PETER QUENNELL
A Matter of Style

*When Peter Quennell speaks of style, he speaks with book, for he is a
master of style himself, as he has shown in a long list of literary studies
and biographies, and some studies that were not so literary. They range
from Shakespeare to Byron to Ruskin. He is at present the editor of the
English magazine, History Today.*

GEORGE MOORE used sometimes to announce, when he was
meditating aloud about the writer's business, that any critic might be
sure of his eternal gratitude if he could help him improve an awkward

sentence by putting a comma in the right place. How odd that announcement sounds today! With the notable exception of Evelyn Waugh—a novelist who was always at pains to write correct, euphonious English—few modern authors have been much concerned with style, and still fewer, I suppose, with problems of grammar and syntax or the minutiae of punctuation. Language is regarded as a means to an end; and the end, of course, is more important than the means.

Style has become synonymous with "fine writing"; and "fine writing," which recalls the work of Walter Pater—indeed, of George Moore himself—is popularly linked with feeble thinking. The deliberate stylist—the man who cherishes words and loves the music of prose—has now been thoroughly discredited. In the crowded democracy of modern letters, he is at best an aristocratic anachronism, at his worst a fascist brute.

The case against style, admittedly, can be supported by some telling arguments. Good writers, we are reminded, have often been imperfect writers. Saint-Simon, for instance, and his great disciple Marcel Proust both overwhelm us with huge unwieldy paragraphs, in which we grope through a labyrinth of relative clauses, at times collapsing or completely losing our way, towards the blessed apparition of a distant full stop. And then there was Balzac, who declared that the main point was not to avoid mistakes, but to possess an imaginative quality "that sweeps everything in front of it."

Samuel Butler, too, another advocate of what Arnold Bennett once called "the higher literary carelessness," remarked that he had never known an author who took the smallest trouble with his style "and was at the same time readable." More recently, H. G. Wells poked elaborate fun at Henry James, typical of the artist who lives secluded from the world "in his stuffy little corner of pure technique." James's books, he said, resembled pompous sacerdotal edifices, where every light is focused on the high altar; and on that altar we see, reverently disposed, "a dead kitten, an egg-shell, a bit of string."

His victim's response, however, was prompt and effective. First, James distinguished between life and art, life being "all inclusion and confusion," art "all discrimination and selection." The artist, when he has chosen his subject, must begin by purifying and transforming it; art, he assured Wells, "*makes* life, makes interest, makes importance." In the chaos of our day-to-day experience, the novelist, who is also an artist, seeks out the tiny golden nugget that, on the anvil of his craft, he can afterwards "hammer into a sacred hardness." James was primarily an artist-craftsman; it did not occur to him that he might one day be considered either as a moralist or as a social commentator.

Most modern literary criticism adopts a very different point of view. Mistrustful of a narrowly esthetic approach, it tends, following F. R. Leavis, to discuss literature as a current substitute for religion and morality. Critics "evaluate" the social content of a book, assume a moral attitude towards its characters. Thus "Othello" is an unsatisfying play because it is built around a "bogus hero." The Moor, Mr. Leavis informs us, reveals "an obtuse and brutal egotism," which soon involves him in the "ferocious stupidity" of an "insane and self-deceiving passion."

Mr. Leavis, it so happens, is himself a rough-and-ready writer; and his example, unfortunately, has proved infectious. If one compares an English literary magazine of today with a similar periodical published 30 years ago, one notices that, whereas reviewers of that far-off period made some attempt to write gracefully—or, at least, amusingly and fluently—the modern reviewer records his opinions like a messenger delivering a heavy package, which he plumps down, with an air of "take-it-or-leave-it," before abruptly turning on his heel. The precious gift of communicating enjoyment—and of writing enjoyably as well as instructively—is seldom found in youthful critics.

No doubt the present distrust of style is due to a misconception of its nature. A man's style, Samuel Butler decided, should resemble his dress—"it should attract as little attention as possible." Style, he implies, is an outward covering, to be buttoned on or taken off. And, in a decently democratic age, who would wish to own a Brummell's wardrobe? Just how misleading was Butler's view becomes evident when we examine the works of any famous English stylist.

Gibbon's style is not to be confused with his lace ruffles and embroidered coat: it was an essential adjunct of his genius, the method he had evolved of shaping his material into a comprehensive literary pattern. His style was the reaction of his personality to the gigantic task that he had set himself, and the weapon by which he conquered it. He developed as an historian by developing his command of the English language. Without a style could he have carried on his story from the polished Age of the Antonines, across a tremendous gulf of centuries, to the crude beginnings of medieval Europe? As I have suggested elsewhere, "more authors learn to think and feel in the laborious process of learning to write than have ever mastered the art of writing under the pressure of urgent thoughts and violent emotions."

A modern writer customarily reverses the sequence: having something he feels obliged to say, he next attempts to produce a literary vehicle by which he can propound his message. For all the verbal license they allow themselves, many authors—particularly young authors—are nowadays instinctive puritans. They resent style because it may distract our attention from the general grimness of their world-picture. Style is a form of self-indulgence; style is escapist and somehow vaguely wicked. If an individual method of expression is required, let it be as unruly and turgid as that of Thomas Wolfe, as muscle-bound as the prose of Henry Miller, as rambling and elliptical as the fantasies of William Burroughs!

Thus from Hemingway's novels contemporary writers borrow his self-conscious stutter, the calculated hesitations that denote the Plain Man doing his damnedest to batter through to clarity; from Lawrence, the habit of endlessly repeating adjectives—"dark-dark-dark" or "soft-soft-soft"—until the reader's critical sense is gradually lulled to sleep by an insistent pounding tom-tom rhythm. To write with ease and grace is always a dangerous sign: the author must be glossing over problems and ignoring issues that he knows he dare not face.

In fact, style is usually an indication of difficulties confronted and problems triumphantly solved. A tolerable style is the product of life-long effort. It takes not only skill but honesty—a high degree of disciplined self-awareness—to compose a single smoothly-running page.

DONALD HALL
An Ethic of Clarity

Donald Hall is a sort of literary man for all seasons. He is a critic, an essayist, a professor of English (University of Michigan). He is the author of a biography of the sculptor Henry Moore. He has written stories for children, has edited anthologies of verse. Most of all he is a poet. One of his poems won the Newdigate Prize at Oxford in 1952. Three years later the first collection of his verse, "Exiles and Marriages," received the Lamont Poetry Prize. Of poets he has said: "One en-

deavor common to all good poets is the lonely art of writing, the endeavor of the spirit which continually doubts itself and involves nothing in itself but the possibility of art."

Ezra POUND, George Orwell, James Thurber and Ernest Hemingway don't have much in common: a great poet who became a fascist, a disillusioned left-wing satirist, a comic essayist and cartoonist, and a great novelist. If anything, they could represent the diversity of modern literature. Yet one thing unites them. They share a common idea of good prose style, an idea of the virtues of clarity and simplicity. This attitude toward style was not unknown to earlier writers, but never before has it been so pervasive and so exclusive.

Style is the manner of a sentence, not its matter. Yet the distinction between manner and matter is a slippery one; manner affects matter. When Time used to tell us that President Truman slouched into one room, while General Eisenhower strode into another, their manner was attempting to prejudice our feelings. The hotel which invites me to enjoy my favorite beverage at the Crown Room is trying not to sound crass ("Have a drink at the bar"). One linguist in discussing this problem took Caesar's "I came—I saw—I conquered," and revised it into "I arrived on the scene of the battle, I observed the situation, I won the victory." Here the matter is the same, but the tone of arrogant dignity in Caesar disappears into the pallid pedantry of the longer version. It is impossible to say that the matter is unaffected. Still, let us say that this kind of difference, in the two versions of Caesar, is what we mean by style. One of the things we *don't* mean by style is grammar.

In the phrase "good writing" or "good style," the word "good" has usually meant "beautiful" or "proficient"—like a good Rembrandt or a good kind of soap. Now it means honest, as opposed to fake. Bad writing happens when the writer lies to himself, or to others, or to both. Probably it is usually necessary to lie to yourself in order to lie to others; advertising men use the products they praise. Bad writing may be proficient: it may persuade us to buy a poor car or to vote for an imbecile, but it is bad because it is tricky, false in its enthusiasm, and falsely motivated. It appeals to a part of us that wants to deceive itself. I am encouraged to tell myself that I am enjoying my favorite beverage when I am really only getting sloshed.

"If a man writes clearly enough any one can see if he fakes," says

Hemingway. Orwell reverses the terms: "The great enemy of clear language is insincerity. . . . When there is a gap between one's real and one's declared aims, one turns as it were instinctively to long words and exhausted idioms, like a cuttlefish squirting out ink." Pound talks about the "gap between one's real and one's declared aims" as the distance between expression and meaning. In "The New Vocabularianism," Thurber speaks of the political use of clichés to hide a "menacing Alice in Wonderland meaninglessness."

As Robert Graves says, "The writing of good English is thus a moral matter." And the morality is a morality of truth-telling. Herbert Read declares that "the only thing that is indispensable for the possession of a good style is personal sincerity." We can agree, but must add that personal sincerity is not always an easy matter, nor always available to the will. "Real aims," we must understand, are not necessarily conscious ones. The worst liars in the world may consider themselves sincere. Analysis of one's own style, in fact, can act as a test of one's own feelings. And certainly, many habits of bad style are bad habits of thinking as well as of feeling.

There are examples of the modern attitude toward style in older writers. Jonathan Swift, maybe the best prose writer of the language, sounds like George Orwell when he writes: ". . . our English tongue is too little cultivated in this kingdom, yet the faults are nine in ten owing to affectation, not to want of understanding. When a man's thoughts are clear, the properest words will generally offer themselves first, and his own judgment will direct him in what order to place them, so as they may be best understood." Here Swift appears tautological: clear thoughts only *exist* when they are embodied in clear words. But he goes on: "When men err against this method, it is usually on purpose." Purposes, we may add, which we often disguise from ourselves.

Aristotle in his "Rhetoric" makes a case for plainness and truth-telling. "The right thing in speaking really is that we should be satisfied not to annoy our hearers, without trying to delight them: we ought in fairness to fight our case with no help beyond the bare facts." And he anticipates the modern stylist's avoidance of unusual words: "Clearness is secured by using the words . . . that are current and ordinary." Cicero attacks the Sophists because they are "on the lookout for ideas that are neatly put rather than reasonable."

Yet when we quote Cicero, the master rhetorician, on behalf of honest clarity, we must remember that the ancients did not really think of style as we do. Style until recent times has been a division of rhetoric.

To learn style, one learned the types of figures of speech, and the appropriateness of each to different levels of discourse—high, middle and low. The study of style was complex, but technical rather than moral. For some writers, Latin was high and the vernacular low, but in the Renaissance the vernacular took in all levels. It is only with modern times that style divorces itself from rhetoric—rhetoric belongs to the enemy, to the advertisers and the propagandists—and becomes a matter of ethics and introspection.

Ezra Pound, like some French writers before him, makes the writer's function social. "Good writers are those who keep the language efficient. That is to say, keep it accurate, keep it clear." We must ask why this idea of the function of good style is so predominantly a modern phenomenon. Pound elsewhere speaks of the "assault," by which he means the attack upon our ears and eyes of words used dishonestly to persuade us, to convince us to buy or to believe. Never before have men been exposed to so many words—written words, from newspapers and billboards and paperbacks and flashing signs and the sides of buses; spoken words, from radio and television and loudspeakers. Everyone who wishes to keep his mind clear and his feelings his own must make an effort to brush away these words like cobwebs from the face.

The assault of the phony is a result of technology combined with a morality that wishes to use this technique for persuasion. The persuasion is for purposes of making money, as in advertising, or winning power, as in war propaganda and the slogans of politicians. Politicians have always had slogans, but they never before had the means to spread their words so widely. The cold war of rhetoric between communism and capitalism has killed no soldiers, but the air is full of the small corpses of words that were once alive: democracy, freedom, liberation.

It is because of the assault, primarily, that writers have become increasingly concerned with the honesty of their style to the exclusion of other qualities. Concentration upon honesty is the only way to exclude the sounds of the bad style that assault us all. These writers are concerned finally *to be honest about what they see, feel and know.* For some of them, like William Carlos Williams, we can only trust the evidence of our eyes and ears, our real knowledge of our immediate environment.

Our reading of good writers, and our attempt to write like them, can help to guard us against the dulling onslaught. But we can only do this;

if we are able to look into ourselves with some honesty: an ethic of clarity demands intelligence and self-knowledge. Really the ethic is not only a defense against the assault (nothing good is ever merely defensive) but is a development of the same inwardness which is reflected in psychoanalysis. One cannot, after all, examine one's motives and feelings carefully if one takes a naïve view that the appearance of a feeling is the reality of that feeling.

Sometimes the assault is merely pompous. Some people say "wealthy" instead of "rich" in order to seem proper, or "home" instead of "house" in order to seem genteel. Years ago, James Russell Lowell ridiculed the newspapers which translated "A great crowd came to see" into "A vast concourse was assembled to witness . . . ." None of these examples is so funny as a Colonel's statement on television that one of our astronauts "has established visual contact" with a piece of his equipment. He meant that the astronaut had *seen* it.

Comic as these pomposities are, they are signs that something has gone wrong somewhere. (My father normally spoke a perfectly good plain English, but occasionally when he was unhappy with himself he would fall off dreadfully; I remember him admonishing me at dinner, "It is necessary to masticate thoroughly.") The Colonel must be worried about the intellectual respectability of the space program, if he resorts to phrases like "visual contact." The lady who speaks of "luncheon" instead of "lunch" is worried about her social status. She gives herself away. Something has gone wrong, and it has gone wrong inside her mind and her emotions.

The style is the man. Again and again, the modern stylists repeat this idea. By a man's metaphors you shall know him. When a commencement orator advises students to "enrich themselves culturally," chances are that he is more interested in money than in poetry. When a university president says that his institution turned out 1,432 B.A.'s last year, he tells us that he thinks he is running General Motors. The style is the man. Rémy de Gourmont used the analogy that the bird's song was conditioned by the shape of the beak. And Paul Valéry said, ". . . what makes the style is not merely the mind applied to a particular action; it is the whole of a living system extended, imprinted and recognizable in expression."

These statements are fine, but they sound too deterministic, as if one expresses an unalterable self, and can no more change the style of that self than a bird can change the shape of its beak. Man is a kind of bird that can change his beak.

A writer of bad prose, in order to become a writer of good prose, must alter his character. He does not have to become good in terms of conventional morality, but he must become honest in the expression of himself, which means that he must know himself. There must be no gap between expression and meaning, between real and declared aims. For some people, some of the time, this simply means *not* telling deliberate lies. For most people, it means learning when they are lying and when they are not. It means learning the real names of their feelings. It means not saying or thinking, "I didn't *mean* to hurt your feelings," when there really existed a desire to hurt. It means not saying "luncheon" or "home" for the purpose of appearing upper-class or well-educated. It means not using the passive mood to attribute to no one in particular opinions that one is unwilling to call one's own. It means not disguising banal thinking by polysyllabic writing, or the lack of feeling by clichés which purport to display feeling.

The style is the man, and the man can change himself by changing his style. Prose style is the way you think and the way you understand what you feel. Frequently we feel for each other a mixture of strong love and strong hate; if we call it love, and disguise the hate to ourselves by sentimentalizing over love, we are thinking and feeling badly. Style is ethics and psychology; clarity is a psychological sort of ethic, since it involves not general moral laws but truth to the individual self. The scrutiny of style is a moral and psychological study. By trying to scrutinize our own style we try to understand ourselves. Editing our own writing, or going over in memory our own spoken words, or even inwardly examining our thought, we can ask *why* we resorted to the passive in this case, or to clichés in that.

When the smoke of bad prose fills the air, something is always on fire somewhere. If the style is really the man, the style becomes an instrument for discovering and changing the man. Language is expression of self, but language is also the instrument by which to know that self.

DENIS BROGAN
"Clio, a Muse"

Sir Denis Brogan, a longtime ornament of Cambridge University and now retired, is one of those scholars who seem to know everything and everybody. *He is, for example, equally at home in American and English history or politics, and has written books to prove it. He knows France and Frenchmen, and again the proof lies in the books that bear his name on their title pages.*

 HE death of Sir Winston Churchill very naturally brought back to mind the brilliant essay of his fellow Harrovian, George Macaulay Trevelyan whom he made Master of Trinity College, Cambridge, the greatest academic gift a Prime Minister of Great Britain has in his power. That essay is of course, "Clio, a Muse." As befitted the son of one brilliant historian and the great-nephew of a truly great historian, Trevelyan was impressed with the need for defending literary history against what Thomas Carlyle called "Dryasdust" and what historians like J. B. Bury approvingly called "scientific" history. Whatever the case with Carlyle, George Macaulay Trevelyan was no enemy of scholarship and some of his own political history has stood the test of time very well. But when he wrote his essay at the start of this century it was quite unfashionable to be concerned about the *method* in which historical results were transmitted, and in some areas and some countries it was almost indecent. Admiration for German scholarship in England and France threatened to crush the old tradition that held history to be the province of Clio. Of course, one of the most brilliant literary historians of the 19th century was Heinrich von Treitschke; but his highly tendentious glorification of the rise of Prussia made people unwilling to see the real merits of his learning and the brilliancy of his narrative style. (I have more than once told students of mine to read the chapter in Treitschke's history on Waterloo, called "La Belle Alliance," to see how history and irony could be successfully combined.)

Sir Winston had no doubts or hesitations about Trevelyan; although he bitterly resented Thomas Babington Macaulay's denigration of his great ancestor, the Duke of Marlborough, he greatly admired Macaulay's style both in prose and verse (and Macaulay's verse was itself a form of historical writing). Sir Winston also admired Gibbon, and the influence of Gibbon and Macaulay can be seen in his own often highly colored and highly individual narrative manner.

It is probably no longer true even in the academic world that there is suspicion and resentment of literary elegance in historical writing; but there is still a willingness to believe that really solid work must be dull. This superstition—for such it must be called—reminds one of Bertrand Russell's gibe that the English think that a man who speaks badly and writes badly must be honest, but that honesty is not as widespread as this belief would suggest. As for the German influence before Trevelyan, the standard of writing German prose is (I am told by good German scholars) not high, and there is in fact no generally accepted norm of stylistic brilliance. Although narrative style was highly developed in England, France, and Italy, yet all suffered from the prestige of German scholarship and the confusion of scholarship with dullness.

In addition to this snobbery, there was perhaps a good reason for being suspicious of certain types of romantic history. James Russell Lowell had a good deal on his side when he claimed that the example of Augustin Thierry had been very bad. Thierry larded his narrative with eloquence, irrelevant description, and moral judgments barely tolerable in his own work and quite intolerable in the work of many of his imitators. The same applied to imitators of Macaulay and, in France, to imitators of Jules Michelet. The same applied to Carlyle, whom I find the most unreadable of great British historians. (It may be pointed out that he is also, indeed, the least read.)

Of course, the dogmatic manner of Macaulay or Michelet, themselves, could be both misleading and maddening. It would be possible to quote from Macaulay firm judgments on topics on which firm judgments are very rash. Men were black or white: William III of Orange was white (a judgment with which I do not agree); Marlborough was black—which infuriated Sir Winston. Michelet grew more and more rhetorical, more and more removed from his early serious scholarship, and more and more tendentious, the older he got. The recent publication of his "Journals" shows some of the psychological reasons (quite unedifying) behind this increasing degeneracy of style and of critical power.

In the United States, scholars and common readers both came to resent the extremely rhetorical, the almost religious eloquence of George Bancroft, and it might well be said that Richard Hildreth, with his clear, lucid, sometimes acid style, was much the better writer.

While it is generally agreed that the greatest of American historians was Francis Parkman—a solid scholar as well as a brilliant writer—he often did overdo, I believe, the picturesque passages: his descriptions of Canadian and American scenery, for example. Yet you cannot understand some campaigns of the Civil War without having an adequate description of the landscape. For example, Gen. John Hood's last desperate campaign in Tennessee would gain a great deal in his own narrative of it if he were topographically accurate, which he is not. It is also important to know about the weather: had the ground dried earlier on the morning of June 18, 1815, Napoleon would probably have won the Battle of Waterloo—although I do not think that would have made much difference in the not very long run. At all events, in the writing of history, Trevelyan recognized, the association between literary brilliance, political prejudice and superficial or disingenuous learning was fixed in the academic and, by mere snobbery, in the public mind.

Yet toward the end of the 19th century, this superstition could have been confuted by two brilliant practitioners who combined in their works historical value and excellent style. One of these was F. W. Maitland, whom most British professional historians think was the greatest of English historians. Maitland wrote on the most complicated questions of feudal history, but he wrote with wit and lucidity and immense learning and there are people who think that "Domesday Book and Beyond" makes better reading than Henry Adams's "Mont Saint-Michel and Chartres." The other example is provided by an amateur whose very great merits are brought back to my mind by the very great faults of the late Douglas MacArthur's "Reminiscences." U. S. Grant's "Personal Memoirs" is a masterpiece of narrative power, of candor and of historical intelligence. But these examples did not shake the snobbery. In the United States, for example, I can remember 40 years and more ago in the Harvard Graduate School being told by one of its most eminent historians (himself an admirable writer) that only one Harvard professor attached importance to the literary merits of a thesis (obviously that exception was Samuel Eliot Morison). There was, of course, a market for dramatic historiography of a rather cheap kind: what the French call *vies romancées* and even *histoires romancées*. There was also a market for rather cheap "debunking."

Works could have a very great influence, of course, without being badly written. It can even be maintained that much of the influence of Charles Beard's "Economic Interpretation of the Constitution of the United States" was due to great literary dexterity rather than to profound scholarship.

How stands the case today, 62 years after Trevelyan's "Clio"? I think we have a good many examples of the happy combination of

literary skill and sound scholarship. I think, for example, that while
Bruce Catton overdoes the lushness of his historical evocations, his
history of the Civil War is dramatic, engrossing and impressive nonetheless. He gains, of course, a great deal by having so intrinsically
dramatic a subject. If the world has steadily refused to read Henry
Adams's "History of the United States of America," it is partly because the average man will not be involved in diplomatic maneuvers
of a remote age even if they were of great importance for the future of
the United States; and the War of 1812 was very largely comic opera,
not to be made really interesting by any literary devices. Only at New
Orleans and only at sea did this absurd squabble rise to the dignity
Clio demands. Perhaps it might be said that the only subject on
which Henry Adams really let himself go with great literary art, if
with some unscrupulousness, was his own life story, and his ingenious
manipulation of the Middle Ages and the early 20th century into
aspects of the Adams epic.

No, things are much better today. I read more printed American history theses than probably any other man alive. Many of them,
it must be admitted, though no worse than the English, are very drab.
But many are in the best sense more critical and much better written
than they used to be. Some of the great historical enterprises, like that
of Allan Nevins, combine style, learning and wisdom in the most impressive manner. Admiral Morison's history of the United States Navy
in the last war is not only a brilliant reconstruction of the greatest naval
war in history, but at moments intensely dramatic: for example, in the
account of the Japanese Navy's approach to Pearl Harbor and in the
account of the final sea battle of Leyte Gulf.

And Sir Winston? In this, as in many other things, he was *sui
generis*. The two lengthy, extremely readable, and extremely valuable
accounts he has given us of the First and Second World Wars are not
mere memoirs or mere academic history either. (After all, Thucydides
was an actor in, as well as a chronicler of, the Peloponnesian War!)
Sir Winston's life of the Duke of Marlborough, published in four
volumes from 1933 to 1938, is not only full of family piety, but of
brilliant evocation of the past, as in the account of the terrible Battle
of Malplaquet. And Sir Winston himself could rise above mere pedan-
tries. The first chapters of his "History of the English-Speaking Peo-
ples" were sent for criticism to a very distinguished ancient historian
and archaeologist. She returned the proofs, having altered the ancient
Queen Boadicea to "Boudicca"—"as she is now called." The proofs

went back to her by return of post. On the margin was this message: "Not by me. W.S.C." This, I think, is the way to rise above even valid pedantry and give Clio, who is a muse, the honors her sisters have earned, of being at least as much a patron of an art as of a science.

LINDSAY ROGERS
Metaphors

Lindsay Rogers, emeritus Burgess Professor of Public Law at Columbia, has drawn his essay from a long association with words and phrases in books that have been part of a professor's life.

NOW IN common usage, "hawks" and "doves" will remain so for some time. The words are short and fit well into headlines. The cartoonists have an easy time with a bird of prey and a pigeon. If the public-opinion pollsters put the appropriate question to a sample, they would find that a large majority would report that the hawks desired to escalate the measures being taken toward North Vietnam and that the doves wished to slow the measures down with the hope of speedily obtaining peace. Dictionaries in their future editions will list these current meanings of hawks and doves.

Metaphors—"The application of names or descriptive terms to objects to which they are not literally applicable"—have been used since men began to communicate their ideas to their fellow men. But metaphors have been more frequent in poetry than in prose. Moreover, they can be bolder; they can be mixed and sometimes contradictory. Hugo restrained himself more than did Shakespeare, but a good many writers and speakers on politics "shoot the works."

Metaphors are also a substitute for thought, and their unskilled or even unscrupulous use may be dangerous when the subject being discussed is political. Mr. Justice Cardozo, when he was on the New York Court of Appeals, warned that "metaphors in law are to be narrowly watched, for, starting as devices to liberate thought, they end often by enslaving it." William Penn did not mix his metaphors: "Governments, like clocks, go from the motion men give them: and as governments are made and moved by men, so by them they are ruined too. Wherefore, governments rather depend upon men than men upon governments." Nor did the legal historian Frederick William Maitland do any mixing when he observed "that at the Reformation the English State put an end to its Roman bride but married its deceased wife's sister."

"How infinite," Sir Winston Churchill once said, "is the debt owed to metaphors by politicians who want to speak strongly but are not sure what they are going to say." Sir Winston once talked of party machines "baying at each other," but others of his metaphorical adventures disclose that sometimes he was quite sure of what he was going to say. On the day after the United States entered the war against Germany and Japan, the British Cabinet considered the text of a communication to Washington. Churchill disapproved. "No," he said "that is the way we talked to her while we were wooing her; now that she is in the harem we must talk to her quite differently." Wendell Willkie's little book "One World" (1943) was mentioned in another British Cabinet meeting and Churchill told his colleagues that the book had been mistitled: it should have been called "Gullible's Travels."

At least three Prime Ministers resorted to metaphors to describe their feelings when they were entitled to occupy 10 Downing Street, and their choices disclosed something of the mental habits of the choosers. On becoming Prime Minister, Disraeli wrote to a feminine friend: "I have climbed to the top of the greasy pole." When he succeeded Disraeli, Gladstone's genre was somewhat different. He confided to his diary: "I ascend a steepening path with the burden ever gaining weight. The Almighty seems to sustain and spare me for some purpose of His own, deeply unworthy as I know myself to be. Glory to His name." The Earl of Rosebery was somewhat facetious and prophesied correctly: "I have taken a piece of gingerbread that is indigestible."

In the reign of Charles II, some newspaper writer used the word "trimmer" in criticism of George Savile, Marquess of Halifax, who was never an extremist and often shifted his attitudes. Halifax took the appellation as a compliment and wrote a pamphlet that has become famous:

"This innocent word 'trimmer,'" declared Halifax, "signifieth no more than this, That if Men are together in a Boat, and one part of the Company would weigh it down on one side, another would make it lean as much to the contrary; it happeneth there is a third opinion of those, who conceive it would do as well, if the Boat went even, without endangering the Passengers."

Fisher Ames suggested that Monarchy and Democracy were different kinds of crafts: "A Monarchy," he told the House of Representatives, "is a merchantman which sails well, but will sometimes strike on a rock, and go to bottom; a republic is a raft which will never sink, but then your feet are always in the water." Tocqueville was pessimistic: "Like the navigator he [the statesman] may direct the vessel which bears him along but he can neither change its structure nor raise the winds nor lull the waters which swell beneath him." Apparently no critic has pointed out that the ship of state, unlike ordinary vessels, can spring a leak at the top.

It is a risky business to analyze and elaborate metaphors when one is arguing and criticizing. In his multivolume "A Study of History," Arnold J. Toynbee sometimes defined his thought by resorts to metaphor and simile and to them alone. "At one point he actually speaks of himself as having carried a simile 'far enough to ascertain' what he wanted to know: but when did a simile ascertain anything?" This question from an eminent reviewer, Richard Pares, who went on to say: "No doubt there are some things which can only be described by a metaphor, but the fewer the better; to define by a metaphor is impossible. Nor do the similes always succeed even in conveying a visual image—for example, what clarity can we gain from the strange simile . . . in which a pig is attached by umbilical cords to a number of people who are all beating it, trying to ride it, and in danger of being led by the nose by it?"

Among those who have discussed American politics, there have been few metaphor users more inveterate than James M. Beck, President Harding's Solicitor General and later a member of Congress. Beck published volumes with the titles "The Constitution of the United States," "The Vanishing Rights of the States" and "Our Wonderland of Bureaucracy." Writing before the financially generous days of the New Deal, Beck disapproved of Federal appropriations granting aid to the states and likened them "to that tragedy on the ocean seas when the Titanic was struck by a submerged ice floe. After the collision, which was hardly felt by the steamer at the time, the great liner at first seemed to be intact and unhurt and continued to move. But a death wound had been inflicted under the surface of the

water. . . . The power of appropriation is such an ice floe . . . and has
inflicted a similar fatal wound to the good ship Constitution."

Mr. Beck looked upon our Constitution as "a flaming beacon and
a Gothic cathedral, like that of Rheims." Then the elaborations proceed along lines that the reader will guess. Foundations seem secure
even though some of the buttresses may be weakened and statuary
mutilated. (Winston Churchill once remarked that he was not a pillar
but a buttress of the church: he supported it from the outside.) Mr.
Beck hoped that, given popular indifference and the innovating spirit
of a restless age, the time would come "when the Constitution would
be as the Rheims Cathedral was after the German bombardments of
1916, a noble but beautiful ruin."

Then Mr. Beck proceeded to elaborate the metaphor still further:
"The high altar of the Constitution is the self-restraint which the
American people of 1787 were wise enough to impose upon themselves, and their posterity, and the rose windows are those great
traditions of liberty which we have gained at an infinite sacrifice of
treasure and life from our English-speaking ancestry."

One of the fellow lawyers who commented on Mr. Beck's books
was Thomas Reed Powell, an ornament of Columbia's Faculty of
Law and Political Science and of the Harvard Law School, who, at
the time of the "court packing" proposal, authored the phrase: "A
switch in time saved nine." Mr. Justice Frankfurter in his reminiscences
says that Reed Powell "speared his victims" in "happy doggerels" that
were privately circulated and in prose that all could read. It was in
prose that Reed Powell dealt with Mr. Beck's metaphors:

"It helps us," he wrote, "to know what the Constitution is if we
know what it is not. Mr. Beck puts it very beautifully when he says:
'The Constitution is neither, on the one hand, a Gibraltar rock, which
wholly resists the ceaseless washing of time and circumstance, nor
is it, on the other hand, a sandy beach which is slowly destroyed
by the erosions of the waves. It is rather to be likened to a floating
dock, which, while firmly attached to its moorings, and not therefore
at the caprice of the waves, yet rises and falls with the tide of time
and circumstances.'

"You might think," Mr. Powell goes on, "that a Constitution
which is all these wonderful things would be sure to last forever
without any help from anything else. But this is not so. Mr. Beck
says that it would not have lasted so long as it has if it had not been
for the Supreme Court, which he says is 'the balance wheel of the

Constitution.' He has a whole chapter which he calls 'The Balance Wheel' and this chapter ends up by saying: 'But always the Supreme Court stands as a great lighthouse, and even when the waves beat upon it with terrific violence (as in the Civil War, when it was shaken to its very foundation), yet after they have spent their fury, the great lamp of the Constitution—as that of another Pharos—illumines the troubled face of the waters with the benignant rays of those immutable principles of liberty and justice, which alone can make a nation free as well as strong.'

"It makes you see," Mr. Powell remarks, "how marvelous the Supreme Court really is when it can be a balance wheel at the beginning of a chapter and a lighthouse at the end." What metaphors could Mr. Beck have found which would have been worthy of use in connection with Mr. Roosevelt's 1937 battle (which he lost) and the war (which he won) and the divisions of opinion in later Supreme Courts?

Mr. Beck concluded his book on the Constitution by noting that, when the original document had been taken out of a State Department safe a few years before, examination showed that the ink had faded. Mr. Beck asked that the American people "write the compact, not with ink upon a parchment, but with 'letters of living light'— to use Webster's phrase—upon their hearts." This, Mr. Powell remarked, "must be a very hard way to write," and suggested that "it would be a good thing to write the ink letters as well as the light letters, because the light might go out before the ink had all faded."

In the Wilson Follett book, "Modern American Usage," there is the suggestion that "there is a domain of fact, namely scientific fact, which metaphor has lately invaded and where it has visibly weakened the hold of common sense. Both scientists and laymen, for example, now believe that digital computers think, have memories, learn, translate, make errors and correct them and succeed each other in 'generations.'" The examples are not numerous enough to let a nonscientist like myself be sure just what this means, but machines have difficulties with metaphorical language.

Some translations I have recently seen are reminiscent of the German version of Shakespeare's famous line: "I will carve my way to fortune with a sword." The retranslation into English made Shakespeare say: "I will make my living cutting meat." One computer turned "out of sight, out of mind" into "invisible and insane," and another made "the spirit is willing but the flesh is weak" become "the whiskey is all right, but the meat has gone bad." But others than computers have special difficulty with words of double meaning,

a good many of which (along with some metaphors) appear in a
jingle which has long been one of my favorites:

> Where can a man buy a cap for his knee?
> Or a key for the lock of his hair?
> Can his eyes be called a school
> Because there are pupils there?
> In the crown of his head,
> What gems are found?
> Who travels the bridge on his nose?
> Can he use in building the roof of his mouth
> The nails on the ends of his toes?
> Can the crook of his elbow be sent to jail?
> If so, what did it do?
> How does he sharpen his shoulder blades?
> I'll be hanged if I know, do you?
> Can he sit in the shade of the palm of his hand?
> Or beat the drum in his ear?
> Can the calf of his leg eat the corn on his toe?
> If so, why not grow corn on the ear?

JAMES A. MICHENER
An Honest Account of
What Transpired

*That the English language can trip even the expert is the moral of "An
Honest Account of What Transpired." James Michener, it is now
almost forgotten, was once a teacher and an editor in a publishing
house. That part of his life has been overshadowed, of course, by his
success in authorship. Twenty years ago he won a Pulitzer for "Tales
of the South Pacific." His novels "Hawaii" and "The Source" made
him all but a national institution. His latest book is "Iberia: Spanish
Travels and Reflections."*

THE telephone call was from my editor at Random House, Albert
Erskine, and it carried a note of urgency.

"I've never asked you for anything like this," Erskine apologized, "but I have this first novel and I think it's bound to be a winner. . . ."

"You want me to read it?"

"More. I want you to give me an endorsement for the cover."

A writer gets many such requests and soon discovers that they are of little significance, for nothing he says will alter the natural life of a manuscript. He is well advised to keep his fingers off the jackets of other people's books.

"This novel is different," Erskine reasoned. "The author is a young fellow of tremendous promise and I don't want him lost in the shuffle of first publication."

Albert Erskine is not only an impeccable editor; he is also a scholar in English literature and the author of a fine text used in many universities, so when he insisted that he had something special, I was obligated to listen. He sent me the book. It was as good as he had said. I enjoyed it and wrote an endorsement.

As soon as my letter reached New York Erskine called me. He was most apologetic. "It's about your blurb."

I started to freeze. This was going to be unpleasant and I thought we might as well get to the heart of it at once. "Albert," I said quietly, "I've given that book a first-rate plug and I can't strengthen it." I had a copy of my statement at hand and read him the opening sentences:

"In his novel 'The Orchard Keeper,' young Cormac McCarthy has written with distinction. His use of words is remarkable, for he lures from them a very special music. His use of nature is uncommon these days and his constant reference to the land and the things that transpire on it is refreshing."

"I can't honestly make it any stronger than that," I said.

"It isn't what you've said that's the problem," Erskine replied. There was a long moment of hesitation during which I had the dreadful thought: "He wants me to make it more sexy." This was wholly unlike Erskine, so I waited.

"You see—" he fumbled in what I deduced was acute embarrassment, —"we're promoting this book as an example of fine writing. Malcolm Cowley, Robert Penn Warren and Ralph Ellison are all praising its style."

"I've said the style was good."

"Correct, but in saying it you use a word . . . well, a word that doesn't exist. At least, not in the way you use it."

I looked at my copy and concluded that unless my typist had made a blunder in transcription I was on firm ground. "The words look all right to me," I said.

"It's *transpire*. The way you use it is not only wrong. It's gauche."

I looked at the word and at the sentence in which it appeared and both looked satisfactory, but Erskine continued: "Since *transpire* is not acceptable would you mind if we changed it to *occur*, which is what you apparently meant?"

Before dashing off to my dictionaries I growled that if I had misused a word in so public a place, please correct it. So now on the jacket of Mr. McCarthy's fine novel appears this statement from me; ". . . and his constant reference to the land and the things that occur on it is refreshing." I am happy to report that the novel was received with precisely the critical applause that Erskine had anticipated. With his novel Mr. McCarthy won both a literary award and an important fellowship to Rome, where he completed a second novel reported to be even finer than his first.

When I got to "The Oxford English Dictionary" I found a fascinating account of the verb *transpire*.

The first recorded use in English writing came in 1597, when *transpire* was used properly as meaning "to pass in the state of vapor through the walls of a body." It was derived from the Latin *trans* (through) and *spirare* (to breathe). This basic definition has continued in use from that time to this, but in 1741 a new meaning began to appear in the works of good writers: "to escape from secrecy to notice," which is how Samuel Johnson defined this upstart meaning, adding "a sense lately innovated from France, without necessity." The novelist Richardson, the epistolist Chesterfield, the statesman Jefferson and the historian Froude all used the word in this way: "I am telling you this in secrecy. Do not let a word of it transpire."

About 1800 a gross misuse of the word developed, apparently in the United States, whereby it came to mean *happen* or *occur*; the first recorded use appeared in 1802, but quickly thereafter one finds writers as diverse as William Lloyd Garrison, Charles Dickens and Nathaniel Hawthorne adopting it, and this definition appears in Webster's dictionary of 1828. The 1933 O.E.D. dismisses this usage as "misused."

Other principal dictionaries support the O.E.D. in condemning the misuses. The 12-volume "Century Dictionary," the best so far produced in America and much missed today, cites four acceptable definitions plus a fifth: "To happen or come to pass; occur. (An erroneous use.).'' To this condemnation is added a quotation from F. Hall: "The penny-a-liners 'allude' in cases where others would 'refer'; and in their dialect, things 'transpire' and only exceptionally 'take place.'"

"Webster's New International, Second Edition" adds its condemnation: "*Transpire* in this sense has been disapproved by most authorities on usage." But prudently the authors add: "although the meaning occurs in the writing of many authors of good standing."

The various handbooks on style that I consulted were uniformly harsh on any who abused this old word.

Fowler in his "Modern English Usage" castigates the new definition sharply as "this notorious misuse," but as acceptable usage he cites only the secondary meaning "to emerge from secrecy into knowledge, to leak out, to become known by degrees." Thus one of our language's strictest purists surrenders the true meaning of the word, accepts a secondary one but condemns a late innovation.

Wilson Follett in his "Modern American Usage" calls *transpire* the "old, rather pompous word for what we now call *leak out*. Accordingly it is not a synonym for *happen, occur, take place.*" He sees no future use for the word whether rightly or wrongly used and recommends, "Use *happen* and *leak* and leave *transpire* to die quietly."

Mitford M. Mathews in his "A Dictionary of Americanisms on Historical Principles" cites Abigail Adams as having written in 1775, "There is nothing new transpired since I wrote you last," but in such a sentence she may have been using the word correctly or incorrectly. Mathews's later citations, however, refer only to the misuse.

It was not until I read that excellent summary of advice to professional writers, "The Careful Writer" by Theodore M. Bernstein, whose job it had been for many years to correct and chastise the reporters of The New York Times, that I came to the nub of the matter. Bernstein says, "The Unknowing, particularly those who tend to reach for the fancy word, think *transpire* means to happen or take place, and they write, 'The treaty looked to the appointment of a governor for the territory, but this never transpired.'" Bernstein's subsequent comment is most compelling: to use *transpire* as a substitute for *occur* is to err trebly in that *transpire* has a specific, clearcut meaning; no other word exists with that same meaning; whereas *occur* has many alternatives such as *happen* or *take place*.

The most representative assault on those who use *transpire* came, however, in Bergen Evans's recent handbook, "A Dictionary of Contemporary American Usage." In a long entry Evans says first: "There is no doubt that *transpire* now has the meaning of 'happen' for many people. But there is also no doubt that a great many other people regard this usage as wrong. Indeed, with some it has become a shibboleth, a touch of literacy and refinement; anyone who uses *transpire* to mean 'happen' is, in their estimation, vulgar, illiterate and contemptible."

Against this battery of evidence one would be ill-advised to misuse a word which has become a touchstone of the higher nicety. To me the strictures were especially relevant because I love the English language and am constantly impressed by what a subtle tool it is, infinite in its possibilities and quite impossible for any but the ultimate expert to master, even in a lifetime of study.

For example, I cringe when people pronounce an otherwise good word as *dimunition*; these days one rarely hears it otherwise. Perhaps because of my stay in the Orient I am unusually attentive to the error *hari-kari*, but this has become so entrenched that I suppose the correct spelling and pronunciation will soon be lost. I like my writers to differentiate between *connote* and *denote*; *centrifugal* and *centripetal*; *bring* and *take*; and especially *imply* and *infer*.

So when I am corrected on a word like *transpire*, I listen, and over the years have cleaned up my usage, at least to a degree. But whenever I am tempted to discard emergent meanings entirely, I move cautiously, because I keep in mind my youthful experience with *amuse*. I suppose that this word, more profoundly than any other, has determined my attitude toward language.

One day when I was a graduate student in Scotland I happened upon a sentence, written about 1800, which made no sense at all: "The canny Scots erected along their shores stone pillars which from the sea would look like men, and this they did to amuse the invading Norsemen." I pondered that statement for some time, trying to decipher why such a ponderous joke as building stone pillars should prove the canniness of the Scots. The only word in the sentence that could be causing my perplexity was *amuse*, and when I looked it up I found the type of entry which is so often informative: "Archaic: to deceive."

This led me to my first extended etymological exploration in English and, working on my own, I uncovered those fascinating bits of information which today the O.E.D. summarizes as follows:

Amuse was borrowed from the French relatively late and meant "to be put into a stupid muse or stare." It was so used in the early 1600's but very quickly acquired a secondary meaning, *to deceive*. For 200 years, in military writing, *amuse* meant *to mislead the enemy* and in general writing, to *delude, cheat, deceive*.

During this time, however, a new meaning was slowly gaining ground and by the opening years of the 19th century had pretty well preempted the field. *Amuse* now *meant to divert, please with anything light or cheerful*; later it came to mean more or less what it means today, to *tickle the fancy of*. For some 300 years the exact meaning of this difficult little word swayed in the balance between etymological purity on the one hand and gross misuse on the other. As so often happens, in English, it was the latter usage that won out, so that today *amuse* means something it was never intended to mean and for which there is no scientific base.

I can imagine the purists of the 17th century warning, "Any man of learning who prizes his reputation will be studious to avoid the error of using *amuse* to mean *beguile*." I can hear the linguistic experts of that day thundering, "To give the fine old word *amuse* the meaning which one hears today in coffee-shops is wrong on three counts. It denies the etymology of the word. It deprives us of a word which has its own precise meaning. And the change is unnecessary in that we already have many words which adequately express the new meaning, such as *beguile, divert, entertain*, and *regale*." On all counts the experts were correct, but the people who spoke English determined that *amuse* should pass over to a new meaning. The original, correct usage was not only diminished; it was positively lost.

Transpire is presently caught up in such a transformation; within the next two centuries I should imagine that its original meaning will be lost. One must agree with Bernstein that this will be regrettable in that the word originally had a precise meaning, whereas its new meaning can be covered by a host of other words. What is especially galling to the purist is that *transpire* seems to have been appropriated as a synonym for *happen* only because it sounds a little fancier. This is a most deplorable reason for using any word, even if it is used correctly. If pressed, I would have to admit that when I praised Mr. McCarthy's novel because it reported what transpired on the land, I was throwing my stylistic weight around, and Mr. Erskine was well advised to throw the word out. It was truly inappropriate for use in conjunction with a book whose merit lay largely in its style.

The major reason why I was willing to drop the word, however,

was Mr. Bergen Evans's warning that if I continued to use it I would
be considered "vulgar, illiterate and contemptible."

But no sooner had I sworn to eschew this vulgarism than certain
amusing things began to, shall we say, happen. A friend called me in
some excitement to say that "Webster's New International, Third
Edition," had an entry on page 2,430 which would interest me. I ran
to our local library and there it was:

"4. to come to pass: *happen, occur*" and the citation for this now
accepted usage was interesting:

"I gave an honest account of what *transpired* — J. A. Michener."

The ultimate in revenge came when one of Mr. Erskine's assistants
at Random House, recalling my humiliation over the McCarthy
blurb, whispered to me, "Have you seen how Mr. Erskine's own dictionary defines the word?" I turned to "The Random House Dictionary of the English Language" and found this preferred definition:
"1. occur; happen; take place." In this most contemporary of dictionaries there was no nonsense about "misuse, error, poor taste or
even contemptible." It was not until I reached definitions 2, 3 and 4
that I found the original meanings of the word. The transformation
that had required 300 years in the case of *amuse* had in this case
transpired in a mere century.

Since I have been made a kind of godfather to this emerging
definition I shall, as a matter of honor, use it at least once in each of
my remaining books, but I shall try not to use it more than once, for
I have been socially intimidated by my betters. Of course, two centuries from now it won't matter, because *transpire* like all other words
in our magnificent, vital, growing language will have found its own
level and nothing that either writers or scholars determine to do about
it will alter that level significantly.

MORRIS BISHOP
Limericks

Morris Bishop is that rarity, a distinguished scholar with a light touch.
He has been a professor of romance languages at Cornell and president
of the Modern Language Association. He has written history and biog-

raphy, translated plays of Molière—and written light verse, some of which is collected in "A Bowl of Bishop."

THE high-mettled, fine-grained, and mellifluous poet, Conrad Aiken, recently beguiled a term in hospital by devising "A Seizure of Limericks." *Seizure* is good; a mild taste for limericks can lead to seizures, addiction, septic logorrhea and compulsive recitation neuroses.

Mr. Aiken's offering brings up again the phenomenon of the limerick. It represents, said Robert Frost, one of those obscure tribal rhythms to which our pulse beat inevitably corresponds. It is the only successful fixed poetic form created by the English (if the English did create it); it is universally recognized, cherished and quoted; yet it is commonly treated as the black sheep of poesy's flock.

The limerick has nonetheless its art. Its form is as rigidly prescribed as that of the Japanese haiku. It must have three loud thumps in lines one, two, and five, two thumps in lines three and four; it must be anapestic in rhythm: ditty-*dum*, ditty-*dum*, ditty-*dum*, though one or two unaccented or hypercatalectic, syllables may be added; ideally the rhyme-word of the first line is unusual, a proper noun, a place name; the second rhyme-word of line two is startling; the concluding rhyme is an explosion. The structure should be a rise from the commonplace reality of line one to logical madness in line five.

A scholarly writer in the Times Literary Supplement has pointed out that "the form is essentially liturgical, corresponding to the underlying ritual of Greek tragedy, with the *parodos* of the first line, the *peripeteia* of the second, the *stichomythia* of the two short lines ('When they said . . . He replied . . .'), and the *ephiphaneia* in the last."

Let us take Oliver Herford's famous one as an example:

> There was a young lady of Twickenham,
> Whose shoes were too tight to walk quick in 'em;
>> She came back from her walk
>> Looking white as a chalk,
> And took 'em both off and was sick in 'em.

This fulfills all the rules, barring the dialogue of *stichomythia*. The prosaic exposition leads to the revelation of the tragic flaw, the vanity of the young lady from Twickenham, which prompted the wearing of overtight shoes; the punishment by fate, retribution for her offense against moral law, resulting in public humiliation. The

awful lesson should give pause to all young ladies who, out of hubris
or overweening, choose shoes too tight to walk quick in 'em.

Curiously, in view of the industry of literary researchers, the history of the limerick is obscure. Some examples of the rhyme-scheme
have been reported in early Latin hymns and French devotional verse
of the 17th century. These are hardly true limericks, however. In
English literature we find no pure limericks in the Middle Ages.
"Hickory, dickory, dock," is a limerick, but it cannot antedate the
period when clocks were in general use. "Tom o' Bedlam's Song,"
(probably of the 16th century) comes close to the proper form.
Shakespeare approached the goal in Ophelia's mad song and attained
it in Iago's song in "Othello":

> And let me the canakin clink, clink
> And let me the canakin clink!
> A soldier's a man;
> And life's but a span;
> Why then let a soldier drink.

Iago explains that he learned the excellent song in England, where
they are most potent in potting.

G. Legman, in an erudite study of the limerick in his recent volume,
"The Horn Book," has found a number of 17th-century and 18th-
century examples, and I have turned up a few myself. Thus Robert
Herrick's "Night-Piece to Julia" is a perfect limerick in form, though
certainly not in substance.

The limerick persisted, then, in England in a dormant state. In the
early 1820's appeared a children's book of pure limericks. "Anecdotes
and Adventures of Fifteen Gentlemen." These came to the attention
of Edward Lear. He says in his introduction to "More Nonsense"
(1872): "Long years ago [about 1834], in days when much of my time
was passed in a country house where children and mirth abounded,
the lines [from the "Anecdotes"] beginning 'There was an Old Man
of Tobago,' were suggested to me by a valued friend as a form of verse
lending itself to limitless variety for rhymes and pictures." Then the
limerick awoke.

But the name "limerick," as applied to the verse-form, remains a
mystery. No one has reported its use before the 1890's. How did the
placid city in western Ireland come into the history of English
prosody? A number of witnesses testified that such a song was familiar
in Ireland, with the obligatory refrain:

> Oh, won't you come up, come up, come up,
> Oh, won't you come up to Limerick?
> Oh won't you come up, come all the way up,
> Come all the way up to Limerick?

This is explained as an invitation to a ship to sail up the wide Shannon to port in Limerick.

Modern students have scoffed at this explanation as mythopoeic. However, a few hours in the library have revealed to me some substantiation. In Kathleen Hoagland's "1000 Years of Irish Poetry" I find some perfect limericks, translated from the Irish. Here is one stanza, to the air of "The Growling Old Woman," by John O'Tuomy (1706-75), who was an innkeeper in Limerick. (Limerick is in Munster.)

> I sell the best brandy and sherry
> To make my good customers merry;
>   But at times their finances
>   Run short, as it chances,
> And then I feel very sad, very.

Edward Lysaght, Esq., "Pleasant Ned Lysaght," was a barrister-at-law on the Munster Circuit about 1800. (His daughter married the Lord Bishop of Limerick.) His "Poems," published in 1811, include a serious celebration of Ireland in limerick form and also a series of limericks in Irish.

These indications, though tenuous, hint that the limerick form was actually existent in the city of Limerick; that it crossed the Irish Sea in the early 1800's; that it was picked up by the anonymous author of the "Anecdotes and Adventures of Fifteen Gentlemen"; and that then, by the mediation of Edward Lear, it came to its glorious efflorescence, even comforting Conrad Aiken on his sickbed.

I like to think that the Great Mother of all our modern limericks was that "growling old woman" who gave the tune to John O'Tuomy.

> Mourned a limerick written by Aiken
> Sometimes when at night I awaken
>   And think but for Lear
>   I wouldn't be here
> O how by that thought I am shaken!

> What is truth said the cynical Pilate
> That ignorant men should defile it?

From the source to the seed
   All nature's agreed,
It is only man's mind would restyle it.

With the critical Randall Jarrell
Few poets presume to quarrell
   So they hate and they hate
   While they wait and they wait
To put him across a barrell.

                               —From Conrad Aiken's
                                 Seizure of Limericks

V
Visitations

PETER QUENNELL*
Literary Sight-Seeing

NOT long ago I was walking through the market-square of Illiers, a small town well off the main road, about 100 kilometers southwest of Paris. Although I had never set foot there before, I felt that I stood upon familiar ground. Yet was Illiers quite the place I remembered? Since my last view of it—in the pages of a masterpiece—it appeared to have undergone a subtle change. Something had faded out of its shapes and colors. It recalled one of the sacred places of childhood, which, if we are unwise enough to revisit them in later life, seem to have grown smaller, meaner, more prosaic.

Still, the Church of Saint-Hilaire answered my expectations—not the whole church admittedly, but at least its ancient tower. That tower continued to dominate Illiers and the wide surrounding landscape. As I had recollected from my reading, it was perpetually intruding its presence—down a street where Illiers meets the river, above a tile-capped gardenwall, slipping its belfry "into every fold of the sky . . . its little iron cock veering . . . in all directions." Nor had its inhabitants changed: "From the tower windows . . . it let fall at regular intervals flights of jackdaws," which wheeled away from it as though their old home above the square had become "of a sudden uninhabitable"; then, their agitation no less suddenly subsiding, settled back again amid its pinnacles and turrets.

* (Mr. Quennell is introduced on page 162)

Illiers, of course, was the starting-point chosen by Marcel Proust for the famous imaginative journey that produced his great novel. On the memorable evening when his journey began—thanks to the mysterious pleasure he received from tasting some crumbs of a *madeleine,* a miniature sponge cake, soaked in a spoonful of hot tea— it was to Illiers, the summer home of his youth, that his newly aroused imagination transported him across the years:

"Once I had recognized the taste of the crumb of *madeleine* soaked in the decoction of lime-flowers which my aunt used to give me . . . immediately the old gray house upon the street, where her room was, rose up like the scenery of a theatre. . . . And just as the Japanese amuse themselves by filling a porcelain bowl with water and steeping in it little crumbs of paper which . . . the moment they become wet . . . take on color and distinctive shape . . . so in that moment all the flowers in our garden and in M. Swann's park, and the water-lilies on the Vivonne and the good folk of the village and their little dwellings and the parish church and the whole of Combray . . . taking their proper shapes and growing solid, sprang into being . . . from my cup of tea."

There are still *madeleines* to be bought at Illiers—"those short, plump little cakes . . . which look as though they had been molded in the fluted scallop of a pilgrim's shell." But the *madeleines* I bought at the local bakery proved to be extremely stale; and I was obliged to scatter their remains across the surface of the River Loire—which Proust in his novel calls the Vivonne—the placid stream that divides Combray-Illiers from the rather uninteresting garden named the Pré-Catelan, once the pleasure-ground of Proust's uncle. It is in the Pré-Catelan, enlarged and embellished as Charles Swann's stately and spacious park, that the narrator first catches sight of Madame Swann, M. de Charlus and Gilberte, Swann's seductive daughter.

Similarly, "the old gray house," occupied by that wonderful invalid Tante Leonie—the house at which Proust and his family used to spend the summer months—has become even grayer and more un-inviting; though today it bears an impressive memorial plaque, and the narrow street has now been renamed in memory of the novelist's distinguished father. But it was not, I reminded myself, a question of what Illiers had lost, so much as of what Proust had added. Imagina-tive artists are constantly transforming their subjects; and Proust, who seldom, if ever, drew a portrait without combining the most revelatory traits of several different human characters, employed exactly the same technique, when he depicted a landscape or a building.

Thus his Church of Saint-Hilaire is a composite edifice. Its tower is the tower that stands today; but the celebrated porch—"black, and full of holes . . . worn out of shape . . . just as if the gentle grazing touch of the cloaks of peasant-women going into the church . . . had managed by age-long repetition to . . . impress itself on the stone"— probably comes from the much more important church of Saint-Loup-de-Naud. The interior of Saint-Hilaire was extensively redecorated some time in the 19th century. It contains no Gothic windows, no precious medieval arras; no sepulchral slabs, emerging from the pavement, threaten to trip up the visitor.

There is bound, I suppose, to be some degree of disappointment in finding reflected on one's own inferior eyes a place with which one has already become acquainted through the luminous vision of a man of genius. But, now and then, the disappointment is slight. Newstead Abbey, for example, retains an extraordinarily Byronic aura; and this is all the more surprising because Colonel Wildman, Byron's Harrow friend, to whom he eventually sold the "melancholy mansion" of his ancestors, carried out, during his tenancy, many extremely ruthless restorations and completely remodeled the old hall where Byron used to fence and box, with a new entry and pitch-pine paneling in the worst traditions of Victorian neo-Gothic.

Yet the ghosts of Newstead seem to have defied him. In the hollow of its desolate wind-swept park, the old Abbey rises up gaunt and gray beside its shivering reedy lake. And, although Wildman disfigured the hall, he did not touch the series of smaller rooms in which the young poet was accustomed to eat and sleep—Byron's bedroom, approached by a twisting staircase that must have tried his lame foot, containing a small bed hung with greenish chintz curtains, beneath a lavishly coroneted tester.

Newstead provided some valuable clues to a proper understanding of the poet's life and work. So does Buriton Manor, if we are concerned with Edward Gibbon. A low, rambling Elizabethan house, onto which Gibbon's prosperous grandfather had clapped a modest Georgian front, comfortable farm-buildings just behind it, and whale-backed downs and "long hanging woods" peaceably encircling it, Buriton was the nursery of Gibbon's genius. It was here that he spent the formative period of his youth after he had returned from Switzerland and had agreed to give up Suzanne Curchod, preparing the ground on which he was presently to raise the gigantic structure of "The

Decline and Fall." At Buriton he learned to know England, which
helped him in due course to focus his impressions of the Roman world,
and developed the studious and sedentary habits that enabled him
to become a historian and a scholar.

During the latter stages of World War II, I myself ventured to
write an essay on Gibbon, published in a book entitled "Four Portraits." Traveling at the time was difficult, and I am ashamed to
admit that I did not visit Buriton until the volume was several years
old, but relied on photographs, printed sources and, to some extent,
on an intuitive notion of how I felt it ought to look.

I was lucky; and, when I saw Buriton lying just below, I was
delighted to notice that my fanciful picture very largely corresponded
to the facts. It is not a method that I should recommend; nor do I
suggest that my slipshod procedures constitutes a valid precedent.

Yet it might be possible, I think, to write a biography without (as
some modern biographers like to do) examining every house in which
the hero spent a few weeks and studying every landscape that he loved
or hated. Such evidence is always worth gathering; but the biographer
who collects it must be enough of an artist himself to re-create his
raw material in imaginative form.

Besides its practical uses, however, literary sight-seeing has many
functions. It increases our sense of the drama of human life,
strengthens our awareness of the indissoluble relationship between the
present and the past. I enjoyed for its own sake my visit to Illiers,
though I have no intention of writing a new book on Proust—that has
already been done by George Painter in his two-volume biography.

And, although I have no professional concern either with Madame
de Sévigné or with Chateaubriand, I mean one day to visit the letter-
writer's country house, Les Rochers, and the poet's Chateau de Com-
bourg near St. Malo. But very often Time has intervened; and it is
an odd experience to visit the scene of some momentous happening
nowadays almost entirely obliterated, or half buried in the 20th
century—the slope of Ludgate Hill where the ill-fated Earl of Essex,
accompanied by Shakespeare's beloved friend Southampton, fought
his last inglorious battle; or the dusky passage, leading off Fleet
Street, at the mouth of which, on June 30, 1784, Samuel Johnson for
the last time bade good-bye to James Boswell.

Johnson, who dreaded death, knew that his end was near; Boswell,
whose spirits were then particularly low, was reluctant to prolong their

parting. "Fare you well," enunciated the old man, as he turned to disappear forever; and Boswell noted the "kind of pathetick briskness" with which he plunged off into the narrow dark passage to seek the shelter of his lonely rooms.

CARLOS BAKER
Hemingway's Italia

As the authorized biographer of Ernest Hemingway, Carlos Baker has traveled widely in search of material and impressions, some of which are presented in "Hemingway's Italia." At Princeton, where he is Woodrow Wilson professor of literature, he speaks also as a novelist and critic.

FOLLOWING Hemingway's footsteps across the European Continent as I did in the fall of '66, is an exercise in revelation of how things change while managing to remain very much the same. It is now years since Hemingway returned from Spain for the last time. Yet he is still a well-remembered presence in all the bullrings—from noisy Pamplona in the north, through the monumental Plaza de Toros in Madrid, and down to the ancient arena of Ronda, among the Andalusian mountains of the south. The imagination need not strain to picture him in a choice seat among trusted cronies, up-ending his wine bottle to the side of his mouth, scratching his beard, adjusting his eyeshade or his steel-rimmed glasses, and watching death avoided and given on a thousand summer afternoons.

So it seems to be wherever else he set foot: beside the Rhone Canal, where he fished for trout in snow-water; inside the spectacular Montafon Valley in the Austrian Vorariberg, where he skied, read, and wrote for two whole winters in the middle twenties. Or in the Closerie des Lilas in Paris, where a brass plaque commemorates his favorite perch at the bar—while outside on its pedestal the sculptured figure of his revered Marshal Ney still flourishes his saber and yells soundlessly into the Parisian air.

One finds him, too, on the battlefields: at Omaha Beach near

Colleville, where with bandaged head and swollen knees he watched seventh-wave infantrymen booted ashore from their landing-craft at 0700 on D-Day; in the Belgian village of Houffalize, where he sat joking with his friend Colonel Buck Lanham while native artisans rebuilt a blown bridge in the astonishing time of 40 minutes; in the gray old city of Luxembourg where he arrived from Paris with a temperature of 104 to be present, rather woozily, at the Battle of the Bulge.

Hemingway's tracks are even more deeply dented along a strip of northern Italy, which he loved so much that he used it as the locale of two novels, nearly a dozen short stories, several poems, 15 newspaper dispatches and two small fables. He returned to it, as to a magnet, after his near-fatal African airplane crashes of 1954. He might have been content to be buried there, like his fictional Colonel Cantwell, under the tall plane trees of a villa along the Brenta—instead of where he now lies, under a sagebrush-covered hill in Ketchum, Idaho, seven thousand miles away.

His adopted Italian domain is bounded by Milan on the west, by Udine on the east, on the north by Cortina d'Ampezzo, and on the south by Venice. It embraces the pleasant Piedmont town of Schio, below the scarred brow of Monte Pasubio, where he drove Red Cross ambulances for a month in 1918. It includes the village of Fossalta-di-Piave, where World War I ended for him one July midnight in the clanging roar of an Austrian trench-mortar. Thirty years later, with another world war behind him, he extended his holdings to include Friuli and Udine, together with the country villas and shooting preserves of some ancient Venetian families. It was here, on the road between Latisana and Codroipo, that his fictional Colonel Cantwell died.

At first, he found that one could not go back. Not, at any rate, with the rapture of discovery. He tried it in June, 1922, in the company of his first wife Hadley. He had spoken to her enthusiastically of Schio, where he had been quartered, with the other young ambulance drivers, on the second floor of a wool factory. He remembered the town as "one of the finest places on earth," and he wanted to spend a night at the Two Swords Hotel, where the food had been superb. But when they took a bus from Milan on June 13, the sky had gone gray with a hint of rain, and he learned, as he would later learn a thousand times, that the nostalgic dream was not the present reality.

Schio had somehow shrunk in the years between. Even the commanding mountains looked "rain-furrowed and dull." The Due Spadi now was only a "small mean inn," where the bed squeaked and the sole light came from a fly-speckled bulb. The wool factory was back in operation—a flow of black muck had polluted the former swimming hole. Ernest strolled down the long twisting main street, looking at the shirts and postcards and cheap dishes in the windows of the shops. He knew enough not to try to find the garden with the wisteria vine where the young American lieutenants had drunk beer on hot nights four years earlier. He tried a drink at one of the bars, but it did not help. "All the kick," he complained, "had gone out of things." The dinner at the Two Swords was reprehensible. Early next morning he and Hadley left in a rented car for Rovereto and a trip round Lago di Garda. It was still raining.

It was not very different at Fossalta-di-Piave, the site of Hemingway's wounding. Hiring a car and driver in Mestre, they went chugging along the straight road that ran like a causeway through the "poisonous green Adriatic marshes that flank all the coast near Venice." Like many a veteran returning to the scene of his wartime exploits, he found the village unrecognizable. In July, 1918, it had been a heap of rubble, one of the first Austrian footholds on the Venetian side of the river. Now he could not identify a single landmark. "All the shattered, tragic dignity of the wrecked town was gone. In its place was a new, smug, hideous collection of plaster houses." Shell-scars on the trees had healed over; the old trenches and dug-outs had vanished without a trace.

He climbed the grassy slope above the sunken road that gave the town its name. The Piave was clean and blue, in color very much like Walloon Lake in Michigan, where he had spent the summers of his boyhood. He watched the slow progress of a cement barge upstream, towed by laboring horses. The bargemen were working just where the Italian parapets had been. Now there was nothing but a smooth green slope stretching down to the quiet waters. Only the river bend was familiar. In a hedge he found a rusty shell fragment, sole evidence of the front where he had lost his right knee-cap and thousands more their lives.

He turned away gloomily. He had tried and failed to re-create a former actuality. "Chasing yesterdays," he concluded, "is a bum show, and if you have to prove it, go back to your old front." In half a dozen

years he would discover how to re-create a vanished past with the story
of Frederick Henry and Catherine Barkley. But he did not know this
as he stood beside Hadley among the rebuilt houses of Fossalta-di-
Piave that hot June afternoon in 1922.

Yet the changes are not, after all, so great as Hemingway then believed. It is true that the "poisonous green marshlands" of the Veneto
have now been largely drained and the reclaimed earth sown to corn-
fields, truck gardens and vineyards. Fossalta, half asleep in the sun,
has a new bell-tower in the central square and a system of grass-covered
dikes to divert floods from the northern reaches of the village. Schio,
the wool town, is now so lively and prosperous that the still active Due
Spadi Hotel seems like an anachronism, its bar-restaurant reeking of
garlic and poor tobacco, its tablecloths enriched with a week-old patina
of spilled wine and gravy.

In most of the ways that matter to the imagination, the great cities
have altered less than the towns and villages. In Milan, where Hemingway recovered from his wounds and fell in love with his nurse, it
is still an easy stroll from the Via Allessandro Manzoni, where the
Red Cross Hospital was, down past La Scala, through the babbling
Galleria, and into the vast dim interior of the unscarred Duomo. Nor
have there been many overt changes at the San Siro track where the
young American lieutenants laid modest bets on the steeplechasing
horses, and where one of them caught the germ of a prize-winning
short story called "My Old Man."

It is likewise with Venice. When their car wheezed to a halt near
Portegrandi that June day in 1922, Ernest and Hadley saw it "gray
and yellow like a fairy city" across the glinting blue of the Laguna
Veneta. It was the same for Colonel Cantwell (and for Hemingway)
half a lifetime later, alighting from a stopped car to gaze over
the lagoon to the square-towered church at Torcello, and the high
campanile on Burano, to the magical city hull-down on the far horizon.

In 1922, he had regretted his attempt to chase his yesterdays. He
had to learn the lesson all over again in 1950, when a whole gamut
of reviewers condemned his Venetian novel, "Across the River and
Into the Trees," as a bathetic descent from his former levels of achievement. What shocked and hurt him most, however, was the knowledge
that his many-layered romantic vision of the city in the sea had not
moved the hearts of others, as, for 30 years, it had never failed to

move his own. This may well be why, though he lived for 11 years more, he never afterwards wrote of Italia, his first love in the order of time among all the countries of Europe.

But his footprints are still there. In Milan and Venice, Vicenza, and Verona, Latisana and Udine, as in dozens of other Continetal locales, he is a remembered presence, whose sharp outlines have blurred very little since his death.

WALTER TELLER
Whitman at Timber Creek

The way men live has always seemed to fascinate Walter Teller. He revealed this fascination in his "Search for Captain Slocum." It lies behind the essays "Whitman at Timber Creek" and "The Outermost House" (see page 210). Something of his own way of life is set out in his philosophical reflections, "Area Code 215: A Private Line in Bucks County."

GOOD nature writing is hard to come by. So is good-natured writing, and these two things may be not unrelated. A rising tide of urbanization produces little of either. Nor does accelerating mobility. The first-rate writer on nature is not chasing the sun or the season. Instead, he localizes. He summons forth the sense of locality, the genius and gist of particular place. He evokes its peculiar characteristics. In tune with the spirit and substance of place, reasonable and also romantic, few have written on nature so well as—and none I think better than—Walt Whitman.

In 1873, when he was 53, Whitman suffered a stroke. Leaving Washington, where he had lived and worked during and after the Civil War, he made his way north, through Philadelphia to Camden. There he broke down, disabled, as he said. Three years later, apparently over the worst of it, he began spending random weeks and months convalescing "at a secluded haunt down in Camden County, New Jersey—Timber Creek . . . with primitive solitudes, winding stream, recluse and woody banks, sweet-feeding springs, and all the charms that birds, grass, wildflowers, rabbits and squirrels, old oaks, walnut trees etc., can bring." His diary of those hours, put down on the spot, contains some of the best prose he ever wrote. He later published it in his little autobiographical book, "Specimen Days."

When Whitman turned "to the primitive winding, aforementioned wooded creek . . . away from . . . the whole cast-iron civilized life . . . to the breast of the great silent savage all-acceptive Mother," he did so as guest of George and Susan Stafford. These "dear and valued friends," as Whitman later called them, lived twelve miles or so from Camden on a farm that George Stafford worked himself.

He had met the Staffords by chance. The Centennial Year, 1876, was approaching, and with it the Centennial Exposition in Philadelphia, the first large international exposition held in America. It seemed to Whitman a likely time to reissue "Leaves of Grass." Since he then was without a publisher, he went to a printing shop in Camden to have an "Author's Edition" set up. There he met an apprentice, Harry Stafford, one of five children of George and Susan. The young man and the lame and aging poet struck up a friendship. Presently Harry Stafford invited his friend out to the farm.

In this fashion Whitman and the Staffords met. George Stafford has been described as hard-working and silent in manner, a local Methodist preacher as well as a farmer. Susan, his wife, is said to have had a "cultured expression and spiritual mind."

The Stafford farm sloped south in a slightly undulating countryside. A fenced lane led past the house and barn through fields to a woodland ravine where a slow stream, widening out, formed a pond. This place, which Whitman called Timber Creek, the world called—and still calls—Laurel Springs. When Whitman showed up at the Laurel Springs farmhouse the Staffords could never be certain—and did not ask—whether he came to stay a couple of nights or three months.

Though Timber Creek has long been part of the landscape carried around in my head, not until recently did my eyes see it in fact. One February day Whitman wrote: "I, too, like the rest, feel these modern tendencies (from all the prevailing intellections, literature, and poems) to turn everything to pathos, ennui, morbidity, dissatisfaction, death. Yet how clear it is to me that those are not the born results, influences of nature at all, but of one's own distorted, sick or silly soul. Here, amid this wild, free scene, how healthy, how joyous, how clean and vigorous and sweet!" Rereading those words on a

February day, I got out a road map, unfolded it, and started out for Laurel Springs.

The landscape one carries around in one's head is sometimes, and not surprisingly, hard to recognize on the ground. While much of the aspect Whitman saw no longer exists—rubbed out, evaporated— the farmhouse, the old Stafford home, is standing, surrounded by lilacs and maple trees on what is called Maple Avenue. Two stories high and well proportioned, it was lately acquired by the state. In due course its faded clapboard will be repainted, the building restored and enshrined.

Maple Avenue, I learned, is the one-time Stafford farm lane, the same that was fenced with chestnut rails and down which cattle and horses and hogs and Whitman, half paralyzed, made their way to the creek. One cannot easily follow in Whitman's footsteps. During the years he navigated those banks, most Philadelphians and Camdenites were bound for the Jersey shore. As traffic increased, another railroad was called for. This one, the Narrow Gauge Railroad, notched through the Stafford farm. Traversing the farm lane with a deep gash, it cut off the farmhouse from the creek and ravine. Finally, and in Whitman's time, George Stafford sold out. He left off farming and went to keeping store. The face of things was changing.

So the farmhouse stands north of the railroad tracks and the long since abandoned narrow gauge line, while south of it Maple Avenue continues. There is a raw unfinished newness about it—bulldozers, pipelines, houses and automobiles going to the edge of the ragged ravine. And still you see remnants of what Whitman saw, the fringe of disheveled shore line, the flat sluggish creek, some big, hard-to-get-at old trees.

Remnants. Farther along the main highway, on the glassed-in porch of a yellow frame house, I met a grandson of George and Susan Stafford. Warren Stafford, 75 years old, said that when he was a boy a stream of cold water as big as this—holding up his hands and making a circle—poured out of the bank near the end of the farm lane. He said he used to drink there, especially on hot summer days; that Whitman had watered there too, but the spring—"sweet-feeding springs," Whitman wrote—eventually had dried up.

If the landscape of Laurel Springs differs from the landscape Whitman called Timber Creek, it was probably always different. Whitman, a poet, inevitably makes his own. The good writer on nature does more than observe. In an important sense he also creates. This is by no means everyone's field. Always subjective, and making no bones about it, the good nature writer includes the human—the most available being himself. Through his personal relationship to nature he creates in part the environment, then takes from it what he requires.

"Come, ye disconsolate, in whom any latent eligibility is left—come get the sure virtues of creek shore, and wood and field. . . . A light southwest wind was blowing through the tree-tops. . . . So hanging clothes on a rail nearby, keeping old broadbrim on head and easy shoes on feet, haven't I had a good time. . . . Nature was naked and I was also. It was too lazy, soothing, and joyous-equable to speculate about. Yet I might have thought somehow in this vein: Perhaps the inner, never-lost rapport we hold with earth, light, air, trees, etc. is not to be realized through eyes and mind only, but through the whole corporeal body."

If waltzing nude in the sun was rare and original in Whitman's time, being able to write about it was probably even more so. But then Whitman did not look at nature in traditional conventional ways. No good writer on nature does. He is more confident than that. He enters into his own arrangements. One of the things that Whitman required of nature would now be called physical therapy. He partook not only of sun and mud baths, and creek-water bathing—his own prescriptions—but he also wrestled with saplings. This latter involved something more than mere traction—"to pull on that young hickory sapling out there—to sway and yield to its tough-limber upright stem —haply to get into my old sinews some of its elastic fiber and clear sap"; these health pulls, as Whitman called them, were part of the "silent delicious medicine" he sought in nature, and found.

Nothing in the natural world is closer to Whitman's heart than a tree. He makes a list—"Trees I am familiar with here"—a common-run pleasant-reading catalogue, nothing competitive about it. As for "The Lesson of a Tree," he would not illustrate it, he says, with either the biggest or the most picturesque. "One lesson from affiliating a tree," Whitman writes, "perhaps the greatest moral lesson anyhow from earth, rocks, animals—is the lesson of inherency, of *what is*, without the least regard to what the looker-on (the critic) supposes or says, or whether he likes or dislikes."

For the reader and writer who contemplate nature, "Specimen Days" is both lesson and teacher. When I was writing my book, "Area Code 215: A Private Line in Bucks County," Whitman was much in my mind, especially his precept concerning free margin: "You must not know too much, or be too precise or scientific about birds and trees and flowers and water craft; a certain free margin, and even vagueness —perhaps ignorance, credulity—helps your enjoyment of these things, and of the sentiment of feather'd, wooded, river, or marine Nature generally. I repeat it—don't want to know too exactly, or the reasons why. My own notes have been written off-hand in the latitude of middle New Jersey. Though they describe what I saw—what appear'd to me —I daresay the expert ornithologist, botanist or entomologist will detect more than one slip in them."

Free margin, I found out, is not all that free. If, as Whitman says, you must not know too much, you must not know too little either. Above all, you must know what is evident to the senses. Free margin is actually a control, a caution, not to make too much of a point, not to be heavy about it. Free margin may be the wonderful margin the great nature writer has over the plodder.

At bottom a nature writer must be a philosopher, a man who keeps watch along a canal, or who knows how to talk to house plants. Good nature writing, like all good writing, is a salvage operation, an attempt to save what is valuable. The scene is changing as possibly never before. When you find urban man in the woods, then established dividing lines fall away. Life is haphazard. You have only really to look at the landscape to see how chaotic life is. On the other side, however, is order. Day follows night. There is the march of the seasons. And truth in whatever form is welcome.

HELEN BEVINGTON
The Way to Little Gidding

In telling of the way to Little Gidding, Helen Bevington has the incomparable touch one has come to expect from her. Consider her volumes of light verse: "Company: Doctor Johnson's Waterfall," "Nineteen Million Elephants," "A Change of Sky." Or "When Found, Make a Verse Of," a collection of poems and the experiences involved in writing them. She is also the author of two volumes of memoirs,

"Charley Smith's Girl" and *"A Book and a Love Affair,"* and is Associate Professor of English at Duke.

I T WAS still winterspring in England, a cold rainy day in early April, and the bus I took, No. 151 to Peterborough, was a big red double-decker like the London buses. Nobody in it looked as if he were on a pilgrimage.

Mr. Eliot says in the "Four Quartets" that you go to Little Gidding from wherever you are. And it is here, in England and nowhere. "If you came this way,/Taking the route you would be likely to take/From the place you would be likely to come from—" you would find it. The place I was likely to come from was Cambridge, since that is where I was, only a few miles from Huntingdonshire where Little Gidding was supposed to be. Yet nobody I asked (at the hotel desk, the bus terminal, the railroad station) had ever heard of it. There was no train connection. I decided to take the Peterborough bus and see how close I could come.

The conductor, puzzled by my destination, offered to consult the bus driver. He returned to say he would try putting me off this side of Peterborough, at a crossroads near Alconbury. Scratching his head, he went off to have another talk with the driver. A minute later he came back to say he had decided on a different crossroads farther on. I asked him pointblank:

"Do you know where Little Gidding is?"

"Not actually, no. Can't say I do," he replied.

"If you came this way, taking the route you would be likely to take, is this the route you would take, do you think?"

"Well now, that I can't say. It might be."

"What about the driver? Does he know where Little Gidding is?"

"He says it might be near Great Gidding."

I didn't ask him if he had ever heard of T. S. Eliot.

Lambing was over in Cambridgeshire, and the fields we passed were full of baby lambs frisking beside their mothers. The conductor stopped at my seat a third time to assure me that he and the driver had the problem licked. He would put me off just beyond Alconbury Hill.

"That should be about six miles from there over to the Giddings," he said kindly, "however you went about it."

We rode on in the rain into Huntingdonshire, passing again

through the little village of Godmanchester that I had visited on this same bus only last week. I didn't yet know how to pronounce Godmanchester, whether the accent was on man or God. But I reflected I had now traveled in England to Chester, to Manchester and to Godmanchester, which should bring me to the end of the prefixes unless there was a Goodgodmanchester somewhere as well. Beyond the town of Huntingdon, the county seat, we joined the Great North Road from London. This side of Alconbury Hill, 23 miles from Cambridge, the conductor came to lean over my shoulder, anxiously scanning the road ahead.

"We can't be far off now," he said, breathing hard on my neck. "I mean, it has to be hereabouts, hasn't it?" Suddenly he rang the bell and cordially put me off at Conington crossroads.

A small wooden sign pointed cross-country to the left:

GREAT GIDDING—4 MILES
LITTLE GIDDING—5¼ MILES

My appetite for this journey had by now considerably waned. To walk some 11 miles back and forth across a flat, forsaken English countryside in the pouring rain appealed to me not at all, not even for Mr. Eliot's sake. I looked around for help and immediately spotted a pub across the double highway, the Crown and Woolpack, where over half a bitter I might consider a way to make this literary pilgrimage in reasonable comfort.

My instinct was perfectly right—the innkeeper had a solution. He had never visited Little Gidding ("I've only lived around here 10 years," he said) and showed no curiosity as to why one would want to go. But he listened thoughtfully.

"That'll do it," he said, "the man from Sawtry," and went to the telephone.

Within 10 minutes, the man from Sawtry arrived in his battered Ford car. A Deliverer, you might say, in the Eliot tradition. Though he had a terrible stutter, he conveyed the idea as I climbed gratefully in with him that there were not two, but *three* Giddings over yonder, and which one did I want?

"Little Gidding," I said. "Have you been to Little Gidding?"

"I s-h-h-h-houldn't think so, ma'am."

"Is there a church there, do you think?"

"One's at S-s-s-s-steeple Gidding."

The country road lay quiet in the rain, with lots of graceful winding turns. Four miles distant, we reached Great Gidding, a sleepy hamlet of yellow stone houses and, the man from Sawtry guessed, about 300 inhabitants. At noon not a soul stirred.

More than a mile beyond we came to a small sign beside the road: "Little Gidding Only." No houses were in sight within the thick grove of trees, but the sign clearly pointed to the right to a narrow muddy lane, lined with potato bags drying on the fences. This we followed in low gear for a half-mile, to where the lane ended abruptly in a farmer's barnyard. There we stopped of necessity. We sat pensive in a silent, empty barnyard, beyond which we could see a pond and a green countryside, nothing more. Two large barns, one on either side of the road, effectually hid the farmhouse.

The man from Sawtry turned in his seat to know if I was well pleased with the trip.

"Where are we?" I asked.

He looked about him in mild surprise and shook his head. He didn't know.

"I don't believe this farmyard is Little Gidding," I said. "Maybe we aren't there yet, would you say?"

Agreeing that we couldn't be, he backed the car out of the barnyard, maneuvered a turnaround, and drove down the potholed lane the way we had come. We went whizzing up the country road a mile farther, till at length we reached another road sign: "Steeple Gidding Only." Here again we turned as directed and followed a muddy lane to its end. Behind a picket fence stood a little gray stone church, surrounded by ancient elms and fallen gravestones in the tiny churchyard.

I got out and went inside the cold, bleak church with its dozen pews and altar, but I found no sign of what I sought, nothing but a dim memorial to Sir John Cotton, 1752. In perplexity I returned to the guide and sadly shook my head.

"This isn't Little Gidding," I said. "I think it must be Steeple Gidding, don't you?"

The man from Sawtry looked completely crestfallen, and for a while we stood uncertainly in the rain wondering what to do. A sudden idea came to him. "I'll ask," he cried and ran off through the field to a farmhouse hidden by the trees, hurrying back almost at once with a broad smile. "Get in," he said. He was a man of few words.

We drove hell bent back to the sign "Little Gidding Only," turned in at the now familiar lane, and splashed our way to the farmer's barnyard. This time on reaching the dead end, we kept boldly on a few feet farther, past the barns into the farmer's cropped field from which we could gaze into his chickenyard. Beyond it, on the other side of the chicken coop, stood Little Gidding.

> If you came by day not knowing what you came for,
> It would be the same, when you leave the rough road
> And turn behind the pig-sty to a dull façade
> And the tombstone.

The incredibly tiny church was gray stone, its façade weathered and dull. A bell hung in the small steeple; a beech wood spread behind. Halfway down the flagstone path stood the tombstone, the simple gray tomb of Nicholas Ferrar. And over the door of Ferrar's church shone the words, "This is none other but the House of God and the Gate of Heaven." Inside, it gleamed like a bright jewel, with shining brass font and lectern, an altar of cedarwood, a stained-glass window of the Crucifixion, and 12 highly polished choir stalls along each side of the chancel. It could be lighted only by candles.

Mr. Eliot traveled there from London during World War II, on a journey to the world's end, seeking peace. Nicholas Ferrar had gone for the same reason. More than 300 years ago, Ferrar had purchased the dilapidated manor house of Little Gidding, where the farmhouse now stands. The little church was being used then to store hay, and the sacristy was a pigsty.

He brought his mother with him, his brother, John, his sister, Susanna, together with their families (Susanna, married to John Collett, had 16 children)—about 30 in all. At the age of 34, Nicholas entered passionately upon the religious life, seeking and finding peace. Three times a day the whole family walked in procession from the house to pray in the church, which they adorned lovingly with silver-fringed tapestry cushions, rich altar hangings, a silk carpet, with their own embroideries and exquisitely bound books of Scripture. On Sunday the vicar of Great Gidding came over to perform the morning service. On Sunday afternoon the family walked across the fields to evensong at the church of Steeple Gidding.

After Nicholas Ferrar was dead, Charles I visited Little Gidding on three separate occasions, the last time as a fugitive in the dead of night, March 2, 1646. Three months later the Puritan soldiers completely destroyed the manor house and despoiled the church, ending their day's work with a huge bonfire. The church was rebuilt in 1714.

The man from Sawtry, relieved, as I was, to find the place and complete the quest, stepped inside with me and couldn't believe his eyes. Dumbfounded, he swore he would bring his wife next time to have a look at it. I returned to Cambridge that afternoon by Bus No. 151, after being picked up on the highway and warmly welcomed by driver and conductor as lost and found.

Next day in the Cambridge library I learned from "The Survey Gazetteer of the British Isles" that the village of Little Gidding consists of a total of 42 souls. I wondered where all 42 were keeping themselves yesterday.

WALTER TELLER*
"The Outermost House"

ON A visit to Cape Cod in spring 1965, I drove out of Eastham to the rim of the dunes, then walked a mile or so up the beach to see the cabin in which Henry Beston had lived and written "The Outermost House."

In his time, no building stood between the cabin and the old Coast Guard Station at Nauset. This is no longer the case. I walked past a lengthening line of camps. Tracks of jeeps, the beach spoilers, stretched ahead. I walked up to the weathered, wren-plain cabin standing now in the lee of the dunes, hauled back twice from the edge of the sea. A low grassy dune rises east of the little house. Beyond lies the beach and horizon of water. Westward the view across Nauset Marsh, across salt hay meadows, extends to the roof lines of Eastham.

I circled the cabin, sniffed the good air, then read a bronze plaque beside the door and wrote the inscription down. " 'The Outermost House' in which Henry Beston, author-naturalist, wrote his classic book by that name wherein he sought the Great Truth and found it in the Nature of Man. This plaque dedicated October 11, 1964, by a grateful citizenry, at a ceremony denoting The Outermost House a national literary landmark." Three names followed: Endicott Peabody,

* (For facts about Mr. Teller, turn back to page 201)

Governor of Massachusetts; Stewart L. Udall, Secretary of the Interior; The Massachusetts Audubon Society.

"The Outermost House" is Henry Beston's account of "A Year of Life on the Great Beach of Cape Cod." Published in 1928, it has been in print ever since. It appeared in England and was translated into French: "Une Maison au Bout du Monde."

The scene of "The Outermost House," the Great Beach, borders the outer coast of Cape Cod from Race Point in the north, the top of the Cape's upraised arm, to Chatham south, at the elbow. "A powerful tribe of Indians, the Nausets, once inhabited this earth between the seas," Henry Beston wrote in his opening pages. "Having known and loved this land for many years, it came about that I found myself free to visit there, and so I built myself a house upon the beach." Constructed by local carpenters from Beston's own sketch, the house "stood by itself atop a dune, a little less than halfway south on Eastham bar." It was only 20 feet long by 16 wide, partitioned into two rooms. If, as he wrote, his house showed "a somewhat amateur enthusiasm for windows"— there were 10—that would be all right, for Henry Beston aimed to see what winds, waves and birds were up to.

The summer of 1927 was waning when he moved in, 39 and single. He intended to spend a couple of weeks, but he "lingered on." Autumn came, and something of moment happened: "the beauty and mystery of this earth and outer sea so possessed and held me," he wrote, "that I could not go. . . . The longer I stayed, the more eager was I to know this coast and to share its . . . life. . . . I had no fear of being alone, I had something of a field naturalist's inclination; presently I made up my mind to remain and try living for a year on Eastham Beach."

And so he stays—alone—and transcendentally watching. "The sand here has a life of its own," he notes. He sees "land birds and moor birds, marsh birds and beach birds, sea birds and coastal birds, even birds of the outer ocean." He discovers need for "a wiser and perhaps more mystical concept of animals." He listens to the "awesome, beautiful, and varied" voices of the sea. He learns firsthand that "it is not good to be too much alone, even as it is unwise to be always with and in a crowd."

He lived very simply, heating his house with a fireplace "crammed maw-full of driftwood," cooking meals on a two-burner oil stove, writing in longhand at the kitchen table. Water came from a pipe driven into the sand. Using a knapsack to carry his groceries, he made weekly trips for "fresh bread and butter." Day and night the Coast Guard patrol would stop to converse and "mug up," for Henry Beston always kept a pot of coffee on the hearth. "The world today," he wrote then, "is sick to its thin blood for lack of elemental things, for fire before the hands, for water welling from the earth, for air, for the dear earth itself underfoot."

Back home, the seasons passed for me as well. When winter came, the outermost house became in my mind a bird refuge for the psyche. I found myself thinking of Henry Beston. What was his Great Truth? To say that he found it in the Nature of Man seemed to me to beg the question a little. I reread his book. "Some have asked me," he wrote in the closing pages, "what understanding of Nature one shapes from so strange a year? I would answer that one's first appreciation is a sense that the creation is still going on, that the creative forces are as great and as active today as they have ever been, and that tomorrow's morning will be as heroic as any of the world. *Creation is here and now* . . . Poetry is as necessary to comprehension as science. It is as impossible to live without reverence as it is without joy."

Twenty years after writing those words, in a new foreword for a new edition of "The Outermost House," Beston wrote, "Once again, I set down the core of what I continue to believe. Nature is a part of our humanity, and without some awareness and experience of that divine mystery, man ceases to be man. When the Pleiades and the wind in the grass are no longer a part of the human spirit . . . man becomes, as it were, a kind of cosmic outlaw. . . . Man can be either less than man or more than man, and both are monsters."

"The Outermost House," it becomes increasingly clear, is tied to enduring values—the kind seldom seen till they show signs of going. Above all, unlike the run of books published in any year, it is a work wholly outside of fashion. What sort of man in 1928—when talking pictures were still new, when Coolidge prosperity was ending—made such a singular gesture and wrote such a time-breaking book?

Born June 1, 1888, in Quincy, Mass., Henry Beston was the son of a physician who had studied in France. His mother was a Frenchwoman, member of what he described as an "old military and Bonapartist" family. He went to Harvard, received his B.A. in 1909, his M.A. in 1911, then turned to teaching. During World War I, he served in the Army, afterwards spent a year in the Navy in "the curious world of submarines." He published his first book in 1919. Several children's books followed. Then came the climactic year as observer-philosopher of the beach. In 1929 he married Elizabeth Coatsworth. They moved to a farm in Maine, raised two daughters and made the farm their home.

It was May, a Thursday morning, and a year had passed since I saw the outermost house. Now I wanted to meet the man who had been loner-in-residence. I picked up the phone, asked the operator to connect me with Henry Beston.

The following Saturday afternoon found me in Maine. Five miles north of Damariscotta, in Nobleboro, I stopped at the general store. The proprietor, Robert Palmer, in reply to my question said Henry Beston lived in the next to last house, a red clapboard farmhouse, out East Neck Road. "He thinks a lot of us and we think a lot of him," Mr. Palmer added.

The author of "The Outermost House" is a man with an eye for beautiful places. His farm lies athwart a stretch of land extending into Damariscotta Lake. Red house and red barn stand high overlooking the water. Behind, on still higher ground, rises a woodland of firs. In a latter-day New England parlor, I met Henry Beston, nobly large and courtly, a well-favored man. Though looking younger than his 78 years, complexion ruddy, mustache and hair iron-gray, he no longer gets around easily.

I asked him how he accounted for the present-day interest in his book. "The interest in nature is growing. People see it's a kind of impossible world and they have to have something else. I wish people would get on more peaceably," he said smiling. A big man with a gentle smile.

Why had he gone to the beach, I asked. "During the war and afterwards," he said, "I saw so many people writing in New York I was anxious to see what a year, more or less alone in the midst of great natural beauty, would mean. Cape Cod has good people—hospitable to wild and unexpected things—so I decided to go there alone. I wanted to be solitary and to have nothing between me and nature."

Was this the whole plan? "I had no particular plan," Henry Beston said. "I thought it would be a gorgeous place to live—with the roar of the surf and a wonderful view to north and south. And to the east, the Gulf of Maine—you would find lobster buoys on that beach that had drifted down from Matinicus Island. I had a little money. I used a handful to build the house. Everything went ahead. It developed in its own way."

Had he been influenced by Thoreau? "No, I think not," Beston
said. "I admire Thoreau but don't care much for him. He wasn't warm
enough."

What books had he taken along? "I had a good clutch of books,"
Beston said. "There were Shakespeare's plays, the Bible, W. H. Hudson and Longfellow, whose poems of rain and sea have always appealed
to me. I had Forbush's three-volume 'Birds of Massachusetts,' wonderful reference books. And the Sherlock Holmes stories. And the
'Rubaiyat'—a great favorite."

He showed me a photograph of himself taken at the time. He was
then half his present age. "I was 6 feet 1½ inches tall, weighed 190—
strong as a bear," he said. "I was a good deal out of doors and a good
deal indoors. I wrote every morning from 9 to 12. I didn't put in any
fake stuff. I told everything truly.

"It was a lonely life out there. Nobody patted me on the back,
but the life had great appeal. The most solitary time was on certain
wild nights. Sometimes I would be inside when a single wave would
crash on the beach and shake the whole house. I always had a fire
going—kept fire on the hearth. I was an old-fashioned person—always
liked a hearth fire. I had a teacher who used to say hearth fire was the
only fire fit for a human." Henry Beston paused, "It was a very happy
year."

Mrs. Beston came in bringing glasses, cakes, and Bristol Cream
sherry. "That's good stuff," he said, as we savored the wine. I thought
of the very first words in his book. "Only a solitary knows how social
and kindly life can be."

"The Outermost House" is an inside story of individual perception—experience written in a manner befitting the man. Henry Beston
believes he wrote "rather an English style." Be that as it may, one
finds in his book dignity, courage and a point of view.

VI
The
Experience of
Literature

CARLOS BAKER*
The Relevance of a
Writer's Life

ONCE upon a time there was a critical concept known as the biographical fallacy. Along with the intentional fallacy and one or two others, it came into prominence in the late 1930's and early 1940's, when the New Criticism was seeking to establish the doctrine of the essential autonomy of the individual work of art. Some of those excellent New Critics held that the prime purpose of criticism was to explore and explain the structures and the textures, the intensions and the extensions, the conceits and the paradoxes in poetry and fiction. The cultural or psychological environments from which the poems and novels sprang were said to be irrelevant. Biography and history were directed to take a back seat, or even to leave the bus. They were supernumeraries.

These gifted critics were in revolt—needful revolt—against excessive critical preoccupation with the social backgrounds of literature. This, in its turn, was a habit of the 1920's and 1930's when the ugly face of economic depression stared like a stuffed bear-head from the wall of every study, and when the Marxist view that literature must serve the ends of the state and the dictatorship of the proletariat was widely if by no means universally entertained.

Like many other instances of reform or revolution, the Neo-Critical insurrection was justified. Cleanth Brooks and Robert Penn Warren,

* (For facts about Mr. Baker turn back to page 197)

with their epoch-making anthologies, "Understanding Poetry" and "Understanding Fiction," powerfully reasserted the right of the work of art to be itself. They performed a notable service in overturning the preciosities of literary "appreciation," and insisting that direct inspection of the esthetic object would yield all that a reader needed to know about it. Neither an author's life, nor his social background, nor his politics, nor his religious views, nor the course of his amours, nor his favorite breakfast menu, had anything finally to do with the thing that really mattered: what he had written, painted or composed. To use any such information in the interpretation or evaluation of a sonnet or a short story or a play was to entangle oneself like a latter-day Laocoön in the serpentine toils of the biographical fallacy.

It was a good idea. The difficulty arose when it was allowed to freeze into a dogma. The New Critics repeatedly, and often eristically, insisted on their point of view. They behaved a little like Socrates, relentlessly interrogating the members of the opposition, backing sophistical pretenders into corners by the cool fury of their logic. The apogee of their position, at any rate for biography, was reached in 1949, when the brilliant critic René Wellek stated flatly that literary biography had no final critical importance: "No biographical evidence can change or influence critical evaluation."

In a way, of course, he was perfectly right. Our sense of the ultimate and timeless value of a work of art depends relatively little upon our particularized knowledge of its creator. What do we know of the life of Shakespeare, for example, that genuinely assists us in the evaluation of his plays? A few dates, a few legal documents, a bald-headed bas-relief, the legend of the second-best bed, a fierce epitaph carved in stone in a church in Stratford, but very little more. What do we really know about Homer that would be relevant to the evaluation of the "Iliad" and the "Odyssey"? And so on through a long list of ancient worthies, the "sons of light" as Shelley called them, whose non-autobiographical works constitute a great part of our humanistic heritage.

Yet (and it is a big word) there are questions in criticism to which biographical knowledge is directly applicable. They usually come in the two preliminary stages before the final act of value-judgment. These are the phases of description and interpretation, where biographical evidence does—and in fact should—change or influence critical judgments. That admirable esthetician, Monroe Beardsley, properly distinguishes between the art object itself and the antecedent conditions that produced it in the mind: the environment, and the personal history of its creator. The art object provides the indispensable *internal* evidence. All the rest, no less useful and no less valuable, represents the *external* evidence. The critic's job of work is to describe, interpret and evaluate the work of art by using both internal and external evidence. This seems to me an eminently sensible way of looking at the matter.

To return to the course of literary history. For ten or twelve years, the polemicists of the New Criticism continued their slingshot barrage, like a company of stalwart Davids bent on destroying the Goliath Historismus. The counterforce began to be felt in the early 1950's. One forthright spokesman for the opposition was Leslie Fiedler, himself a talented debater. He opened an essay in 1952 by saying that "a central dogma of much recent criticism asserts that biographical information is irrelevant to the understanding of poems." This dogma, said he, was "one of those annoying clichés" put forth by "the intellectually middle-aged" as if it were still a "stimulating heresy."

It is now over 15 years since Mr. Fiedler whipped the anti-biographers and summoned them back to the raft. There, at present, they seem to be living in amicable association with History and Biography. This recrudescence of an old friendship has made criticism somewhat more complicated than it was in the 1940's, when all a man needed to set himself up as Pontifex Maximus Scriblerus was wit, sensibility, imagination, a gift of gab, his bare hands—and a poem or a story to analyze the hell out of.

Up to a point, I would hold with Fiedler. Both the biographer and the critic are in similar businesses, though their mail goes out under different letterheads. The business is revelation. The primary task of the biographer is to select important details from multiple sources and to arrange them in an orderly and illuminating narrative. What is illuminated is the subject, a man at his chosen work (and play) in all his cultural environments. The biographer must assume that "the best poetry is what happens."

The critic's primary task also involves selection, multiple sources, and the goal of illumination. What is illuminated as a result of his labors is not a human life, but the origin, development, meaning, and value of works of art. Although the paths followed by the biographer and the critic are clearly not the same, they inevitably intersect. Where they do not intersect, they run parallel. When they seem to diverge sharply, the divergence is probably an illusion. For no esthetic object

is ever divorced completely from its creator. It is his. He is in it—
for better or worse. Or, to put the matter in terms supplied by Wallace
Stevens: "It is often said of a man that his work is autobiographical
in spite of every subterfuge. It cannot be otherwise."

Stevens continues in the same essay with yet another pertinent
comment. "The truth is," says he, "that a man's sense of the world
dictates his subjects to him and this sense is derived from his personality, his temperament, over which he has little control and possibly none, except superficially." I remember a remark of William
Faulkner's, made in my hearing some years ago. "A writer writing,"
said he, "is like a man building a chicken coop in a high wind. He just
grabs onto any board he can and nails it down fast." And where does
he get his board but from his "sense of the world," from the range of
his past experience, from his sudden, flashing decision that this, and
no other, is the board that belongs in this place at precisely this point
in his narrative?

Close knowledge of a writer's sense of the way the world is put
together, to say nothing of the details of his experience, can help the
critic to correct some of those misapprehensions to which he may
have been led by his own highly personalized response to a work of art.
As a result of reading the letters (the best form of autobiography) of
Wallace Stevens, my conception of "The Emperor of Ice Cream" has
undergone subtle and valuable alterations. Lawrance Thompson's
splendid biography of Robert Frost has colored my rereading of a
whole host of long-loved poems. In criticism it is always better to
know the facts than to dream up fanciful associations and analogues.
Leon Edel's life of Henry James illuminates a thousand hitherto dark
corners in the fiction of the master. Biography remains ancillary—
the quick handmaiden in the house of criticism—to the serious
study of a man's works. But the critic cannot dispense with that assistance.

A practical problem comes to mind. Not long ago, an East Indian
critic sent me a letter of inquiry about one of Hemingway's early
stories, "The Battler." The story tells of an encounter between Nick
Adams and a down-and-out prizefighter in a hobo jungle near Mance-
lona, Mich. The fighter's name is Ad Francis. Ad might well be short
for Addled. Being punchdrunk makes him perpetually belligerent. He
is obviously laying plans to "cool" young Nick Adams when Bugs,
Ad's polite and kindly Negro companion, taps him with a blackjack

on his already well-beaten cranium. In the most gentlemanly possible fashion, Bugs then suggests that Nick would do well to leave before Ad comes to. My Indian friend was under the misapprehension that Ad and Bugs were homosexuals. He did not know that Hemingway had invented the figure of Ad Francis from two real-life professional boxers, Bat Nelson and Ad Wolgast, while the wise and patient Negro was modeled on the man who "looked after" Ad Wolgast during his decline.

Hemingway himself had long since rejected the notion that Ad and Bugs were homosexuals. It may not be wrong, as our man in India argued, to read the story as if they were. Yet the portrait of the Negro takes on a new dimension of selfless loyalty, resourcefulness and gentle humor if his character is interpreted in the light of Hemingway's intention. My Indian friend is still pondering that critical issue. And well he might, for it is an issue involving description, interpretation and (I believe) evaluation.

Was the concept of the biographical fallacy, as Fiedler suggested, merely a negativistic dogma masquerading as a heroic heresy? Probably not. For in warning against excessive reliance on external evidence, the New Critics led us to pay positive attention to the evidence provided by the work of art itself. This was a palpable advantage, but the real fallacy lay in stopping the bus there and inviting History and Biography to take their leave. For biographical and historical information, judiciously brought to bear on a work of art by a sensible critic, is always relevant to the important business of understanding poetry and understanding fiction.

HARVEY SWADOS
Writers of the Thirties

Harvey Swados is a novelist ("The Will," among others), a writer of short stories, a critic, a teacher at Sarah Lawrence, and, as the following essay makes plain, something of a literary historian. Of his anthology, "The American Writers and the Great Depression," Granville Hicks has said: "So far as the written word can ever serve to give people

*some inkling of an experience they have not shared, this is the book
that shows what the Depression was like."*

I N THE course of a year's reading (and rereading) to prepare an
anthology on American writers and the Great Depression, I met with
two basic reactions among those with whom I discussed the matter:
that the thirties were a kind of tail end to the Golden Age of the
twenties, or that its writers were an untalented lot better left in limbo.
Both of these extreme attitudes, I discovered as I read on not only
among the novelists and poets but among the critics as well, derived
not so much from a fresh knowledge of the work of the thirties as
from memories or reverberations of the judgments the critics of the
period had passed on their contemporaries. Thus, those writers all
but ignored at the time of their work's appearance—Daniel Fuchs,
Nathanael West, James Agee—are now only haltingly received, along
with those once well-reviewed but later forgotten, like Henry Roth.

The critics of the period tended, if they were Marxists (and this
included many of the leading academics), to reserve their accolades
for those who were writing about the underdog with the proper mixture
of indignation and revolutionary optimism. As a result, they system-
atically undervalued writers like William Faulkner and F. Scott Fitzgerald, who held to concerns established before the advent of the
Depression. And they overvalued books like Michael Gold's "Jews
Without Money" (1930), a sentimental caricature not only because
its version of American Jewish history leads in a straight line to the
Revolution, but because it invokes Mother as the guardian of revolutionary morality:

"Mother! Momma! I am still bound to you by the cords of birth.
I cannot forget you. I must remain faithful to the poor because I cannot be faithless to you! I believe in the poor because I have known you.
The world must be made gracious for the poor! Momma, you taught
me that!"

This incantatory prose can be seen as the forerunner if not the
model for later rebel voices whose verbiage no longer impresses us
quite as it did in the thirties and forties: Clifford Odets ("See this
ankle, this delicate sensitive hand? Four hundred years to breed that.
Out of a revolutionary background! Spirit of '76! Ancestors froze at
Valley Forge! What's it all mean! Slops! The honest workers were
sold out then, in '76. The Constitution's for rich men then and now.
Slops!") and Arthur Miller ("Attention must be paid.")

Those critics who, like Alfred Kazin, were not Marxists, had no difficulty in demolishing the pretentious claptrap published by proletarian novelists in the decade following the appearance of "Jews Without Money." Mr. Kazin's "On Native Grounds" (1942), precocious though it was, includes among its other virtues a devastating indictment of those writers whose strike novels revealed both poverty of imagination and lack of literary staying power. The book also includes incisive exposures of the weaknesses of writers like John Steinbeck and John O'Hara who failed to fulfill their early promise, yet have survived to enjoy great popular vogue three decades later. Unfortunately readers in the sixties still tend to think in terms of Mr. Kazin's more general strictures (which he would doubtless now disavow) on "the decline of the novel all through the period, a moral and physical decline," and of John Chamberlain's 1938 verdict: "Beyond Hemingway, Lewis, and Dos Passos, beyond Farrell and Wolfe, the fiction of the thirties that one remembers is sparse indeed." These readers forget that critics often couple reverence for the safely dead with lack of respect for the confusing and contradictory work in progress of their own contemporaries.

Well, what does remain? What do the writers of the thirties have to tell us now? It ought to be said, for one thing, that if the postwar writers have sought in their own various ways to answer the question: Who am I? then the Depression writers struggled to answer an equally important question: Who are we?

If the latter query is seldom asked nowadays, except by those whose answer seems to be that we are all either ridiculous or crazy, it does not follow that the artist who persists in posing it is either hopelessly outdated or as unworthy of the attention of the intelligent reader as the commercial novelists who have seized upon it in recent years for crasser purposes. Nor should a persistence in asking the question be taken to mean that the artist's concern for the shape and definition of our society has foreclosed the possibility of his examining even the most private dreams and longings of those who do, after all, function not only as individuals alienated to a greater or lesser extent from their fellows, but also as members of a society.

Perhaps we need to be reminded that not writers alone, but painters obsessed with their own changing and dissolving image—Rembrandt, Edvard Munch, Max Beckmann—did not thereby shrink from the effort to capture an image of their world as well.

We need to be reminded too that, while much of our current

experience can be apprehended as bizarre, meaningless and absurd, gifted American writers, not merely political hacks, have strained to deepen our understanding of society as an evolving organism, rather than as a random collectivity of atomized individuals. We have rediscovered Henry Roth's "Call It Sleep," which succeeded far better than "Jews Without Money" in relating the preceding generation to the immigrant experience, and also to the hard but challenging world of young people coming to maturity in the Great Depression. But there was also Jack Conroy, whose "The Disinherited," in addition to being a *bildungsroman* of a young revolutionary, was an ode to the hero's miner father, and to his widowed mother, who took in washing in their Missouri coal town so that he might go to school. And there was Edward Dahlberg, who told the tough but, in its way, epic story of his mother, the immigrant itinerant lady barber, in two fascinating novels, "Bottom Dogs" and "From Flushing to Calvary" (reworked into an autobiographical narrative, "Because I Was Flesh," published in 1964), which found her son entering the literary world as a revolutionary leftist. (Indeed all of these writers who apotheosized their mothers were deeply involved during the Depression with at least the literary aspects of the Communist movement, without thereby destroying their talents.)

We still pay lip service to, and perhaps some of us still read (certainly we should) John Dos Passos' "USA," but not many of us are even aware of the ambitious performance of Josephine Herbst, who also published a panoramic trilogy during the thirties, and whose memoirs, when finally completed, will bring to our attention once more a literary craftsman of tumultuous vitality. The strike novel, on the other hand, or the novel of the underdog, we have tended to dismiss utterly as nothing but a vehicle for worn-out sloganizing. Thereby we have cut ourselves off from those creative figures who not only rejected the values of bourgeois society, but attempted to understand it and to ascertain at least inferentially what might replace it. Robert Cantwell's second novel, "Land of Plenty," is still a powerful and edifying work. The young writer presented his Pacific Northwest lumber mill as a microcosm of Depression America, with the lights going out and the inhabitants groping toward a solution of their problems—in this case, the night-shift workers, brought together by a power failure, deciding to strike.

Similarly, Nelson Algren's first novel, "Somebody in Boots," which sold 750 copies in 1935 and is hardly known today, is a relentless exploration of the social reality of the hobo world of the thirties, which refuses to pretty up its hero to make him conform to the stereotype of the virtuous proletarian. If it demands rereading, Tom Kromer's "Waiting for Nothing," published the same year, cries out for rediscovery. Written on scraps of paper as its author, a victim of the Depression, bummed across the country in boxcars and afoot, it is a Gorkyesque cry from the lower depths, the remarkably honest, unvarnished, nonpolitical utterance of a man who barely survived to tell us of certain American horrors.

What is more, when we speak of these writers we must remember that we have not even named—much less done minimal justice to—all those others who, like Daniel Fuchs in his Brooklyn novels, Erskine Caldwell in his Georgia stories, and many others, played substantial roles in an era that was far richer than its contemporary critics have allowed.

While political conviction or philosophical commitment may have influenced the Depression writers' choice of subject matter and stylistic manner, at their best they transcended politics. The intensity of their concern sprang from a richer and deeper source, a desire to wed their craft not alone to an examination of the solitary intellectual but to an interpretation of the bewildering complexity of American life. This was, we need to be reminded in the sixties, not simply the celebration of "the little people," either in the amateur biologist's manner of John Steinbeck or in the more pompously patronizing manner of the radio dramatists; nor was it simply the potent naturalism of James T. Farrell or the tedious naturalism of the less gifted and more dogmatic. It was rather a continuation of what had been seen a hundred years earlier in Europe as well as in America as the fundamental task of the literary artist: laying bare the corpus of modern society with every tool at the artist's disposal.

Perhaps the noblest expression of the era is to be found in such perdurable poets as Horace Gregory, and in the James Agee-Walker Evans collaboration, "Let Us Now Praise Famous Men." Located, so to speak, in the summer of 1936, but not published until 1941, and not seriously read until after Agee's death in 1956, this study of Southern tenant farmers expresses in quintessential form everything most ardent and unafraid about the creative men of those years. It is a humane and unselfishly impersonal examination of American life, not just of the artist's wounded psyche (although that is to be found too), the like of which we have hardly experienced on the American literary scene in the decades that have elapsed since its appearance. This radicalism, this humanity, this searching not for absurdity but for meaningfulness, not for individual dissolution but for the profoundest kind of comradeship—this is what animated the best writing of the Depression years, and this is what the record of those years by the best of its chroniclers has to offer us.

BRIAN GLANVILLE*
The Sporting Novel

I T WAS a winter night and the train had just drawn into the glass cavern of St. Pancras Station. I had been North that Saturday, covering a football match. Southampton had been playing in the Midlands, where they'd lost. I saw their team when I stepped on the platform. They were good-tempered and reconciled, disappointment gone by now. As I walked with a couple of the players, a third came up behind me, laughing, tall and blond. At first I didn't recognize him, but I placed him as he spoke as Tony Knapp, a center-half who had once nearly played for England.

"That book of yours," he said, "there's a bit of language in it, isn't there? A bit of bad language?" And then, less jocular, "That's it, though, that's professional football! That's how it is! Here, sign it for me." And, to my surprise, he opened his case, produced the book —my football novel, "The Rise of Gerry Logan"— and got me to autograph it.

It was a sort of fiat, and there had been others—by Geordie footballers from the prolific North East, a Scottish international from the Glasgow Gorbals, players from Manchester and London. Yet I'm still convinced that the sporting novel, in essence, must either be proletarian or a fantasy; either a "This Sporting Life" or "The Natural." My own was neither. If it worked at all, it worked as a tour de force,

* (Mr. Glanville is introduced with another essay on page 62)

distilled out of a long, intense knowledge of the professional game, the dressing rooms, the planes, the endless railway trips—and out of a mélange of other people's voices.

Short stories about sport are another thing again. Here, the ventriloquism, the tour de force, need not be maintained at such length. Thus, we have Ring Lardner's germinal tales of baseball—"Hurry Kane," "Alibi Ike," "My Roomy," "Letters From a Busher" and Hemingway's "Fifty Grand" and "My Old Man." Neither of these writers attempted a full-length sporting novel. The explanation seems to me less that the world of sport, which always mattered so much to Hemingway, could not sustain one, less that their background knowledge was inadequate (Lardner traveled for years with the White Sox), but that they were essentially writers of middle-class origin.

The proletarian novel still has some validity, if only because realistic books about the working class can be written with passion and authenticity solely by those who have grown up within that class. For years, this hard fact deterred me from writing a football novel, though I had published many short stories dealing with the sport. Despite my journalistic contacts, I felt that I lacked the first-hand knowledge displayed by such a writer as David Storey, in his novel "This Sporting Life."

There was a clear authenticity about the Rugby League milieu and the mining background of Mr. Storey's hero. This, in turn, was guaranteed by his own experience. He was a miner's son who became an art student. He traveled North on week-ends to play for the Leeds Reserves, thus making enough money to go through school. It was, however, a freakish concatenation of circumstances. Many creative writers have made their way up from—or out of—the working class, but they haven't played games as professionals. Whether it will happen again seems extremely doubtful. Despite greater social mobility in Britain and Europe, despite the high wages paid to soccer stars, professional sport largely remains a working-class preserve.

Even when it isn't, as in the case of cricket, the chances that a good amateur player, however expensively educated, will also be a creative writer, are immeasurably remote. Cricket, a haven for the belletrist and the literary romantic, has yet to produce serious fiction about the professional game. Yet throughout its history, that game has been full of distinguished amateurs—Cantabs, Oxonians, Etonians —while the dressing-room of any county team is dense with character, idiom and repartee.

Here, we find one of the reasons why professional sport can appeal so strongly to the writer; it is a matter of language. Virginia Woolf, superficially the most isolated of writers, was in fact both catholic and sensitive enough to appreciate the importance of Ring Lardner. As long ago as 1925 she wrote "Mr. Lardner does not waste a moment thinking whether he is using American slang or Shakespeare's English. . . . Hence, incidentally, he writes the best prose that has come our way. Hence we feel at last freely admitted to the society of our fellows." She also believed that Lardner used baseball where an English writer would use society, as "a clue, a center, a meeting place for the diverse activities of people whom a vast continent isolates, whom no tradition controls."

Scott Fitzgerald saw it quite differently. "However deeply Ring might cut into it," he notes, "his cake had exactly the diameter of Frank Chance's diamond."

These points of view were complementary rather than contradictory. The world of sport is exciting precisely because it is closed and artificial. The drama it produces is at once regular, arbitrary—and, in human terms, limited. Certain themes have a validity larger than sport itself; the waning of the body, the rivalry between old and young, the imminence of injury and death. Go beyond those themes —which Lardner did not—and you are entering an essentially working-class world, whose assumptions and myths you have either grown up with or you haven't. In Lardner's case, there may be a deeper explanation. Alan Ross, himself a celebrated writer on cricket, has suggested that Lardner "at least made a pact with himself that the arena in which complex feelings between men and women were fought out was one about which he preferred not to comment. . . . He kept the private and therefore most essential part of his life out of his work."

Lardner divined and exploited the possibilities latent in the speech rhythms of the American working class, using them as narrators, setting them down in their own terms of reference. In the United States, the seam is particularly rich; Peter Ustinov has envied the American playwright for the various kinds of immigrant English which lie close to his hand. In Britain, the linguistic problem is depressingly immediate. Most writers come from, or settle down in, the middle class. It is nearly 30 years now since Orwell lamented the deadness of middle-class speech; a point had been reached, he felt, where it could be used in fiction only for parody. Middle-class and upper-class English speech is no less stultified today, so that the uninhibited rhythms of the football and boxing world are a grateful oasis. A writer who is also a sporting journalist is perpetually invigorated and delighted by what he hears.

But there is, as I have suggested, another perfectly legitimate way to deal with sport, and that is in terms of myth and fantasy; in a word, from the viewpoint of the fan. Bernard Malamud has brilliantly exploited these possibilities. In his baseball novel, "The Natural," he divines the unconscious need, both collective and individual, which has made professional sport possible and necessary, which has created its heroes and its legends. We are used to the documentary novel about sport, show business, Hollywood and the rest. We are inclined to forget that all these have another, surface reality in which perhaps their true importance lies.

Lardner hints at this in the bitter conclusion of "Champion," when an editor refused to publish the truth about the vicious protagonist, because he is still champion, and a public hero. From an immediate, moral point of view, the editor was wrong and was no doubt actuated by commercial motives. From a wider point of view, he may have been right, may even have apprehended that the public needs its fables and delusions.

In "The Natural," Malamud draws both on recorded event and the jargon of popular sports writing. At the beginning, his hero is shot by a nymphomaniac—as certain sports stars have indeed been shot. At the end, having thrown a game, he's accosted by a boy with the words which, apocryphally, were spoken to Shoeless Joe Jackson, after the Black Sox scandal: "Say it isn't so, Joe." There is no pretense at naturalism; even at realism. Told to knock the cover off the ball, Malamud's hero goes to bat and does precisely that. His bat, Wonderboy, is what you will—Excalibur, a phallic symbol. His ultimate downfall is caused, in the most direct and demonstrable sense, by greed; he is lured into overeating.

Thus, whether Malamud has the detail of the baseball world right is beside the point. The book is true in terms of myth, in terms of the compensatory function which all professional sport fulfills in our tame, urbanized experience.

The middle-class writer who cannot, or prefers not, to treat sport in so original and elliptical way, has a solution in the shape of the journalist narrator. The device has been used frequently enough— most notably, perhaps, in Budd Schulberg's boxing novel, "The Harder

They Fall." It is valid because here, in the persona of the sporting journalist, the middle-class writer can delegate himself, a legitimate, even an organic, function. The journalist is an essential figure in professional sport, which could scarcely survive without him, and he can lend, besides, a dimension of moral objectivity.

The nemesis of the journalist narrator, on the other hand, is precisely that he *is* peripheral. Because he is outside the conflict, that conflict can never take on true fire and significance. Too many things are said and done which he will never hear or see; the characters are forever passing out of his world, and slamming the door to their own. It was for this reason that I rejected the device while writing my football novel, though I had used it so often in short stories.

In the meanwhile, boxing has produced more good fiction than any other sport. This is because it comes nearer to the bone than any other. Soccer, baseball, basketball, cricket are essentially formal elaborations, artificialities. Aggression may be at the bottom of them, but it is sublimated. When the sublimation breaks down, when footballers start kicking one another instead of the ball and baseballers throw punches, we may see what the game is really about; we aren't seeing the game itself. Boxing, on the other hand, is undisguised aggression; its apotheosis is the knockout. Its very popularity can be traced to the damming up of aggression in society at large, and its ritualization in boxing. It is significant that many boxers, however sober their adult lives, spring from an adolescence of delinquency, reformatories. Aggression, in such cases, has not been purged. It has merely been put to socially permissible uses.

Yet the world of professional sport as a whole is closer to the bone. Hemingway, with his tormenting need to prove his masculinity, was naturally attracted to bullfighting and boxing. Courage and cowardice are *leitmotifs* in the conversation of any British soccer team. Love, of course is missing; dressing-room talk is all of "crumpet" and conquests. It is only when the dressing-room door closes behind him that the athlete passes into the fully adult world: and there, the writer is too often socially disqualified from following him.

JOHN BOWEN*
The Novel As...

ONCE upon a time, a novel might begin, "Once upon a time."
Novels began, "London. Michaelmas Term lately over, and the Lord
Chancellor sitting in Lincoln's Inn Hall," or "Miss Brooke had that
kind of beauty which seems to be thrown into relief by poor dress,"
or (after, to be sure, a little prefatory matter on the nature of authorship) "In that part of the western division of this kingdom which is
commonly called Somersetshire, there lately lived, and perhaps lives
still, a gentleman whose name was Allworthy."

Nowadays it's not the fashion to consider novels in terms of "Once
upon a time." What a novel directly says is often considered less
important than what a novel is. Well—perhaps not *less* important.
Let us say that we cannot truly know what a novel says until we know
what it is—as one might say, "Let me only know what you are, and
I shall know what to expect from you." So we play "The Novel As"
game—the novel as therapy, as a toy, as a tract. One might, I suppose,
make a small critical reputation with an article on "The Novel as
Yorkshire Terrier." Perhaps someone has already done it about the
novels of J. B. Priestley.

"The novel as therapy"! I say "therapy" and not "hobby" (though
many novels are written as mere hobbies, and rewarded about as well)
because "therapy" is more than a matter of passing the time; it is self-
expression. This notation that self-examination is not only healthy
but good in itself is a notion I've found to be held more by people
of student age than by teachers and practicing novelists. Students and
would-be novelists get into a fine rage if one speaks to them of form
and selection, because these only get in the way of self-expression. The
true self is raw like "On the Road," and there's a great deal of it.
And if one should ask a self-expresser, "Why should anyone else be
interested in your expressing yourself?" he will reply, "Because I am

* (For facts about John Bowen, turn back to page 69)

a unique human being made in the image of God." This is literary democracy, and there is no answer to it except to go away quickly.

I would not myself take the self-expressers seriously, except that there are those who have taken the work of Henry Miller and Jack Kerouac seriously enough to praise it, and that the young take this notion of art seriously because they would like to be writers or painters, but don't see why it should be difficult. And also because "the novel as therapy" is not so far from a much more intellectually respectable idea, which is "the novel as eyeglasses."

This last is a development of the more powerful conception of "the novel as tract." When all those eminent people went into the witnessbox at the Old Bailey and spoke up for "Lady Chatterley's Lover," they were not concerned with it as a story but with "the quality of its moral ideas." In this they were true followers of Matthew Arnold, who looked to literature to supply what he could not find in religion. The notion that the value of a novel is to be assessed in terms of "the quality of its moral ideas" is still widely held in Britain, although there is reaction against it, and manifestly it was held by Lawrence himself, so that it was a reasonable defense.

One reason for the reaction is that too rigorous a consideration of moral ideas leads one into judgments that seem to be at odds with common sense. Shakespeare will do because his moral ideas are ambiguous enough to allow disagreement amongst judges, but how does one judge Dickens?—while the moral ideas of Tolstoy and Dostoevsky are often downright silly. Hence the more convenient concept of "the novel as eyeglasses."

In it, one is concerned not with moral ideas but with the "unique vision." The novelist is not a teacher, but a servant. The readers are the masters. They pick through the goods at the Literary Optician's, take up Virginia Woolf, try her on, see the world for a while *through* her, so add her vision to their total experience of life, along with the visions of S. Richardson, G. Greene, W. M. Thackeray, and all the rest. The readers get, with each new pair of glasses a fuller, deeper vision of life, while the novelists write on, each bound forever in the blinkers of his "unique vision."

It is an attractive concept, but perhaps a little close to our earlier idea that the uniqueness itself is in some way good. Much further from both "the novel as tract" and "the novel as therapy" is "the novel as toy." This is the extreme reaction against Arnold. Now the novel is not a moral object at all, but an esthetic object. We don't admire pictures or pieces of music for their moral qualities, so why judge a novel by such qualities? What we expect from a work of art is a subtlety of symmetry, inventive decoration, economy and judgment in the use of tools and the medium. Let us admire a novel for the color of its prose, its wit, its truth to form. It is a delicate and ingenious toy, fashioned to delight and exercise the esthetic senses. Now Firbank and Evelyn Waugh come to join a rather denuded Dickens and Henry James, while Melville and Dreiser drop out of the game.

But when we reach "the novel as a game," then Melville returns. This is a subdivision of the "toy" concept. The Emperor's Nightingale has become a game like "Diplomacy," in which the novelist makes his own rules, but binds himself to follow them, and the reader must work out the rules from the evidence of the novel.

Another subdivision is the "novel as love-object," suggested by Brigid Brophy, writing about Mlle. Francoise Sagan in The London Magazine. "One's wish for the work of art," she wrote, "is not that it should be understood, but that it should be loved"—not loved by others merely, or even preferably, but by oneself; one writes the novel to please one's own self-love. "Just as it is more lasting, so it is more beautiful than one's original self. It is a receptacle for one's own narcissism, which is often so ill-served by one's proper Ego."

"The novel *as* . . ." It is endless and enjoyable, but does it help one either to write novels or to read them? I think that remembering that novels begin "Once upon a time" does help to write them. It reminds the novelist that he is telling a story to other people and that he must use every device of toy and game if he wants to keep them listening. The story itself, when he has done telling it, may turn out to be, not quite a tract or a pair of glasses, but an object that stands for, that represents, his "unique vision"—an object that, having a life of its own (which is obviously not "real life") nevertheless allows his readers to continue their engagement with "real life" with an increased understanding of what it is and what it could be about.

W. H. AUDEN
A Novel by Goethe

For more than a generation Wystan Auden has been a distinguished figure in the world of letters: poet, essayist, translator, librettist, teacher. His verse has brought him awards of many kinds. George VI presented him with the King's Gold Medal for Poetry. He has won a Pulitzer Prize, a National Book Award, the Bollingen Prize for poetry, the Guinness Award, and the National Medal for Literature.

ONE WOULD like to think that the fate of a book is determined solely by its merit but, now and again, one is forcibly reminded that this is not so. Mere chance is just as important. A few years ago, the Henry Regnery Company of Chicago published a new and excellent translation—the only readable one I have come across—by Elizabeth Mayer and Louise Bogan of Goethe's novel, "Elective Affinities." If merit were the decisive factor, this publication would have been an important literary event. As it was, not one of the major newspapers or journals, so far as I know, gave it a review. It is not as if Goethe had written in French, in which case a reviewer might have argued that most readers would prefer to read the novel in the original; everyone knows that, in America and England, very few people are fluent in German. I can only conclude that the average reviewer had prejudged Goethe as a boring writer without having read him.

He is very mistaken. "Elective Affinities" is not only a minor masterpiece, but also one of the most extraordinary novels ever written. Most novelists start from the particular, in character and event, and only when their novels are finished, does their general human significance emerge. Goethe seems to have done the opposite, to have started with certain ideas about the nature of human beings which he felt important, and then to have invented characters and events to illustrate them. It is generally held, and with good reason, that such a procedure is fatal; the characters will be mere puppets, their actions artificial and incredible. Yet, somehow or other, Goethe succeeds; his characters and their story are as interesting and alive as his ideas. "Elective Affinities" could only have been written by someone who was, first, a great poet with a great poet's talent for embodying general ideas in concrete forms, and, second, a mature man with a very wide range of human experience to draw on—Goethe was 60 when he wrote it.

His title is taken from a phrase current in his day among chemists, and the way in which he selects his characters, brings them together, separates them, reminds one of a controlled scientific experiment. Like a scientist, and like a poet, Goethe is extremely neat and economical. His cast of characters is kept to the minimum necessary for the action; even the most minor ones contribute directly to it. The major characters who exemplify the personal aspect of human nature are, Edouard, a rich landowner in early middle age; the Captain, his friend since schooldays, who has to earn his living; Charlotte, Edouard's wife; and Ottilie, the orphaned daughter of Charlotte's best friend, and now her ward.

In their youth Edouard and Charlotte had fallen in love with each other, but Edouard's father persuaded him to marry a rich woman older than himself, whereupon Charlotte married a man whom she admired but did not love, by whom she has a daughter, Lucille. After the death of their respective spouses, Edouard renewed his suit. At first, Charlotte, sensing that his passion was more imaginary than real, was reluctant and even tried to interest him in Ottilie, but, finally, gave in. When the story opens, they have been married less than a year. Again, against her better judgment, Charlotte allows the Captain and Ottilie to come live with them. Presently, Edouard begins to fall in love with Ottilie, and simultaneously Charlotte and the Captain are strongly attracted to each other. In their various responses to this situation they reveal their characters.

The Captain, a practical, not very imaginative, but honorable man, and Charlotte, a sensible woman who knows how essential continuity and order are to a satisfactory human life, resolve to renounce each other rather than break up the marriage. Edouard, on the other hand, behaves like a spoiled and utterly selfish child who, if his wish of the moment is not immediately granted goes into a tantrum; so long as he gets what he wants, he doesn't care what mischief it may do to others, including Ottilie. In Edouard, Goethe has drawn one of the most devastating portraits in fiction of a man whose life from beginning to end is "unauthentic." Ottilie, beautiful, but hysterical and emotionally inclined to passive masochistic devotion, is the born victim. In the end she starves herself to death.

There are many memorable scenes. In a chapter which must have shocked his contemporaries, Goethe describes an act of "psychological" adultery; Edouard goes to bed with Charlotte, but both husband and wife imagine themselves in the arms of another. The outcome of this night is that Charlotte becomes pregnant and therefore doubly determined to save the marriage. Later, in a scene which reminds one of E. M. Forster, Ottilie upsets a boat, and the child is drowned. The effect of this on Charlotte is to make her willing for the first time to agree to Edouard's demand for a divorce, but now Ottilie, stricken with remorse, swears she will drown herself if a divorce takes place.

Goethe never lets us forget, as some novelists do, that love is by no means the sole interest of human beings. Since we are not born with instinctive modes of behavior, the teacher-pupil relationship, for example, is of essential importance to our lives. Also, Man is a maker who constructs a human world of artifacts which outlast the death of the individual, and Man is a player of games. So Goethe's characters spend much time landscaping, building, gardening, discussing the problems of education, playing chamber music and charades, and in such activities they often unwittingly reveal their natures even more clearly than in their scenes of passion.

Always too, as Thomas Hardy does, Goethe keeps us aware of the background of Nature and the seasoned cycle behind the personal, the social and the worldly, of the hills which will outlast a human race, the trees which will outlast a human generation and the flowers which live for but a few months. Hence the significance to us of our birthdays, the celebration of which play an important role in the novel. Once every year, at the same season, we celebrate both our personal uniqueness—the fact that each life is a story in which each moment is a new beginning—and our mortality—the fact that, as bodies, we are born, grow old and die. That Edouard should dislike being reminded of his own birthday reveals two things about him: he is a spoiled child who wishes to be the center of attention on every day of the year, and he is afraid of age and death.

"Elective Affinities" is full of subtle psychological insights of this kind, some of them startling when one remembers the date at which the novel was written. In his perception that apparent accidents, as when the Captain forgets to wind his watch, are significant, Goethe foreshadows Freud, and in his description of the periodic headaches from which both Ottilie and Edouard suffer, he shows a remarkable understanding of what are now called psychosomatic symptoms.

We live in a very different society from Goethe's, but from a careful study of "Elective Affinities," a young novelist could, I believe, learn a great deal. As for the general reading public, they will be depriving themselves of a very interesting and pleasant experience if they fail to read it.

VII
Portraits,
Appraisals and
Reappraisals

CAROLYN HEILBRUN
A Modern Among
Contemporaries

An Edwardian like E. M. Forster (who through longevity also became a 20th-century Georgian and Elizabethan) belongs in the scholarly province where Carolyn Heilbrun is most at home. She is Associate Professor of English at Barnard.

THE Edwardian age, looking before and after, is probably the shortest "age" in history. Even after scholars, ignoring King Edward's death in 1910, have extended it down to the guns of August, it lasts 13 years and 7 months at the most. With World War I, all changed, much ended. What we are now beginning to believe is that almost everything that happened in the first half of the 20th century to literature, art and music began (if anything can ever be said with historical accuracy to "begin") in that brief Edwardian age. All the great moderns, whose major works were published near the beginning of World War I, or shortly after, reached maturity in those years. In 1914, for example, Joyce and Virginia Woolf were 32; Lawrence was 29; Eliot was 26. The great art of the modern period was to be the work of those whose ideas had been formed in the years before the war.

G. M. Young called those 13 years "that flash Edwardian Epilogue" to the Victorian age, and so, for the most part, they have continued to appear to social and literary historians. It has often been observed that society glittered, during the "epilogue," with a special brilliance —Edward enjoyed good food and beautiful women and all things French, so for a brief time England too relished its own stability served up with French sauces. Only recently, in memoirs and history, have we accounts of the period which seem to suggest that in ideas, as in food, the seasoning was particularly vibrant.

This was—one may as well say it—the last time of simple happiness. Progress seemed possible, scientific salvation sure. Only James and Conrad and Forster possessed the "imagination of disaster," and this only in their work. James turned to Edith Wharton and said: "Summer afternoon, summer afternoon; to me those have always been the two most beautiful words in the English Language." The Edwardian age was the summer afternoon for England. It was the summer afternoon in which, amid the social manifestoes of Wells, Bennett and Galsworthy, E. M. Forster bowed in, ever so graciously, ever so kindly, ever so unobtrusively, the great modern British novel.

"Where Angels Fear to Tread," Forster's first novel, published in 1905, is not one of those mountains of a book against which scholars, critics and the ambitious young hurl themselves with all their prowess and ingenuity, their literary maps and climbing equipment. Precisely because it is not a "big" work, it has not been over-discussed and analyzed. One tends to overpraise a long book (as Forster says) because one has got through it. Getting through "Where Angels Fear to Tread" is an effortless task; one feels almost frivolous at its completion.

Forster titled his first book prophetically, for his fools rushed, undeterred by the rattle of teacups, right into the modern novel. Lionel Trilling finds Forster irritating in his "refusal to be great," and Forster's first novel represents him in this. Yet its slight story of an inhibited and undeveloped English man and woman who go to Italy, meet death and passion, and return, their lives but not their hearts unchanged, speaks of sexuality, moral impulses, the tragic vision—the whole world of modern fiction. Philip, the Englishman, at the close of the novel looks at Caroline Abbott and knows her "to be transfigured, and to have indeed no part with refinement or unrefinement any longer. Out of this wreck there was revealed to him something indestructible." Revealed, throughout the years, also to us.

Forster not only refuses to be great; he does not, even more annoyingly, seem amenable to the pummelings of academic theorists. Those who chase him across the fields of scholarship are likely to find that he has climbed a tree, or turned into one (as in his stories); the reader hears only the thundering of academic footfalls. Trilling alone has written brilliantly of him, recognizing him as one of those few authors who continue to give a reader the sensation of having learned something. Sensations of learning and feeling were Forster's specialty, as they were Lawrence's.

It may seem strange, as we pick our way today across the troughs of pornography, to recognize in Forster one of the first who faced and honored the claims of sexuality, and who, moreover, saw sexuality, as Lawrence did, to be passion touched by the fire of intellect. Gino, in "Where Angels Fear to Tread," for all that he is beautiful, even sacred, knows only lust. But there is Caroline Abbott's feeling for the lusty Italian: "I'm in love with Gino," she tells Philip at the end of the book, "don't pass it off—I mean it crudely—you know what I mean. So laugh at me." "Laugh at love?" Philip asks, and is transformed.

"Where Angels Fear to Tread" nestles, in any literary history, almost unnoticed among the other "Edwardian" works, each of which sounds a brassier note: the novels of Wells and Bennett, the plays of Galsworthy and Shaw, Hardy's "Dynasts," Butler's "The Way of All Flesh," "Peter Pan," that exercise in aborted sexuality which Rupert Brooke could not see often enough. Conan Doyle in 1905, the year of "Where Angels Fear to Tread," resurrected Sherlock Holmes, in whom inspiration coincided, Edwardian-fashion, with rationality. Yet it was none of these writers, extending 19th-century modes of thought and feeling into the confident prewar years, who foretold the age to come. Arnold Bennett's "Old Wives' Tale," the most "Edwardian" of books, is not, if one thinks of Forster's rushing fools, going anywhere at all. Conrad's "Heart of Darkness," James's "The Wings of the Dove," Forster's four early novels—*there* is the modern world.

Wells, Bennett, Galsworthy, Shaw, were famous for the fervor with which they set out to reform society, and especially those relationships the Victorians, and many before them, had held sacred: motherhood, fatherhood, marriage, God and His worshippers. It has become one of the clichés of modern literature that all the old standards had gone pop in everyone's face, like so many inflated paper bags. What few enough noticed, though Forster had seen it, was that the loss of the old commandments did not leave chaos, only an order rather more complete.

Modern literature, like "Where Angels Fear to Tread," was to be, for the most part, a literature of encounters; encounters which did not receive the sacraments, but which were sacramental for all that. The meeting of Marlow and Kurtz in "Heart of Darkness"; the meeting of Philip and Caroline with Gino in "Where Angels Fear to Tread"; the meeting of Milly with Densher and Kate Croy in "The Wings of the Dove." And in the years of greatness ahead the meeting of Bloom and Stephen in "Ulysses," of Lily and Mrs. Ramsay in "To the Lighthouse," of all Lawrence's lovers who confront one another beyond the range of a tidy marriage. The Edwardian age, in so far as it was modern, realized what Keats had guessed: that there was no certainty but the truth of imagination, that, if old claims were no longer sacred, the heart's affections now were holy.

Stephen Spender has distinguished between modern and contemporary literature, seeing Wells, Bennett, Galsworthy, Shaw as "contemporary," like Amis, Wain, Braine, Osborne in England today. "Contemporaries" write of current problems, of how the world may be changed, practically changed into something fairer, more bearable. The "Moderns," Spender tells us, are those whose artistic imaginations work, as the unconscious works, in metaphor. The "moderns" reform nothing; iniquities do not feel the blast of their disdain. But the moral impulses of the reader, his awareness of what it is "to conceive life as a tragedy," in Yeats's words, these the "modern" writers inspire, breathe life into. Modern; but no more modern than Conrad in 1902, James in 1904, Forster in 1905.

In an article written after Forster had celebrated his 80th birthday in 1959, one of his young friends at Cambridge University was quoted as saying: "Most elderly people are apt to talk a lot about there being no men or books or plays like the ones when they were young, and they may be right, but it's infuriating all the same. [Forster] doesn't make that sort of comparison. Then, what is so fearfully gratifying is that he always seems to want—really to want—to know what you feel about things." Which seems to suggest that Forster, no more than his novel, has aged. Or rather, for he would certainly loathe an untruth—all human beings age—Forster not only experienced the modern vision a good deal earlier than most; he has retained it longer.

ANDREW TURNBULL
Perkins's Three Generals

There were literary giants on the earth during the period in American letters that Andrew Turnbull has made his own. He has written about three of them in the accompanying essay. He is the author of a life of Scott Fitzgerald, who was once a neighbor, and has edited Fitzgerald's letters. His most recent book is a biography of Thomas Wolfe.

IT SEEMS worthwhile to consider F. Scott Fitzgerald, Ernest Hemingway and Thomas Wolfe conjointly as public figures, because their fame during their lifetimes has been crowned by that much rarer thing, literary survival, and because they emerge from the lost world of the twenties and thirties as a sort of triad or covey, emulous and even rivalrous, yet bound together through all their squabbles by an editor named Max Perkins—"our common parent," as Fitzgerald called Perkins in a letter to Wolfe. These writers, who in their separate ways combined artistic authority with the glamour of great actors or politicians, considered themselves an élite. If you go through Fitzgerald's letters, you will find that next to Hemingway, who was an obsession with him, the writer he discusses most is Wolfe—much of what he says is critical, to be sure, but if he hadn't felt Wolfe was important, he wouldn't have given so much thought to the futile business of trying to reform him.

Hemingway once remarked that Perkins had had three guys—Scott, Tom Wolfe and himself—and I am told by a member of Perkins's family that after Wolfe and Fitzgerald died, Hemingway in one of his more sadistic moments said to Perkins, "You realize you're through, don't you? All your generals are dead." Wolfe, who didn't bother much with his contemporaries, nevertheless had great respect for these other two. He was strong for "Tender Is the Night" when the critics were running it down, and in Hemingway he admired qualities he himself lacked—Hemingway's "superb concision, his ability to say one thing and suggest ten more."

Before turning to the causes and effects of the public attention bestowed on these three novelists who wanted to be king, let me sketch in their overlapping reigns. By all odds the easiest and most instantaneous success was Fitzgerald with "This Side of Paradise," published in 1920, when he was 23. Hemingway was 27 before he achieved a comparable notoriety and Wolfe an old man of 34. In the public mind Hemingway began to edge past Fitzgerald with "The Sun Also Rises" in the fall of 1926, though the actual take-over had occurred a year and a half earlier at that confrontation in the Dingo Bar so cleanly etched in "A Moveable Feast." Here comes Fitzgerald, the jaunty, delicately handsome Ivy Leaguer, who has just published "The Great Gatsby" while pulling down huge sums from the magazines, in quest of the relatively unknown but not unsung Hemingway, whose only work between covers is the little Paris edition of "In Our Time."

From the start Hemingway has this faculty of making you go to him, of meeting you like a skilled tactician on *his* terrain. Right away his mild curiosity about Fitzgerald becomes superiority, because of Fitzgerald's mawkishness, his sloppy drinking, his rudeness to waiters, his embarrassing praise of Hemingway's work, and other violations of The Code. Ashamed of his potboilers, Fitzgerald bows to the integrity of a writer whose approach is quite different. Where Fitzgerald morbidly stands aside to probe and analyze and speculate, Hemingway is a healthy animal enjoying experiences which enter his subconscious and become a part of him, and are later distilled in his fiction. His geniality, however, is mixed with a guardedness, a secretiveness, and understandably so, because his new, highly sophisticated art is still a fragile fetus that needs defending. Then, too, Hemingway is a competitor. Back of his warmth and niceness and generosity up to a point, one senses a feeling vis-à-vis Fitzgerald of "I can take this guy."

And take him he did in the fall of 1929 with "A Farewell to Arms," which got superlative reviews and far outsold any volume of Fitzgerald's. That season Wolfe's first novel, "Look Homeward, Angel," appeared, selling a modest 12,000 copies, but establishing Wolfe with the intelligentsia, for he began not like Fitzgerald, with a sweeping popular success, but like Hemingway, as a writer's writer and the object of a cult. During the thirties he overtook and usurped Hemingway, becoming really famous with "Of Time and the River" in 1935. Though basically nonpolitical and impervious to ideology, Wolfe was a workingman's son whose roughhewn, down-to-earth appeal suited the decade of social consciousness, during which Hemingway's reputation declined. Hemingway's nonfiction had a vein of ranting self-indulgence, and "To Have and Have Not" in 1937 wasn't much of a novel.

By then, Fitzgerald, who had led the pack in the twenties, was dog-paddling way back in the rear somewhere, and Wolfe's behavior toward him showed genuine concern. After Fitzgerald's essays in Esquire about his "crack-up" and hideous exposé of his condition in The New York Evening Post, Wolfe took the line that if Fitzgerald was bent on professional suicide, it was dastardly of others to help. Hemingway's contribution was the "poor Scott Fitzgerald" business in his story "The Snows of Kilimanjaro"—a pointed and gratuitous assertion that Fitzgerald was washed up, partly because of his infatuation with the rich.

In fairness to Hemingway it might be added that his intimate feelings about Fitzgerald seem to have been more kindly and respectful than what has gotten into print then or since, but he didn't do much about it, while Wolfe went to see Fitzgerald several times and tried to buck him through. Wolfe died in 1938, and Fitzgerald faded out in Hollywood, the Spanish War meanwhile having recast Hemingway in his Byronic role and restored him to legend. The overwhelming critical and commercial success of "For Whom the Bell Tolls" made him once again *the* artist-novelist of his generation—that is, until Faulkner's work began to filter down in the forties. By then Hemingway also had to put up with Fitzgerald's eloquent ghost.

The literary fame and immortality which Fitzgerald, Hemingway and Wolfe wanted above all else had in each case a way of getting mixed up with other kinds of renown. Fitzgerald came at the postwar effervescence he christened "The Jazz Age" as an artist seeking material, and got drawn in as a participant, for he had always been a show-off, a merchant of astonishment, and here was a chance to shine on a national scale. Pretty soon he was the myth of the advertisements—youth, beauty, money, early success—and he believed in these things so hard that he endowed them with a certain grandeur. But his hour was brief in that tinsel world. He didn't have much fun after Gatsby, after 1925, when his drinking and his wife's aberrations began to get out of hand.

Incidentally, Hemingways's theory in "A Moveable Feast" that Zelda was Fitzgerald's undoing seems to me a half-truth, because it overlooks how much she helped him. An original of rare distinction, as her letters and her flawed novel proclaim, she had given him a great deal of material by unexpected word and deed, and was really an arm of his talent, her sane strangeness and her orphic flights echoing the depths in him. Hemingway also failed to understand Fitzgerald's capacity for love and commitment, his backing of one frail individual against eternity, which seemed foolish to Hemingway, who was more hardheaded in his personal relations.

In any event, Fitzgerald's later life was a long penance for that first, wildly intoxicating draft of public acclaim which upended his career and made him a malcontent, though whether his work suffered in the absolute sense, who is to know? He seemed destined for the extremes, and perhaps the surfeit of success followed by the surfeit of failure wrung out of him the most that he had to say.

To me the interesting thing about Hemingway's rise was his power of dominating and impressing before he had much work to stand on. He reminds one of Lenin the way he galvanized those around him with his belief in himself and in the revolution—the revolution of the word, that is. He was always a celebrity, even in obscurity, his life beginning and ending in legend. In the Gerald Murphy set on the Riviera, Fitzgerald, Dos Passos and MacLeish were older and more established, yet Hemingway was the one they all looked up to, fusing as he did the artist with the American ideal of the red-blooded, 100 per cent male. Not only his passion for war and sports but his over-all resourcefulness and know-how took the curse off being a poet.

Outside their writing, Fitzgerald and Wolfe were impractical, somewhat defenseless men whom women constantly sought to mother, but no one was going to mother "Papa," a selfnomer Hemingway began using as far back as 1932. Another source of his wide appeal was a strain of violence that spoke to something in the American temper, and a style which on the simplest level had a good deal in common with the sock and biff of our journalism. Add in the expatriate mystique, his speaking for the Lost Generation of which Fitzgerald was not a part. As Hemingway wants us to know in "A Moveable Feast," Fitzgerald went abroad like a summer visitor or tourist, while Wolfe's outlook during his European jaunts of the twenties was more or less that of a graduate student on his *wanderjahr*.

Hemingway's initial strength lay in his dedication. He scorned cheap publicity. He wouldn't debase his stuff to make it sell and got furious at exaggerations of his exploits in puffs and press releases. How then in later years did the artist get swallowed up in the legend? Was it because his fictional protagonists—Nick Adams, Jake Barnes, Frederick Henry and Robert Jordan—were vehicles for his own adventures? Or was it the result of the megalomania which Fitzgerald ascribed to Hemingway in the thirties? Or did the legend take over by default, because the talent was waning? That literary lepidopterist, Sainte-Beuve, says that often 15 years fills out a career, or the span between "In Our Time" and "For Whom the Bell Tolls." Whatever the explanation, one cannot avoid the feeling that somewhere along the line Hemingway ate his publicity and became a travesty of his former self. Never completely though, and that his pathos and his grandeur. Part of him knew what was happening. As he said in his Nobel Prize speech, the writer grows in public stature as he sheds his loneliness and often his work deteriorates.

Perhaps I might bring in here without irrelevance my one glimpse of Hemingway. When I was doing research on Fitzgerald, I heard indirectly that Hemingway didn't want to discuss him, but in the fall of 1959 he was on the same ship coming back from Europe, so I wrote him a note. When he didn't answer, I went up to first class a few times to see what he looked like. Now and then he toured the deck by himself in a plaid shirt and a sleeveless leather jacket, speaking to no one and looking furtively away when another glance met his. A Belgian woman who had been watching him said to me—most aptly I thought —that he had the air of a false patriarch. There was something staged and put-on about him, and yet a great dignity flowed from his tall, lurching frame and his sad mask of a face.

The last day out he wrote that he'd be glad to see me, but that he didn't have anything to say about Scott, as he himself was writing about him. When we met, I was struck by the meagerness of his bare forearms and the near delicacy of his features above a froth of beard, and the red-veined whites of his eyes which took you in with a kind of grazing diffidence. I remember his saying, with reference to some boyhood memories of Fitzgerald I had published, that "Scott wasn't always nice like he was with you kids"—that he could be unjust in the heat of the moment, and then go home and sort it all out in his notebooks and letters. I am glad I had this contact with Hemingway, who seemed shy and wistful, with something inexpressible in his glance. At

this point he wasn't the blusterer one might have conjured up from
his dealings with Fitzgerald, and later I thought of some lines in "Richard II":

> For you have but mistook me all this while:
> I live with bread like you, feel want,
> Taste grief, need friends: subjected thus,
> How can you say to me, I am a king?

Because it came to him more slowly perhaps, but also, I think, because of a fundamental simplicity and breadth of vision, Wolfe of
these three writers was the least disrupted by fame. Far from turning
his head, the praises that were heaped on him—and Perkins said he
had never known anything to equal Wolfe's fan mail, that he opened
people's eyes "to the richness of the world and they worshiped him for
it, in gratitude"—such accolades as these only made him try all the
harder. For his life was ruled, as an artist's should be, not by satisfaction with past achievements but by a sense of how much remained to
be done. He lacked discipline, it is true, but in the sense of living in
and for his work and nothing else, he was more disciplined than Hemingway or Fitzgerald.

His legend and his cross, the thing that focused attention wherever
he went, was his enormity in all the senses of the word; not just his 6½
feet and 250 pounds when the race was a little smaller than it is now,
but his capacity for food and drink and talk and joy and sorrow and embarrassment. Chairs were always cracking under his bulk, and when
he made one of his normal gestures in a crowded living room you expected half a dozen people to fall down. Wolfe was an ego and he
liked to be the center, but he resented the sideshow aspect of his popularity, for he wasn't a circus freak—that misses it. The final impression
he created was one of strangeness, of a visitor from Mars, of a gigantic,
suffering misfit paradoxically crossed with Everyman. Fitzgerald and
Hemingway set a style, people wanted to talk and act and be like them,
but no one wanted to be like Wolfe, though in a sense he was more of
a celebrity than the others, with a greater potential hold on the country.

Wolfe had, said Fitzgerald, "that flair for the extravagant and
fantastic which has been an American characteristic from Irving and
Poe to Dashiell Hammett," and of course Wolfe believed in a neo-
Whitmanesque America in capitals, which to Hemingway and Fitzgerald was rubbish. Not to Perkins, however. "[Wolfe] was wrestling,"

wrote Perkins after his death, "as no artist in Europe would have to with the material of literature—a great country not yet revealed to its people. . . . It was this struggle alone that in a large sense governed all that he did."

HERBERT MITGANG
Carl Sandburg

Herbert Mitgang was a friend of Carl Sandburg and edited the recently published "The Letters of Carl Sandburg." A man of many skills, he is a novelist ("The Return"), a biographer ("The Man Who Rode the Tiger," a life of Judge Samuel Seabury), a historian ("Lincoln As They Saw Him"). He is a member of the editorial board of The New York Times.

WHEN Carl Sandburg collected seven books of poems into one in 1950, he wrote: "It could be in the grace of God, I shall live to be 89, as did Hokusai, and speaking my farewell to earthly scenes, I might paraphrase: 'If God had let me live five years longer I should have been a writer.'"

He did live into his 89th year. In the last decade of his life, I had the good fortune of observing him in small towns on the Illinois prairie, in his birthplace at Galesburg, in Lincoln's New Salem, at Civil War battlefield sites, in his North Carolina home. That is where I remember him most at ease. . . .

At twilight, the poet-biographer-historian-journalist-novelist-autobiographer-troubador (which one is he? does it matter?) looks dimly out of the window of Connemara Farm, where he lives on 120 acres in a comfortable Civil War-era clapboard house that once belonged to the Confederacy's Secretary of the Treasury. He wears an old newspaperman's green eyeshade. Outside cardinals and Carolina wrens dip and swirl around a dozen wooden landingstrips; in the distance the sun streaks purple lines across Pisgah National Forest at the eastern gateway of the Blue Ridge Mountains. It is a place to write a poem.

He has lived here with his wife and daughters for 20 years, with frequent forays around the country and world—to Lincoln's New Salem, for a televised walk through the prairie years; to Moscow with his brother-in-law, photographer Edward Steichen, to show the Russians "The Family of Man" exhibit; to Hollywood, that other foreign land, to lend expensive counsel to a movie about Jesus Christ, a strange turnabout until it is recalled that he was a film critic for the Chicago Daily News in the early 1920's; to Washington, a private citizen addressing a joint session of Congress on the meaning of Lincoln for today—and making his point best at the end by shaking only one hand, that of Chief Justice Earl Warren, whose civil rights decisions (and enemies) won Sandburg's greatest respect.

Connemara Farm is a real working farm. His wife, Paula, is undoubtedly the only Phi Beta Kappa graduate of the University of Chicago who breeds goats that produce excellent milk, assuming you like goat's milk. But the main product raised here is words. The quiet comfort of Connemara Farm resulted from Lincoln words—a million and a half in the biography and related works touching on the Lincoln testament.

The two-volume "The Prairie Years," the four-volume "The War Years," and the combined one-volume version of both continue to sell in the tens of thousands in hardcover, paperback, Book-of-the-Month club dividends and premiums and foreign-language editions. It is still hard to imagine that he was nearly 50 when he published "The Prairie Years" and 61 when "The War Years" appeared. Fortunately, both were written before a modern educator might have labeled Sandburg a late bloomer or, worse, a latent under-achiever.

The master of Connemara Farm has slowed down considerably. No new books will come from here; the best that can be expected is an occasional cutting remark that helps to put America in perspective or some stiff-necked person in his place, or both. His autobiography, "Always the Young Strangers," only took him to 1898, when he enlisted as a private in the Sixth Illinois and served in Cuba and Puerto Rico during the Spanish-American War. The second volume, which he titled "Ever the Winds of Chance," started to reach a fascinating episode in his life, when he became a district organizer for the Socialists in Milwaukee. "I planted a few soapboxes in the State of Wisconsin," he says, recalling the time in the early 1900's when he and his young bride mounted the platform for the profane causes which are now sacred in the United States. But "Winds" is unfinished; the book (to use a Lincoln phrase) winked out.

His last book, "Honey and Salt," appeared on his 85th birthday. It was a collection of poems filled with more kindling than fire; a quiet "love"—of words, of nature, of mankind—was often repeated. "People are going to say," he told me then, "that Sandburg's been practicing writing poetry for 85 years—and this ought to be a heller!" The high point of its publication was a party at which some of his friends paid him tribute.

Justice William O. Douglas of the Supreme Court fondly remembered how the poet has translated "The past is prologue" as "You ain't seen nuthin' yet." John Steinbeck, fresh from the Nobel Prize ceremonies, muttered with affection, "This is not a speech. It's more in the nature of a toast. Carl, all of us could have learned from you and, thank God, some of us have. Thank you for living." The gracious comment brought to mind Ernest Hemingway's own statement upon receiving word about his Nobel—that Carl Sandburg was more worthy of it than he.

There are other unwritten books in him which age will not let out. A subject that intrigues him is Lincoln's self-education. Several years ago, when we were walking around the prairie country in Illinois, he examined a textbook on surveying that Lincoln had mastered before studying the law. Sandburg marveled at the complex mathematical equations that Lincoln comprehended. "I hope some day to do a small book about the education of Abraham Lincoln," he said. Sandburg's reason was rooted in his oft-repeated remark that his Lincoln biography was probably the only book written by a man whose father couldn't sign his name about a President whose mother couldn't sign hers. "I lived with Lincoln across fifteen years of writing but I was never bored or lonely," he said. "Can you think of a better companion?"

Now and then a flash of the old Sandburg that delights or sets teeth on edge breaks through the book-walled rooms at Connemara Farm. He picks up the newspapers and reads a headline: SECRETARY MC-NAMARA CALLS FOR MORE NEW BOMBERS. Sandburg comments: "I thought he had enough." He flips a page and spots a Sears advertisement YOUR HOME ENTERTAINMENT CENTER. Reading both aloud, his resonant intonations and pregnant sneers leave no doubt that he thinks some things in the news are bunk. But all Ralph McGill columns and Herblock cartoons are appreciated.

The mail brings a dozen requests for his signature, often from students attending one of the 13 schools in the country named after him. "I like to call them up," he once said impishly, "just so I can hear the operator answer 'Carl Sandburg High School . . . .' " Much of the fan and request mail goes unanswered. "If I wrote letters," he explained, pointing to a shelf of 30 titles, all reading Carl Sandburg on their spines, "would I have ever written those books?"

Yet there is a special responsibility felt here toward school-children. Paula Sandburg carries the main burden. "When teachers write in to ask for an explanation of a poem," she says, "I am inclined to think of Robert Browning's reply. He would write, 'When I wrote that poem, God knew what it meant and I knew what it meant. Now only God knows.' "

Among all the books, she thinks that "The People, Yes" comes closest to expressing the thoughts felt most deeply by the Sandburgs, herself included. In a real sense, the unfinished autobiography of Carl Sandburg can be found in that book's catch-as-catch-can "stories and psalms . . . sayings and yarns . . . streetcrowds and sidewalk clamor . . . with interludes of midnight cool blue." It is a kind of proletarian paean, written in the unifying Depression years when the blue eagle of the N. R. A. fluttered bravely, yet with a timeless celebration of the American dream.

Where does Sandburg stand in American letters? Among establishment literary critics and book reviewers, about where they place our two living Nobel Prize winners—Pearl Buck and John Steinbeck—which is not very high. His cultured enemies might well agree wth the words of a folk song he used to sing during one of his lecture-recitals: "I have been a nice boy and done what was expected,/ I shall be an old bum loved but unrespected." A Tree is Best Measured When It's Down (as Sandburg called his chapter that followed Lincoln's death), but he himself has been chopped at ever since his first Chicago poems came out a half-century ago.

"Ezra Pound thought Carl had a great natural talent," Paula Sandburg recalled, "but that he ought to get some education, preferably at a school like Princeton. Ezra probably did not know that Carl had graduated from Lombard College in Galesburg, where he lived. I think he wanted to turn him into an Imagist. He advised Carl to read Walter Savage Landor and learn to follow Latin and Greek lyrics. Carl had read Landor long before Ezra advised him to, and he was aware of poetic traditions in many countries, including Japan. 'Fog' is in the Haiku tradition. Anyway, Carl decided to stick to his own style."

Sandburg's vers libre served to free poetry from its self-imposed strictures among his contemporaries. If nothing else, he helped to open new areas of thought and the most commonplace subjects for modern poets. If he does not please today's literary quarterlies and eightlies, he still pleases the people he has celebrated, who go on. And more, he has the admiration of distinguished poets. Speaking of "The People, Yes," Mark Van Doren commented, "You read his book, and you realize that although he's doing nothing but quoting Americans, somehow or other he has composed that work. Sandburg is particularly convincing because, among other things he is humorous."

And says MacLeish: "At a time of great doubt and skepticism in the country, Sandburg somehow had a sense of an optimistic temper, a temper of belief and assertion which later demonstrated itself. He is the poet of the American affirmation, a singer of the city where no one before him thought song could be found, and the voice of a prairie country which had been silent until he came."

Edmund Wilson has been the severest critic of the historian and biographer. "There are moments when one is tempted to feel that the cruelest thing that has happened to Lincoln since he was shot by Booth was to fall into the hands of Carl Sandburg," Wilson wrote in "Patriotic Gore." He cited the romantic and maudlin passages at the beginning of "The Prairie Years." What Wilson failed to disclose was that this started out as a book for children, and later grew into a kind of epic to be read and pondered instead of being only a respectable library citation.

Furthermore, both "The Prairie Years" and "The War Years" appeared before many new Lincoln findings were made and before the rich Robert T. Lincoln papers were opened. Combining the early and Presidential years into one volume, Sandburg cut out many grainy passages, inserted much of the latest research, and produced a mature work that blends his own style of writing with a great deal of solid scholarship. The four-volume "War Years" (which Wilson fails to mention in his "Gore") with "The Prairie Years" remains the most influential biography written about any American President.

And "influence" may be the operative word in any assessment of Sandburg. Robert Sherwood had wanted to write a play about Lincoln's early life for some 15 years. Reading and re-reading "The Prairie Years" enabled him to get started. "Can't open this wonderful book without feeling a rush of emotion to the imagination," Sherwood said. The result of Sandburg's serving as guide to "the main sources of

Lincoln lore" was Sherwood's drama "Abe Lincoln in Illinois." Many another journalist who has broken out of the narrow column-rule measure into wider fields of creative writing has been inspired by this peculiarly American stylist—this flawed Whitman of our time. That is the long view at twilight from Sandburg's mountain top that runs roughly between the unfinished North and South and is deeply imbedded in the American land.

GORE VIDAL
John Horne Burns

For literary versatility—and output—few if any contemporary American writers can match Gore Vidal. His first novel, "Williwaw," was published in his twenty-first year and was followed by others in rapid succession. He is an essayist. He has written for Hollywood, for TV, for Broadway ("Visit to a Small Planet," "The Best Man," "Weekend"). His novel, "Washington, D.C.," was one of 1967's best sellers, and was followed in 1968 by "Myra Breckinridge."

IN 1947 "The Gallery" by John Horne Burns was published, to great acclaim: the best book of World War II. That same year Burns and I met several times, each a war novelist, and each properly wary of the other. Burns was then 26 but looked older, with a receding hairline above a face striking in its asymmetry, one ear flat against the head, the other stuck out. Burns was a difficult man who drank too much, loved music, detested all other writers, wanted to be great (he had written a number of novels before the war, but none was published). He was also certain that to be a good writer it was necessary to be homosexual. When I disagreed, he named a half-dozen celebrated contemporaries, "A Pleiad," he roared delightedly, "of pederasts!" But what about Faulkner? I asked, and Hemingway? He was disdainful. Who said *they* were any good? And besides hadn't I heard how Hemingway once. . . .

I never saw Burns after 1947. But we exchanged several letters. He was going to write a successful play and become rich. He was also going to give up teaching in a prep school, and go live in Europe. (He had been stationed there during the war.) He did achieve Europe, but the occasion of the return was not happy. His second novel, "Lucifer With a Book" (1949), was perhaps the most savagely attacked book of its day. Outraged, and with good reason, Burns exchanged America for Florence. But things had started to go wrong for him, and Italy did not help. The next novel, "A Cry of Children" (1952), was bad. He seemed to have lost some inner sense of self, gained in the war, lost in the peace. He disintegrated. Night after night, he would stand at the Excelsior Hotel bar, drinking brandy, eating hard candy (he had a theory sugar prevented hangover), insulting imagined enemies and imagined friends, and all the while complaining of what had been done to him by book reviewers. In those years one tried not to think of Burns; it was too bitter. The best of us all had taken the worst way.

In 1958 when I read that he was dead, I felt no shock. It seemed right. One only wondered how he had achieved extinction. Sunstroke was the medical report. But it being Burns, there were rumors of suicide, even murder; however, those who knew him at the last say that his going was natural, and inevitable. He was 37 years old.

Twenty-one years ago the American Army occupied Naples and John Horne Burns, a young soldier from Boston—Irish, Puritan, un-awakened—was brought to life by the human swarm he encountered in the Galleria Umberto, "a spacious arcade opening off Via Roma. . . . It was like walking into a city within a city." From this confrontation Burns never recovered. As he put it, "I thought I could keep a wall between me and the people. But the monkeys in the cage reach out and grab the spectator who offers them a banana." It was the time when cigarettes, chocolate, nylons were exchanged for an easy sex that could become, for a man like Burns, unexpected love. He was startled to find that Italians could sell themselves with no sense of personal loss and, unlike their Puritan conquerors, they could even take pleasure in giving pleasure; their delight in the very fact of life persisted, no matter how deep the wound. Unlike "the Irish who stayed hurt all their lives; the Italians had a bounce-back in them."

"The Gallery" (reissued in paperback by Bantam Books) is a col-lection of episodes called "Portraits" and "Promenades"; a study of men and women brought together in one way or another by the fact of the Galleria and war. The characters, some shadowy, some startlingly brilliant, have sex, make love, lose themselves, find themselves. A young soldier retreats into visions of himself as Christ; a major in censorship builds himself a bureaucratic empire; a Catholic chaplain quibbles with a Protestant chaplain; a soldier grimly endures the V.D. ward and wonders how he could ever have loved the girl who put him there; and Momma, a genial Italian lady, presides over the Galleria's queer bar, finding her charges mysteriously simpatico, quite unlike the other conquerors.

Finally, it is not so much what these characters do as the effect that Naples has on them. One discovers the "difference between love and Having Sex." To another, "It seemed that in our lethargic and compassionate caresses we were trying to console each other for every hurt the world had ever inflicted." To the demented visionary: "These people . . . are all in search of love. The love of God, or death, or of another human being. They're all lost. That's why they walk so aimlessly. They all feel here that the world isn't big enough to hold them. And look at the design of this place. Like a huge cross laid on the ground, after the corpus is taken off the nails."

In the classic tradition of Northern visitors to the South, Burns is overwhelmed by the spontaneity of the Italians. Even their rapacity and cruelty strike him as being closer to some ideal of the human than the moral numbness of the American. He contrasts Italian delicacy in human matters with the harshness of our soldiers and their often pathological loathing for the "inferior" races they were forced to deal with, an ugly side to the American in World War II that has not been much written about. Though Burns tends to give too much to the Italian sensibility and too little to that of his countrymen, the point is valid: We were the barbarian army from the great northern plains; they were the civilization beside the southern sea.

Burns's style is energetic, very much that of the 1940's, with distracting attempts at phonetic spelling for dialect ("furren" for "foreign," and made-up verbs ("he shrilled"). Burns's ear for dialogue was not always true; his dislike of those speaking often came between him and accuracy. He was also sometimes operatic in his effects (penicillin hurled at the Galleria: symbolic revenge). But when he is good, the style has a compelling drive that displays the national manner at its best. "Their faces complemented one another as a spoon shapes what it holds," thinks a character who has "contracted a bad case of irrelevance."

Of the well-known books of the war, I have always thought that only Burns's was authentic. To me the others were redolent of ambition and literature, and their talented authors have since gone on to better things. But for Burns the war was genuine revelation. In Naples he fell in love with the idea of life. And obtaining a sense of his own identity, he saw what life might be. That the vision was a simple one makes no difference. It was his. "There'll be Neapolitans alive in 1960. I say, more power to them. They deserve to live out the end of their days because they caught on sooner than we how simple human life can be, uncomplicated by advertising and Puritanism and those loathsome values of a civilization in which everything is measured in terms of commercial success." His indictment is now a cliché, but it struck a nerve 20 years ago. Also I suspect he never understood his own people very well; nor do I think he would have been so entirely pleased by the Neapolitans of 1960 who, in their relative affluence, have begun to resemble us.

But the spirit of his revelation remains true. "For I got lost in the war in Naples in August 1944. Often from what I saw I lost the power of speech. It seemed to me that everything happening there could be happening to me. A kind of madness, I suppose. But in the 28th year of my life I learned that I too must die. Until that time the only thing evil that could be done to men would be to hurry me out of the world before my time. Or to thwart my natural capacities. If this truth held for me, it must be valid for everybody else in the world."

Burns hurried himself out of the world before his time. But he had had his moment. And now that the war we lived through is history, we are able to recognize that the novel he wrote about it is literature. Burns was a gifted man who wrote a book far in excess of his gift, making a kind of masterpiece which will endure in a way that he could not. Extreme circumstances made him write a book which was better than his talent, an unbearable fate for an ambitious artist who wants to go on, but cannot—all later work shadowed by the splendid accident of a moment's genius. I suspect that once Burns realized his situation, he in fact chose not to go on, and between Italian brandy and Italian sun contrived to stop.

As for the man, Burns had the luck to know, if only briefly, what it was to be alive with all senses responsive to all things; able to comprehend another person and to share that truth which is "valid for everybody else." Describing a soldier much like himself, even to the first name, Burns shows us a man discovering himself for the first time in the act of love on a hot August night. But then, love made, he is too keyed-up to fall asleep, too restless with discovery; and so he is soothed and comforted in the dark, and the whispered Italian of his companion strikes the note of epitaph: "Buona notte e sogni d'oro. . . . Dormi, John."

PETER QUENNELL*
Evelyn Waugh

My FIRST meeting with Evelyn Waugh must have occurred well over 40 years ago, some time early in the nineteen-twenties, when I was living at home in a small English town named Berkhamsted, and attending the local grammar school, where Graham Greene's father, Charles Greene—Graham himself attended the school—was established as the headmaster.

Several successful writers inhabited Berkhamsted, among them the celebrated Victorian storyteller W. W. Jacobs, a renowned professional humorist with one of the most lugubrious faces I have ever seen. I knew his family and often visited his house; and I was presently excited to learn that his eldest daughter had just become engaged to the daring young rebel Alec Waugh, author of that highly controversial novel "The Loom of Youth." Alec soon appeared in Berkhamsted, looking as cheerful and rubicund as he does today; and he was quickly followed by his brother Evelyn, a slight, curly-headed, dandified figure wearing a colored waistcoat and carrying, I seem to remember, a pair of lemon-yellow gloves.

Some years later, when I arrived in Oxford, Evelyn Waugh, still slender, alert and dandified, came round to Balliol to call on me. The novelist's future biographers—no doubt he will have more than one—should pay special attention to the varying circumstances of youth and early manhood. Between the time he left Oxford and the moment he emerged as a rising literary artist, he managed—how or for what reasons a critic can only guess—almost completely to transform his character.

The juvenile Waugh had been carefree, gay and affectionate—

* (Other essays by Mr. Quennell appear on pages 162, 193)

though in his cups he sometimes revealed a strain of anarchic desperation. The adult Waugh was somber and cross-grained, and treated most of his fellow human beings as villains, cranks or pestilential boobies. His coreligionists found him warm-hearted; I am told that he frequently did good by stealth. But to doubt his beliefs or question his prejudices was immediately to be thrust outside the pale. Nobody was so fond of drawing a line; and the lines that Evelyn drew gradually cut him off—much, it must be conceded, to his own satisfaction—from nine-tenths of the modern world.

His Oxford period, itself, fell into two separate phases. During the opening phase he occupied airy and agreeable rooms, where he was surrounded by his drawings and woodcuts—he was then an industrious amateur draftsman—and by the Nonesuch editions of the English classics. Then he experienced a sudden reverse, sold most of his books and objects of art at an uproarious private auction, and retreated into the darkest and dingiest quarters in the whole of Hertford College. There he become a dishevelled bohemian, took to lunching off hunks of bread and cheese and swallowing huge draughts of beer, and after dark often made Oxford ring with Falstaffian chants and objurgations.

In those days he was a vehement anti-Papist; and he also conducted a noisy personal feud against various dons whom he particularly disliked. His moods were wild. On one occasion, having, in my absence, found his way into my rooms at Balliol, he finished a bottle of champagne that I had been unwise enough to leave behind, and, leaning from my fourth-floor window, above a quiet stretch of urban pavement, launched the empty bottle in the general direction of an inoffensive passer-by. I am sure that he meant to miss; luckily he did miss—though by a rather narrow margin. Seeing a bottle explode beneath his nose, the pedestrian hurried to the porter's lodge, where he delivered an impassioned protest. He was heavily fined by the college authorities. Had Evelyn's aim been a little more deliberate, his subsequent history, I suppose, might have taken a somewhat different turn.

As it was, once he had said good-bye to Oxford, he went through a period of obscurity and tribulation. He was poor, in disgrace with his father and, though he was fond of drawing and carpentry, revealed no particular aptitude for any kind of profitable employment. He tried journalism; he was briefly a schoolmaster, but withdrew from the school after (he informed me) making facetious advances, on his way home from a convivial evening, to the stout and unattractive matron whom he encountered in a bedroom passage.

Then, just when his friends had begun to despair of him, he underwent a further change, fell in love, proposed, was married and set up as a contented householder, in a small, pretty flat in an un- fashionable district of London, furnished with an array of odd and charming ornaments. The habits of dandyism returned; I remembered, at evening parties, his conspicuously stiff and gleaming shirt-front. His wife was as small and neat as himself. Side by side I thought that they resembled a pair of decorative pouter-pigeons.

His first marriage, alas, was very soon to break down. The circum- stances were humiliating; there is no doubt that he suffered deeply; and from this disaster he seems to have taken refuge in new beliefs and a new attitude towards the world that he continued to maintain until he died. I become aware myself of the transformation at a fairly early juncture.

Walking up St. James's Street, I came face to face with him, ac- companied by a rather grand young woman, his round pink features surmounted and almost eclipsed by an impressive top hat. I paused; his greeting was distant. In some confusion I admired his buttonhole —naturally, a small orchid; at which he pulled it out and suggested I might like to keep it—not, however, as if he were making me a gift, but as if he had been distributing largesse to a needy old acquaintance. I forget if I refused or accepted. The great man nodded, smiled and passed on.

From that moment our friendship declined—partly, I must admit, because I had reviewed his biography of Dante Gabriel Rossetti less enthusiastically, or more critically, than he thought I should have done. But by that time the persona was firmly in place; and nothing— neither literary fame nor the success of his second marriage, which turned out to be as happy and prolific as his first marriage had been brief and barren—ever persuaded him to drop that strange disguise. Of all his books, one of the most revealing from a biographical point of view is "The Ordeal of Gilbert Pinfold," his own lightly fictional- ized account of how, in later life, he had once driven himself, by his reckless abuse of sleeping-pills and alcohol, right to the dizzy verge of a nervous breakdown. He describes his persona at length, remarking, not without a touch of malicious glee, that many people found him "formidable," and that his victims were apt to exchange anecdotes about his intimidating and aggressive manners.

Formidable he certainly was; and here I can add a characteristic

story. Soon after he had returned from a journey to Hollywood, I was
sitting beside a distinguished film-magnate—who, I ascertained, had
undertaken to arrange his visit. What had he thought of the novelist,
I inquired. Mr. Waugh, he replied, in sorrowful tones, had gravely disappointed him. Why had he been disappointed? Well, it seemed that
he had engaged for the celebrated visitor an especially splendid apartment in a particularly fine hotel. The apartment was to have been
vacated a day before he reached Hollywood. Then disaster struck.

The previous occupants had been a delightful old married couple.
The old man suddenly collapsed with a crippling paralytic stroke. The
pair had been much loved; a wave of grief and consternation swept
through the entire hotel. It had become clear that the invalid could
not be moved, at least for another few hours, when Mr. Waugh appeared at the hotel desk, looking very fierce and very authoritative,
wearing his London bowler hat and grasping a tightly-rolled umbrella.
The tragic situation was explained; profuse apologies, of course, were
tendered. Mr. Waugh refused to budge an inch; he continued loudly
to demand his rooms. "And do you know what he said?" I was asked.
"All Mr. Waugh would say was 'Your guests' health is no concern of
mine!'"

Such was the Waugh persona at its most outrageous. So elaborate
and so forbidding was its development in later years that, if he were
ill-disposed, his face came physically to suggest some kind of painted
mask or visor—bulging eyes, threatening sandy eyebrows, pendulous
high-coloured cheeks, pursed mouth and heavy florid jowl. But one
must bear in mind the element of self-parody. He loved to exaggerate
his own disguises, and enjoyed playing the role of pantomime demon-
king in which he had once decided he would cast himself.

As a journalist, he issued bizarre pronouncements, publicly re-
gretting, for example, that the Spanish Armada had failed to conquer
England and thus—at no matter what expense of life and liberty—
restore his native land to the authority of the Roman Catholic religion.

He had never, he announced, cast his vote in an election; the
Queen should be allowed to choose her own advisers. The modern
Welfare State was a pathetic farce; the care of the sick and old and
destitute was "no concern" of any proper government.

Yet the novels showed us a different man. Although some of his
prejudices crept into his imaginative work, there he usually had them
under good control; and his professed contempt for humanity had

little effect on his method of drawing and analyzing human character. Nor did the world-weariness he so often advertised ever extinguish his prodigious sense of fun.

True, the atmosphere of his later books—especially his admirable wartime series, "Men at Arms," "Officers and Gentlemen" and "Unconditional Surrender"—is dark with despair and disillusionment; but he could always find room for a comic intruder; and the vulgar and ridiculous Apthorpe is almost as sympathetically depicted as an earlier hero, the incomparable Captain Grimes.

In an obituary note, Graham Greene, with his usual generosity, called Evelyn Waugh "the greatest novelist of my generation." I believe he was right. No English novelist who lived and worked during the first half of the 20th century has made a more distinctive contribution to the literature of modern Europe.

There are three standards, I assume, by which we can judge the lasting merits of a work of fiction. Has the novelist introduced us to imaginary men and women, who seem afterwards to have become a permanent part of the world in which we live? Has his view of life changed or modified our own—so that, having read his book, we look at existence through slightly new eyes? Have his style and his method of narration had any real influence upon the ancient art of writing?

If these questions are applied to Evelyn Waugh, the answer in each case must be a bold affirmative. He was not an innovator; he distrusted innovations, and appears to have been perfectly content with the structure of the English novel as he found it. What he added were not fresh tricks of style—he was a soberly accomplished stylist—but a far subtler type of originality. Great imaginative talents generally arise from a conflict; and the hidden conflicts that made him so strange a man may also have helped to shape an extraordinarily gifted writer.

HORACE GREGORY
Edwin Muir

A reviewer of Horace Gregory's "Collected Poems" described him as "a classicist who has employed his spirit not to avoid the confusing modern world but to clarify and enrich it," and so he has in a lifetime devoted to verse and criticism and teaching. Literary awards have marked his years. In 1965 he received the Bollingen Prize for Poetry.

IN ANTHOLOGIES and studies of contemporary poetry it is the unexpected poems and poets who are increasingly evoked. Of these the least heralded, yet most rewarding, and even now perhaps the most enduring, is Edwin Muir (1887-1959): his best poems are short, and in contemporary company, resemble no one else's. The poems stand quite alone, and in their outward dress, innocent of fashionable 20th-century devices. Read carefully, their character is both traditional and unique.

And who was Edwin Muir? In answering that question one begins to describe the unusual nature and source of the poems he wrote. He and his wife, Willa, were generally known as the gifted translators of the tales and parables of Franz Kafka into English; it is not too much to say it was they who made Kafka famous. Muir's limited celebrity from his own writing came very late, and at no time in his brief career of about 15 years was he other than a soft-spoken, slender, shy, self-effacing man. The extraordinary thing about him was the youthful, almost saintly brilliance of his gaze glancing through the surrounding veil of his modesty. In the early 1950's, on his short visit to the United States, it was as though the external Muir, a man of letters and mild-voiced lecturer, shielded and half-concealed an internal presence, the best of 12th-century Scottish poets.

The internal Muir, the poet, whom his wife was fond of calling "an extremely early Christian," was born on a farm in the Orkneys, that low-hilled chain of islands, off Scotland, not far from Norway, where the provinces of the Scandinavians and the Scots-Irish almost touch each other. Rich as these unfamiliar farmlands were in spoken myths and legends, the Orkneys were not known for raising poets. Muir was a singular child of that environment, and from it springs his "An Autobiography," published in 1955, as well as the 1965 revised edition (with a preface by T. S. Eliot) of his "Collected Poems." The autobiography provides a valuable backdrop to the poems, a far better exegesis of their visionary content than a conventional critical analysis would yield. If the best of the poems are not as well known as they should be, the self-told story of his life gives us a few of the causes why.

The writing and publication of Muir's poems came late in his

career. During his adolescence the migration of his family south to
Glasgow was a journey into brutish slums, ill-health and death. The
elder members of the family were wiped out and beyond his rural
schooling, Muir's education was of his own finding, his native taste,
and his austere, though imaginative, discernment. He earned his keep
by holding precarious clerkships in beer-bottling and bone factories
and last in a shipbuilder's office—all this an unlikely apprentice-ser-
vice for a future poet and literary essayist.

In these surroundings, it was not extraordinary that he became
converted to Socialism; what was unusual was his quick discovery
that Marxism was not for him, and with this conviction, he turned to
A. R. Orage's startling periodical, The New Age, which advocated
Maj. C. H. Douglas's Social Credit. This choice was significant, for
Orage was an editor of vivid perceptions and fine intuitions: with
the same insight with which he guided Muir, he encouraged the early
work of T. S. Eliot, Ezra Pound, Dylan Thomas and Katherine Mans-
field. When young Muir wrote him, asking for advice, he freely gave
it, and accepted a weekly column of Muir's prose for The New Age.

Meanwhile, the poet in Muir had made independent soundings and
discoveries in Scottish and English poetry, and among English poets,
Wordsworth's example of plain speech that articulated feeling "too
deep for tears" left its mark. Wordsworth as model was a warning
against the use of emotional trivialities and Scottish provincialisms
in verse. Such teaching was excellent for Muir, and so was the discipline
of verbal simplicity. The only harm that came from Wordsworth's
influence (and this is a reason why some readers have underestimated
Muir) is the colorless, atonal utterance that damps his poetry whenever it falls short of its best.

Muir had begun by writing prose. As he wrote later, "I produced
. . . a sort of pinchbeck Nietzschean prose peppered with exclamation
marks. I should be astonished at the perversity with which, against my
natural inclinations, my judgment . . . I clung to a philosophy so little
suited to a clerk in a beer-bottling factory, if I did not realize that it
was a 'compensation' without which I should have found it hard to
face life at all." In 1920 H. L. Mencken reprinted Muir's "Nietzschean
prose" from the columns of The New Age under the ironical title "We
Moderns" in a little green book. As Muir in 1954 was glad to confess,
his "We Moderns" had long fallen out of print, yet between the lines
of its affected style and wit, there was an intelligence that never con-

fused the humane values of poetry and art with those of power politics.
His brief Nietzschean fever thoroughly inoculated him against all future contamination, either from the Fascist right or the Communist
left.

Encouraged by Orage, the Muirs, husband and wife, ventured to
London, and then into Europe, on a career of translations from the
German and of literary journalism. Unlike most such writings, Muir's
reviews and critical pieces had a particularly serious and inquiring air;
he was well prepared to make his discovery of Kafka. In this country,
his prose caught the attention of Van Wyck Brooks, literary editor
of The Freeman, who persuaded him to contribute his middle-Euro-
pean travelogues to that journal, including his sketches of Prague. It
was through their experiences in Europe that Muir was able to shake
off the last vestiges of Scottish provincialism and to find his place as
a citizen of the world, unique of his kind, with the visionary eye of a
poet.

At an age when most poets had lost their first flush of inspiration,
Muir had just begun. His published verse is without juvenilia; no
youthful or experimental imperfections mar its lines; to the present
reader, its only flaws are shadows cast by Wordsworthian matter-of-
factness and lack of color, but when the shadows vanish his poems
have an air of eternal freshness, an "early-Christian" touch and truth-
fulness that Giotto's frescos have, as in the following lines from his
"The Annunciation":

> The angel and the girl are met.
> Earth was the only meeting place.
> For the embodied never yet
> Traveled beyond the short of space.
> The eternal spirits in freedom go.
>
> See, they have come together, see
> While the destroying minutes flow,
> Each reflects the other's face
> Till heaven in hers and earth in his
> Shine steady there. He's come to her
> From far beyond the farthest star. . . .

No poet of our day has been able to emulate the merits of the
Scottish Border ballads with the quiet authority and distinction mastered by Edwin Muir. At their best his lines have the concentrated
action and clarity of "Sir Patrick Spens," as well as Robert Burns's "The

trumpets sound, the banners fly,/The glittering spears are ranked ready . . ." and Sir Walter Scott's "Proud Maisie is in the wood,/ Walking so early;/Sweet Robin sits on the bush,/Singing so rarely." This is of the same power of vision and art that began to enter Muir's poetry in 1934. Note these lines on heraldic beasts:

> Who curbed the lion long ago
> And penned him in this towering field
> And reared him wingless in the sky?
> And quenched the dragon's burning eye,
> Chaining him here to make a show,
> The faithful guardian of the shield?
>
> A fabulous wave far back in Time
> Flung these calm trophies to this shore
> That looks out on a different sea.
> These relics of a buried war,
> Empty as shape and cold as rhyme,
> Gaze now on fabulous wars to be.

Something very like a hint foretelling World War II may be found within these lines, but quite as important as the warning is the transcendental quality of Muir's imagination. There is metaphysical tension and strength in "The Animals," a vision that probably had its source in a memory of childhood on the farm:

> They do not live in the world,
> Are not in time and space.
> From birth to death hurled
> No word do they have, not one
> To plant a foot upon,
> Were never in any place.
> For with names the world was called
> Out of the empty air,
> With names was built and walled,
> Line and circle and square,
> Dust and emerald;
> Snatched from deceiving death
> By the articulate breath.
> But these have never trod
> Twice the familiar track,
> Never never turned back
> Into the memoried day.
> All is new and near
> In the unchanging Here

> Of the fifth great day of God.
> That shall remain the same,
> Never shall pass away.
>
> On the sixth day we came.

Nor as he changes the setting to a Greek environment is his vision less penetrating. Here is the deep vista of "Orpheus' Dream":

> At last to turn our heads and see
> The poor ghost of Eurydice
> Still sitting in her silver chair,
> Alone in Hades' empty hall.

The same depths are reached in "The Horses," one of the poems T. S. Eliot greatly admired, where there is a sight of our world returned to "long-lost archaic companionship" after the devastations of the next great war, a look forward into a future that closely resembles mankind's beginnings.

Among Muir's very last poems, there is the strange and magical fable, "The Two Sisters," which recreates in modern poetry the sense of destiny so often felt in rereading elder Scottish songs and ballads:

> Her beauty was so rare,
> It wore her body down
> With leading through the air
> That marvel not her own.
> At last to set it free
> From enmity of change
> And time's incontinence
> To drink from beauty's bone,
> Snatching her last defence,
> She locked it in the sea.
>
> The other, not content
> That fault of hers should bring
> Grief and mismanagement
> To make an end of grace
> And snap the slender ring,
> Pulled death down on her head,
> Completed destiny.
> So each from her own place,
> These ladies put to sea
> To join the intrepid dead.

Surely here is proof enough that Muir in casting off mere provincial mannerisms and dialects has made his own language that restores the strength of Scottish tradition (which for centuries has held its own in metaphysics) and given it universal character and meaning.

HORACE GREGORY*
A. D. Hope

To ALL outward appearances the scene today in British poetry is gray and chilly. New poets are always there and always welcome, but none has had time to grow to full stature and take the center of the stage. This decade is, I think, a period of transition, or another changing of the guard. The scene is somewhat as it was in the nineteen-twenties, when famous and elder British poets seemed to stand in the background while a young poet, Roy Campbell from South Africa, and two arrivals from America, Pound and Eliot, came to the front. Though some readers then regretted what seemed to be a wintry picture for the future of indigenous English verse, invaders from other shores were endowing the tradition of British poetry with a new lease on life. They were making the old world new; this required magic and it worked.

During the mid-nineteen-forties, they were followed by two others who became well known: Dylan Thomas from Wales and Edwin Muir from the Scottish Orkneys. More recently still, another has arrived. He is A.D. Hope from Australia, whose first book of poems was published in 1955. Among his contemporaries he steps forward as a silver-tongued, if sometimes violent, prophet of doom.

In his fiery moments he is not unlike the South African, Roy Campbell, but such echoes are, I think, less the result of literary influence than a likeness of temperament. Their poetry also has an affinity in its choice of large themes as well as an acknowledged debt to Baudelaire. But far more than from any other source, Hope's verse takes its prece-

* (Something of Mr. Gregory is set forth in the note that accompanies his essay on page 264)

dent from the masters of satire in the British tradition. With his "Collected Poems: 1930-65," Hope moves clearly into view.

What a relief it is to read a poet who is not ashamed to admit that he is a well-educated man! How refreshing it is to find a poet who does not plead that he is mentally confused or ignorant! (In the United States, even such well-established poets as William Carlos Williams and Robert Frost pretended to be less cultivated, less well read and more homespun than they actually were.)

Hope does not believe that "poetry is primarily self-expression," but, on the contrary, it is "principally concerned to 'express' its subject and in doing so to create an emotion which is the feeling of the poem and not the feeling of the poet." In other words, Hope is warning his readers that his poems are not the confessions of a patient on a couch in a psychiatrist's office.

He is also, I think, reminding us that some few of his poems have the detachment, wit, skill and polish of 18th-century verse. Hope's "Lambkin: A Fable," a theological fable of a strayed black sheep, has more profound sophistication than any fable written by John Gay, the author of "The Beggar's Opera" and a master in the genre. "Lambkin" is too long to quote, but the following poem, "Coup de Grâce," illustrates the dark humors of Hope's light verse:

> Just at that moment the Wolf,
> Shag jaws and slavering grin,
> Steps from the property wood.
> O, what a gorge, what a gulf
> Opens to gobble her in,
> Little Red Riding Hood!
>
> O, what a face full of fangs!
> Eyes like saucers at least
> Roll to seduce and beguile.
> Miss, with her dimples and bangs,
> Thinks him a handsome beast;
> Flashes the Riding Hood Smile;
>
> Stands her ground like a queen,
> Velvet red of the rose
> Framing each little milk-tooth,
> Pink tongue peeping between.
> Then, wider than anyone knows,
> Opens her minikin mouth

Swallows up Wolf in a trice;
Tail going down gives a flick,
Caught as she closes her jaws.
Bows, all sugar and spice.
O, what a lady-like trick!
O, what a round of applause!

"Collected Poems: 1930-1965" has an extremely wide geographic scope and range of feeling. The distance traveled is literally from New South Wales to New England, and from here to Rome as well as points between, and back to the Pacific. At the other end of the spectrum from Little Red Riding Hood are Hope's love lyrics. Among them there is the splendid "Chorale," and if there are echoes of Yeats and Auden in its recital, no matter, the poem exists in itself. Its opening lines are:

Often had I found her fair;
Most when to my bed she came,
Naked as the moving air,
Slender, walking like a flame.
In that grace I sink and drown:
Opening like the liquid wave
To my touch she laid her down,
Drew me to her crystal cave.
    Love me ever, love me long—
    Was the burden of her song.

Perhaps no poet of our time has a clearer vision than Hope of the narcissism implicit in the legend of Don Juan. That particular self-love that so often seizes romantic poets has an atmosphere of fatal terror in Hope's poem "The Damnation of Byron," and since Byron is one of his acknowledged masters, "The Damnation" has special pertinence and force.

Hope is not alone among living poets in his appreciation of Byron's "Don Juan," with its underlying motifs of self-imposed exile, of restless travel and of sturdy discontent with Western civilization. Since the writing of "Don Juan" came after Napoleon's defeat at Waterloo, Byron as Juan was a postwar poet in much the same sense that some poets are today, including Hope. In this sense also Hope is a cosmopolitan poet who is as quick to ridicule middle-class suburban life as he is to overturn placid acceptance of Darwinian progress. It is the Byron of Byronic satires whom Hope enjoys and emulates. As for the famous legend of Don Juan, Hope does not carry his speculations into

mythico-psychology too far. The limitations are briskly stated in his
satire "The Return From the Freudian Islands," where "clothes to the
Analytic Eye became/Fantasies, furtive symbols of the skin," and as
for Freud,

> Long time he mused before The Sacred Id,
> Long prayed, before he finally began
> And, purged, impersonal, uninhibited,
> Produced at last The Basic Freudian Man.

I am fairly certain that Hope draws his conclusions less from Freud
than from some of Freud's own sources in ancient literature, both
Biblical and Greek. As for Hope's affinity with Byron, I believe he
shares with the elder poet perhaps an ancestral Scottish, but surely
Calvinistic sense of Original Sin. The wage of the candid sexuality in
his satires is always death; even as a lover takes a girl out to dinner,
her aboriginal image rises before his eyes:

> Delicate, young and cradled in delight,
> You take your seat and bare your teeth to bite—
> What is my courage then to suffer this
> Miracle of your metamorphosis!
> For in that instant I behold the jaws
> Of the most terrible of carnivores
> Tear at its prey; the ravening human packs
> Pull down their terrified victim in its tracks;
> The wit, the charm, the grace, the pride of life
> Adore the bloody edges of a knife!

On similar but more general themes Hope turns from these bal-
anced measures of the heroic couplet to the rollicking light verse of
his Calliope, who says:

> "But what I have to tell embraces
> Much more than Marx or Malthus guessed.
> The future of the human race is
> Somewhat precarious at best.
> The day when mere survival places
> All other values to the test
> May not be far away; indeed
> Man's deadliest instinct is to breed.
>
> "And breeding as he does unchecked
> By Nature, Law or Common Caution,
> No cornucopia can expect
> To pour forth plenty in proportion,

Nor human skills for long perfect
New means to eke his dwindling portion:
Since self-control is too much bother,
They'll end by eating one another . . . ."

And what is Hope's view of his native Australia?

Yet there are some like me turn gladly home
From the lush jungle of modern thought, to find
The Arabian desert of the human mind,
Hoping, if still from the desert the prophets come,
Such savage and scarlet as no green hills dare
Springs in that waste, some spirit which escapes
The learned doubt, the chatter of cultured apes . . .

It well may be that Hope is a close relation of the prophets he has
in mind. If so, his erudition is such that he can afford to be amused
at "the chatter of cultured apes," and he has also created a kind of
oasis in the writing of powerful and often savage light verse. His strictures on the conduct of technocratic man have a universal ring. At
the very least, Hope has shown us that his prophet of doom has tough-
minded intelligence and passionate wit—and that he glitters when he
walks abroad.

MARK HARRIS
Alan Swallow, 1915-1966

*Although Mark Harris's lines have been cast in academic waters, most
recently at Purdue, it is as a humorous novelist with a bite that he is
best known. Examples: "The Southpaw," "Bang the Drum Slowly,"
"Wake Up, Stupid."*

ALAN SWALLOW died at 51 in Denver on Thanksgiving Day,
1966. He was a publisher and teacher. As publisher he was also editor,
printer, first reader and final word, laboring mainly alone out of the
house he lived in on a quiet street. He carried his books himself to the
post office.

As teacher he taught that the judgment on literature must be based upon the text. Beware of paraphrase. Prejudice would never do. Dumb subjectivity was out.

His books and his students, dispersed across the country now— mainly in college English departments—have worked their effect not only upon American literature but upon our general thought: minds well trained in literature begin to understand the world as well. Himself poet, he was the unacknowledged legislator.

Yet I think he never held in his own mind so grand a role for himself. He never so much enunciated principles as lived them out. As publisher, he didn't believe in smallness for its own sake. Rather, his talent for practical recognition assured him that the qualities he preferred in books were more likely to go over small than big. He was no dreamer. He published for his own taste, and he knew he was a minority.

Over the years some of the work he published gained remarkably in audience, profiting author and publisher not in its first weeks but in its further years, and after a quarter of a century he talked in numbers large enough to surprise him, embarrass him, and cause him to wonder whether he had become too efficient. One estimate holds that he reached a recent peak in sales of 70,000 books a year. In his own words, his production of titles in 1965 had built to "the stupid level of 50."

He never published a book he didn't like. Thus he never fell into self-contempt. His faith in young writers gave them faith in themselves, and his interest in each was in the present book; he never thought of writers as prospects, as comers, or as future things. He published several older writers at the far ends of their lives, after commercial publishers had set them adrift.

Swallow was raised on a ranch in Wyoming, and he was sufficiently habituated to solitude to form very early in his life a contentment with the companionship of books. I have heard that he was accustomed to read while driving his tractor, with the result that, once at least, in the depths of preoccupation, he drove through the wall of a barn. Years later, among fellow-professors and talkative students, he was slow at repartee and banter, giving the impression of a man either humorless or a little deaf. Indeed, his eye was for the page, and his ear was inner. Thus the idea of making books, both as objects in themselves and as the natural means of discourse, was the logic of his life.

He played high-school football at Powell, Wyo. In physique he was powerful, and his eyes were sharp. His hair was sandy blond, afterward gray. He distinguished himself as an undergraduate at the University of Wyoming, and from there he went to Louisiana State University, where he came beneath the influence of Southern Agrarianism and the New Criticism, assimilating them to his thinking, as he had already taken to himself the Renaissance and the American West. His loyalties were personal, never doctrinaire. He was no man's disciple, nor did he seek disciples of his own among his students.

I knew him best when I was his student at the University of Denver, and I fought him all the way. The text between us (Modern Poetry, winter quarter, 1949) was Oscar Williams's "A Little Treasury of Modern Poetry," offensive to me because I didn't like it. But when students said to Swallow, "I don't like it" or "I like it," his reply was that we were then speaking not of the poem but of our own raw states of mind. To students raised to "appreciate" literature—to like what one liked and to dislike what one disliked—this was shocking. It deprived us of our prejudices, our mindless safety and the comforts of our assumptions.

Moreover, the poems were filled with mysteries that forced us to work. These were "difficult" poems, at first glance meaningless; the rhythms were new; they didn't rhyme. Swallow never told us the thing we learned as time passed: You must go to the poem, not the poem to you.

Thus he taught us to read by the same method he taught us to write, at a time when programs in "creative writing" were a radical addition to academic life. The procedure in his classes in writing was simple. Someone submitted a manuscript, and Swallow read it aloud in a detached voice, without emphasis or assistance to the text. The class offered criticism. Presumably the author was anonymous, but of course we always had an idea whose manuscript it was, and we frequently attacked or defended not the work but the person. Our minds were made up in advance. The great test lay in learning—for, again, he never told us—how to hear the work itself apart from person, how to receive the work of a fellow-student as if it were an accepted classic.

Often we moved in a body from his classroom to his house, gathering place for students, for Denver writers and for literary visitors from a distance. There we met notable men as diverse as J. V. Cunningham and James T. Farrell and gained a sense of connection with the world of achievement. Our sense of his method we carried with us, and it has come to be one of the principal characteristics of literary study in America. Most of Swallow's students became teachers, some became writers; some both. The idea of the campus as a right place for writers to teach and for teachers to write is commonplace now, like the spirit of the New Criticism. The idea has had, at least, its fair test.

His method must have been the method of liberated readers in all ages. The separation of mind from prejudice is the root of justice. To have carried that ideal into the hazardous field of American book-publishing was noble folly. Publishing is a practical matter. Books sell by name or subject matter. Mere excellence is seldom enough. Little wonder that Swallow was constantly in search of storage space for books he never sold. It was all very well to build a better mousetrap, but when mousetraps were books you'd need distribution, salesmen, hyperbolic advertising, publicity, floods of reviews, cocktail parties and subsidiary tie-ins. Finally it might be desirable, as recent trends reveal, to merge yourself with a big house of business whose estimate of books calculates only their cost.

In the distant east of America, in the eye of The Trade, Swallow was seen as a specialist in regional books about the West. It was a way of dismissing him, in spite of the truth that he published a wide range of general fiction, poetry and criticism. The Eastern professional liked to call him a Western amateur.

Not that he didn't know it. Not that he didn't care. He would have sold a billion copies if he could. He never railed against the East, nor condemned commerce, but steadily maintained his own version of loyalty—as he had at the height of the period of Senator McCarthy, when the private definition of loyalty required special courage.

Thirteen months before his death, in a circular letter "to my authors and friends," he told of complex problems of health. Of his publishing business he wrote: "Of course I could sell part or all; there are values worth 'buying,' if someone wanted them merely to exploit them for a return and let much go by. But so far I have turned aside even the smallest approaches of that kind and will continue to do so. I would rather see it dispersed in another way than to have that happen. . . . I shall have to tackle it another way. Yes, cutting back some titles will help and will permit me to get caught up a bit more. . . . But 'cutting back' is not so easy as it sounds, and not so advisable as it sounds on the surface. I have many obligations to authors, and to my mind, at least, it is important to fulfill them insofar as I can—as a person of large energy, I *can* do much."

I visited him last in Denver—summer, 1965. We took farewells in

front of his house. His four automobiles were parked in a row. I had
always thought his manner of driving reckless, and I avoided riding
with him. He had, also, a passion for motorcycles. He suffered serious
injuries in a motorcycle crash. Treatment was complicated by an ailing
heart. He took to crutches, but he defied all advice to slow down. In
his last letter to me he believed he had found a new drug which "makes
the difference." It was 4 o'clock in the morning. "I think I'll make it
through tonight all right and then be okay."

He made the night, and some months more, but he never cut back
and never sold out.

SYDNEY HYMAN
De Gaulle, Author

*Sydney Hyman once made Washington and American politics his
beat, and it was in that course of duty that he wrote "The American
President" and other books. In recent years he has lived abroad.
Against that background he wrote his essay on President de Gaulle.*

ALEXIS DE TOCQUEVILLE laid it down as a rule that the qualities in a writer that make for great literature can make for great
disasters in a statesman. He had in mind the French literary intellectuals who, before the French Revolution, clamped their political ab-
stractions on the French mind, and with bloody results. Later, in
1848, Ralph Waldo Emerson looked at another French revolution—
where literary intellectuals were again in the lead—and doubted if the
results would be worth the trees that went into the barricades.

It is still too early to say whether Gen. Charles de Gaulle—who is a
writer as well as a statesman—is beyond the reach of de Tocqueville's
rule or Emerson's doubt. The passing years alone can reveal what the
days now hide about the bright or bleak side of his policies. As of this
point in time, however, it seems clear that de Gaulle's traits as a writer
and statesman are much the same. It also seems clear that he carries
in the marrow of his bones the tradition of French literary intellectuals
who have worked on the uneasy frontier where art and politics meet.

There are, of course, as many differences of nuance among French literary intellectuals as among the kinds of French cheese. But to speak of the matter in the singular, the French literary intellectual has a distinctive habit of mind which shows up in his political polemics.

Thus, for example, he is strong on the negative side of any dispute, strong in his assault on that which is—but rather weak in shaping a durable basis for what he wants to build, when existing things have been cut down. Further, he finds it hard to believe that any sequence of political events can happen "naïvely." Rather he thinks of politics in apocalyptic terms as a thing of "plots" and "conspiracies," promising a sudden end or beginning, a sudden ruin or salvation, a sudden darkness or flashing revelation.

At the same time, and in a contradictory way, he tends to forget that the object of politics is justice, not esthetics. He tends to overlook the immensely difficult task politics is burdened by, when it must prudently apply general principles to concrete cases and controversies. His natural inclination is to judge such cases and controversies by the canons of art, and he will often praise or condemn a political leader more for his "style" than for what he actually does in the formidable world of yes and no decisions. On the same grounds, he will "pose" himself toward politics, as though its questions were less important than the prospect that his own pose will appear as a work of art.

One more touch. The French literary intellectual, in his polemics, is never at a loss for opinions about anything in the world. He expresses himself in ways that sound logical, precise and comprehensive— though at times the facts forming his first assumptions were invented according to convenience by his vivid imagination alone. The rest of the world may be anchored to history, where nothing is true except the facts and the dates, but he takes his own stand on the high plane of poetry, where everything is true except the facts and the dates. On that high plane, he feels free to say to the rest of the world: "I know, and you don't." He is all the more free to say this, since he feels that France itself—a great, autonomous work of art—is by right the center of the universe, and the source of its light.

The evidence linking de Gaulle with these traditional impulses rests on something more solid than the fact that many leaders of French letters—like André Malraux and François Mauriac—are among his most ardent admirers. The more solid evidence is in the body of de Gaulle's own writings.

In his "War Memoirs," for example, de Gaulle was both Achilles and Homer as he lived, related and interpreted his experiences in World War II. But first and foremost, he began his account with a vision of France stated in political-esthetic-apocalyptic terms.

"The emotional side of me," he wrote, "tends to imagine France like the princess in the fairytale or the Madonna in the frescoes, as dedicated to an exalted and exceptional destiny. Instinctively, I have the feeling that Providence created her either for complete success or for exemplary failure." The vision, however, did not stand on its own. He promptly related it to a personal hope, fine in itself, but which needed the precondition of national trouble if it was to be fulfilled. For, said he, while he did "not question that France would have to go through gigantic trials," from his youth onward, his own interest in life "consisted in one day rendering her some signal service."

Now turn abruptly to his book, "The Army of the Future," published in 1934. In this technical study, which set forth the case for an élite army corps equipped for mobile warfare, de Gaulle synthesized pieces of military doctrine he had picked up from more seminal military thinkers in other countries. But the high quality of the writing made it seem that the concept of a mobile armored force was itself distinctively his own, and universally applicable.

It was left to the Germans to prove the concept successfully at the expense of France, and this fact, in turn, helped lay the basis for de Gaulle's reputation as a prophet who knew how to lip-read history better than any other leader of his time. The French did in fact fail to use their available armor as he had urged, and the failure compounded all the other reasons for the sudden French collapse. One point, however, was later overlooked in the portrait of de Gaulle the prophet (drawn by his own or by other hands). It was that the successful application of the concept of mobile armored warfare against France did not thereby make it universally valid. Elsewhere in the course of World War II, and in subsequent major wars, what de Gaulle had to say in "The Army of the Future" proved to be only half-right, or all wrong, depending on differences in local conditions.

This is not to deny de Gaulle the proper credit that is his due. Perhaps, through a natural flow of his artistic temperament, he leaped over the doctrinal rigidities of the Maginot Line mentality that made a captive of so many other prewar French military theorists. Where they were enamored of the idea of masses of men waiting in concrete tunnels to receive the blow of the enemy, he envisioned the army of the future as one equipped for "maneuver and attack, mechanized, armored, composed of picked men."

Moreover, it required a man with de Gaulle's artistic temperament to strengthen the polemical side of his case by wedding the facts about the internal combustion engine to a passage drawn from the prose writings of the poet, Paul Valéry. The passage de Gaulle quoted read: "We shall see the development of enterprises carried out by chosen men, acting in crews and producing in a few months at a time and place unforeseen, shattering results."

The vision, again, was apocalyptic. But de Gaulle, again, was not through, once he had stated it. He must relate himself to it. And so he did, though in a way that concealed the personal destiny to which he aspired. He reasoned that the future army, with its "aptitude for surprise," would unfold a "shifting drama" of mechanized warfare, "filled with unforeseen hazards and split-second opportunities." It would thus need a new type of leader out front, who would set an example of what needed to be done.

"If evolution," de Gaulle continued, "were destined thus to favor the rise of those who, in the tragic hours when the storm sweeps away conventions and habits, are the only ones to remain on their feet and to be, therefore, necessary, would not that be all to the good?" It remains to be added here that when all this was published, de Gaulle recruited a number of literary intellectuals who joined his side in the small polemical war the book triggered, and which saved both it and its author from obscurity.

De Gaulle's subsequent book, "The Edge of the Sword," had for its centerpiece an analysis of military leadership and the relationship between the soldier and the statesman. Here, once more, the author can be seen analyzing himself and drawing his own portrait, though he covered the project under the alias of figures known to world history.

His approach to the profession of arms and to war was not that of a Gen. William Tecumseh Sherman, who held that "War is hell." The de Gaulle approach began with a salute to the esthetic side of the matter. "The self-sacrifice of the individual for the sake of the community," said he at the outset of the book, "suffering made glorious— those two things which are the basic elements of the profession of arms —respond to both our moral and esthetic concepts. The noblest teachings of philosophy and religion have found no higher ideals." He thus had no need to ask any further questions about whether wars could be unjust, or whether the demands for sacrifice could be for immoral ends. "Esthetic" swallowed the word "moral," and no further trace of the latter appeared in the book, except in shipwrecked form.

The esthetic note was particularly marked when de Gaulle reconstructed what went on in the mind of an effective military commander. He drew on the writings of Henri Bergson about the nature of perception, then added in his own voice: "There is a close analogy between what takes place in the mind of a military commander when planning an action, and what happens to the artist at the moment of conception. The latter does not renounce the use of his intelligence. He draws from it lessons, methods, and knowledge. But his power of creation can operate only if he possesses, in addition, a certain instinctive faculty which we call inspiration, for that alone can give the direct contact with nature from which the vital spark must leap."

The true leader, like the great artist, he observed further on, "is a man with an inborn propensity which can be strengthened and exploited by the exercise of his craft." To the effective exercise of his craft, "prestige" was a prerequisite, and to this end, the leader must artfully settle an air of "mystery" on himself. How? De Gaulle's answer foreshadowed his own pose in the future. "In the designs, the demeanor, and the mental operations of a leader," he wrote, "there must always be a 'something' which others cannot altogether fathom, which puzzles them, stirs them, rivets their attention." In his dealings with subordinates, he must enhance his authority "with an attitude of cold dignity." He must be governed by "a determination to give nothing away, to hold in reserve some piece of secret knowledge which may at any moment intervene; and the more effectively from being in the nature of a surprise."

In the years immediately before World War II, de Gaulle wrote and delivered many polemical speeches in different French forums in order to make known his views about the needs of the French Army. But it was not until the events of World War II hurled him onto English soil and before a B.B.C. microphone that he had a chance to give full play to his gift of eloquence. Here, too, he began his long series of "painful" collisions with Winston Churchill, but he did not begrudge him a supreme accolade in his own "War Memoirs." "Churchill," he wrote, "appeared to me from one end of the drama to the other as the great champion of a great enterprise and the great artist of a great History."

On what grounds? Because Churchill made sound, practical judgments from within a narrow range of brittle options? Because events might have proven him right and de Gaulle wrong in their clashing positions? It is hard to find where, if anywhere, de Gaulle answered yes to either question. The accolade sprang from an esthetic reaction to Churchill's supreme mastery of language. Wherever Churchill was and whatever his audience, wrote de Gaulle, "the original, poetic, stirring flow of his ideas, arguments and feelings brought him an almost infallible ascendancy in the tragic atmosphere in which the poor world was floundering."

But de Gaulle, in his wartime dealings, was no less effective in contriving a piece of artistry that gave him an ascendancy of his own—and which he kept alive in his polemics to the French people after the war. First, there were the "élite" French who rallied to his person. They had, he wrote, "a taste for risk and adventure pushed to the pitch of art for art's sake." Backed by such men, it was made clear to all, including French generals senior in rank, "that General de Gaulle . . . was outside the ladder of rank and invested with a duty that knew no hierarchy." He was to be, in other words, an autonomous work of his own art.

As such, he contrived his effects with such great care that the persona he deliberately assumed became indivisible with his inner self. Thus he wrote: "The fact of embracing for my comrades the fate of our country, for the French multitude and the symbol of its hopes, and for the foreign image of France indomitable in the midst of her trials, was to dictate my bearing and impose upon my personality an attitude which I could never again change. . . . Our greatness and our strength consisted solely in intransigence concerning the rights of France."

The polemic of intransigence was powerful enough to fuse many things together, so that the terms "I," "General de Gaulle," "de Gaulle," "France," "The French Nation" and the "French State" seemed to be so many eagles growing out of the same stiff neck. It was powerful enough to cloud the truth that "the rights of France" were restored to her primarily by the force of American and British arms and political policy. It was also powerful enough to obscure a wartime and a postwar truth down to the present day that intransigence repeatedly had to give ground, either because it was at odds with reality, or because it was a thing of form alone with no material substance to back it up—except when the task was to tear down some tottering things in being.

Still, the habit of intransigence continued, and to the wartime legend, there was added the postwar polemics by de Gaulle against the "Anglo-Saxons"—as though England and the United States were jointly the country of King Harold before the Norman invasion. It would be wrong, however, to ascribe to de Gaulle's own writings the very strong current of anti-Americanism now running through the writings of other French literary intellectuals. They are anti-American for a different reason, and the reason goes well beyond their views about the conflict in Vietnam.

A new scientific and technological society is taking shape in France, and the literary intellectuals, who are not used to dealing with mathematically exact things and facts, find their preeminence threatened by developments within France which they do not understand—and, in any case, can't control. And who in the world is the archetype of a scientific and technologically oriented society? America is. Who serves others as a measuring stick for the changes achieved or to be attained by such a society? America does. Hence the literary intellectuals must attack America as a surrogate object for the things they hate, feel threatened by and can't grasp within France itself.

What de Gaulle has done, as a powerful writer occupying a statesman's office, is to purify the attack by raising it to the plane of patriotism in the service of the "true" France.

ANTHONY BURGESS*
The Politics of
Graham Greene

I HAD better begin by making my own position clear. I come of an old though not particularly distinguished Lancashire Roman Catholic family, one that held to the faith through the Reformation and had its quota of undistinguished martyrs. It was Royalist during the Civil War and hid its quota of undistinguished Royalist leaders in huts in Lancashire cloughs, and supported the Pretenders after 1688. There are several such families in England, particularly in the northwest, and

* (We have met Mr. Burgess on page 85)

they have made less mark in modern Catholic literature than have the converts.

There is a tendency in old Catholic families to record a number of apostasies with the coming of the days of toleration, though—as Evelyn Waugh demonstrates romantically in "Brideshead Revisited" —deathbed reconciliations are very common; with the intellectual scions of the old Catholic families the faith rarely fires the imagination as it does with new converts, even where the faith burns at all. The English Catholic novel in our own age is almost entirely a product of conversion.

Of the English Catholic novelists, Graham Greene (a convert) is by far the most interesting, since he is probably the least orthodox. The implied doctrines of his novels approach Jansenism, which has been repeatedly condemned by Rome. Cornelius Jansen, founder of the theological school whose most famous and brilliant adherent was Pascal, came too near to Calvinism to be orthodox: he found too much semi-Pelagianism in the "laxist" Jesuits; he affirmed and reaffirmed the more "rigorist" doctrines of St. Augustine.

In Jansen, original sin was not mere "imputation"; it expressed itself in the depravation of nature (whose order was, contrary to official teaching, distinct from the supernatural order), in appetite and in concupiscence. The horror of the natural world is one of the most fascinating aspects of Greene's fiction. Sin is not cool and intellectual matter for theological dissertations; sin is expressed in the joyless sex of "Brighton Rock," with its broken toenails in the bed; the carious landscape of "The Power and the Glory"; the hell of Haiti in "The Comedians."

A religious faith should beget its own politics. To adhere to a political system that denies God is not possible to the Christian, though some Christians have used doublethink to reconcile the contradictions. Thus, both Italy and France have their Communist Catholics, and England had a distinguished Anglican dean who clung to Marxism against all official remonstrances. In such instances one does not have to look beyond the expediency of the nominal; one cannot hold opposed beliefs and maintain total orthodoxy in both.

The political positions of most English Catholics have been dictated as much by the instinct for survival as by matters of doctrinal compatibility. They were Royalist almost to a man in the Great Rebellion, and, with the Parliamentary victory, they suffered for two kinds of faith. They naturally supported the Jacobite cause, and they had no economic stake in Whiggism, though they had good grounds for being favorable to 19th-century liberalism. Many Catholics today find it possible to be socialists, since British socialism—with its slogan "pragmatism"—does not insist, as does pure Marxist doctrine, on a materialistic interpretation of history. And yet any political ideology that rejects original sin and believes in moral progress ought strictly to be viewed with suspicion by Catholics.

Deeper than party politics lies the whole question of national allegiance. The British State tolerates the Roman Catholic Church, but the Roman Catholic Church, being a supranational body, has no representation in the Establishment: there are no Roman Catholic Bishops in the House of Lords, though it was found possible to put the Methodist minister Donald Soper there. To honor the monarch is to acknowledge the hegemony of the Church of England. Catholic patriotism must necessarily be of a qualified kind, since not only is the present involved but also the past, the remembered wrongs of history. These latter are, to the really embittered, incarnated or lapidified in the cathedrals and churches which, once Catholic, are now Protestant.

No Catholic novelist is able to resist the temptation of underlining the architectural squalor of the churches where his heroes or heroines hear mass. But the real historical wrongs are not easily forgotten. There is a significant passage in Greene's "The Heart of the Matter." When the Colonial Secretary says, "The Roman Catholic Syrians are claiming they are a persecuted minority and that the police are in the pay of the Moslem Syrians," the Catholic convert Scobie replies: "The same thing would have happened the other way round—only it would have been worse. Parliament has more affection for Moslems than Catholics."

Graham Greene's self-expatriation—once intermittent but now, it seems, permanent—could never be interpreted as a failure of devotion to England. The Jansenist in him is led to the places where the squalor of sin is exposed in its rawest forms. But, unlike Evelyn Waugh, who fictionally identified himself with the fortunes of English Catholics tied, by land or family bonds, to England, Greene is concerned with the Catholic soul working out its salvation or damnation in isolation; the furniture of England is a distraction and an irrelevance.

Admittedly, two of his finest novels—"Brighton Rock" and "The End of the Affair"—have English settings, but they are not the English settings of the ordinary bourgeois English novel; we have the jungle of gang warfare in the first and the jungle of the Blitz in the second. A parochial England, one in which party politics can be an important concern, hardly seems to Greene a suitable stage for the enactment of spiritual drama. Moreover, his Catholicism reveals, with every new book, its international character. The enemies of the true belief walk the great world, not the parish. The politics of Greene are world politics.

In "The Power and the Glory" we observe a local revolution in a small and remote state, but the lineaments of the new dispensation are familiar and international: the cult of the spiritual holds back the people, whose true enemies are the priests; the great goal is material prosperity; the leader knows best. The progressive slogans are, as always, accompanied by retrogressive enactments, best symbolized in prohibition. The imperfect priest on the run from the state police searches desperately for a bottle of wine with which to say mass. He procures one, only to have it drained by corrupt and hypocritical representatives of the new order, who toast human progress in it. It is "human progress" that is the shibboleth of the antichrist, and it does not matter which political ideology is committed to it. American democracy and Russian Communism alike profess the same goal, but at least one knows where one stands with a materialistic philosophy that openly avows its materialism.

In "Our Man in Havana" the American Consul-General speaks at the Traders' luncheon: "He spoke of the spiritual links between the democracies—he seemed to number Cuba among the democracies. Trade was important because without trade there would be no spiritual links, or perhaps it was the other way round. He spoke of American aid to distressed countries which would enable them to buy more goods and by buying more goods strengthen the spiritual links. . . . It had been a great pleasure for the American Consul-General to be invited to this lunch today and to meet the leading representatives of European trade and so strengthen still further the spiritual links." This is harmless enough. Greene's reputation for anti-Americanism did not begin here. It started with that still very topical novel set in Saigon.

"The Quiet American" is a work of fiction told in first-person narrative, and it was wrong of some commentators to identify the narrator with the author—a most implausible identification, anyway. With a first-person narrative there is no obligation on the author's part to be fair, just, dispassionate; and the anti-Americanism of the book springs from the natural jealousy and vindictiveness of the narrator.

On the other hand, there is no doubt that the image of the American campaign in Vietnam accords pretty well with Greene's own view: the Americans may mean well, but they are naïve, and in any case benevolence is dangerous if it is an expression of a twisted view of the desirable life. Greene, being a writer, hates semantic tyrannies, and he considers that too many Americans respond adversely to the term "Communism" without giving themselves a chance to examine the referent of the term. Evidently, some aspects of Communism cannot rationally be rejected, but it is the very irrationality of official American policy that earns Greene's scorn. Dubbed anti-American, he is assumed by pro-Americans to be anti-democratic and pro-Communist, but the issue is not as simple as that. The issue essentially involves religion and, in the endless cold war, matters of spiritual faith seem to have no role.

But to a Catholic there can be no real taking of sides. Americanism is bad in that it is fundamentally hypocritical. Talk of the "free world" often means an obsession with American security, American trade, the augmentation of an American-led community dedicated to more and more feverish material consumption; it does not necessarily mean the spread of democratic rights. Greene finds this hypocrisy best, or worst, manifested in the Haiti of "The Comedians." The tyranny of "Papa Doc" and the terrorism of the *Tonton Macoute* are more hideous than anything that Soviet Russia can provide, but, since Haiti does not invoke the forbidden name of Communism, America will be friendly.

It is hard to find worse evil than that represented in Haiti, but America—though she may wrap her materialistic doctrines in the language of spiritual aspiration—is not in the least concerned with evil. Remembering the Jansenist dichotomy, we can regard all politics as belonging to the natural order which never touches the supernatural. But America, transmitting her power throughout the world, pretends that she is crusading; this is the unforgivable hypocrisy.

Communism is hypocritical with its claims to free the enslaved, and its own aims are as materialistic as those of Americanism. But the fact that spiritual values are actively resisted under Communism saves its adherents from the bigger hypocrisy. Moreover, a political doctrine that is committed to improving the material lot of the people, yet signally fails to do so, seems to have been visited by an ironical paraclete; it is not yet clogged with butter and drowning in Coca-Cola vats; it is nearer the angels than it wishes to be. The sordid *mise en scène* that best expressed the sinfulness of the natural order is probably easier to find on the other side of the Iron Curtain than on this side of the Atlantic. A place that seems to breathe sin is, paradoxically, spiritually healthier than an aseptic garden city.

Almost the closing passage of "The Comedians" sums up the relationship between the Greene and the Red so admirably that it asks to be quoted at length. The martyr Dr. Magiot, who has had the courage to resist the evil which that other doctor represents, leaves a letter to the narrator in which he attempts to reconcile the anomalies of his own position:

"I have grown to dislike the word 'Marxist.' It is used so often to describe only a particular economic plan—in certain cases and in certain times, here in Haiti, in Cuba, in Vietnam, in India. But Communism, my friend, is more than Marxism, just as Catholicism—remember I was born a Catholic too—is more than the Roman Curia. There is a *mystique* as well as a *politique*. We are humanists, you and I. . . . Communists have committed great crimes, but at least they have not stood aside, like an established society, and been indifferent. I would rather have blood on my hands than water like Pilate. . . . I implore you—a knock on the door may not allow me to finish this sentence, so take it as the last request of a dying man—if you have abandoned one faith, do not abandon all faith. There is always an alternative to the faith we lose. Or is it the same faith under another mask?"

Dr. Magiot is "committed"; the other main characters are not; they are the "comedians" of the title, confusers of acting with action. But, in an evil world, it behooves a man to defend or promote the good, even at the risk of making a mistake: "I would rather have blood on my hands than water like Pilate." It is the "established society" that is most likely to talk about ideals and yet act as though the consumption of materials were the end of life. The Communist state is still in the process of "becoming," as is the kingdom of heaven, and—since in an evil community good can be brought about only through revolution—its techniques are apter for killing evil than are those of an affluent and settled democracy. "Communism is more than Marxism." In Vietnam, Communism can mean an agrarian reform sorely needed by a backward and ignorant people: Americanism—the doctrine of the towns—means teaching that same people to develop the urban appetites of the consumer.

Whether one accepts these notions or not, they seem implied in the later fiction of Graham Greene. A Catholic must accept that any kind of political commitment is dangerous, since no *politique* can coincide exactly with the Christian *mystique* (though a Jansenist will not worry too much about that kind of dichotomy). Yet if Christianity can no longer provide appropriate modes of political action, where can the committed Catholic look? Only to a system with a faith, even if that faith is heretical.

If some Catholic novelists have been able to resist the big troubling theme of commitment, that is because they have remained the products of English parochialism. Evelyn Waugh's broken reed of a Catholic in "Men at Arms," Guy Crouchback (broken, I mean, as a man, not as a believer), meets the postwar world in Yugoslavia and does not like it. Scott-King, who is not a Catholic but may be taken as speaking for his creator, thinks it a bad thing that schoolboys should be made to learn about Modern Europe. All of Greene's later heroes enter, of their own free will, a bigger and more terrible world than Modern Europe.

British politics are too small for Greene, and, in "A Burnt-Out Case," one has the feeling that British people are also becoming too small for anything but satirical treatment. The journalist Parkinson, the one representative of both his races in the colonial Congo, is a bloated joke. His opportunist and materialistic philosophy—a sort of parodic Americanism—is qualified by an inability to do anything with the truth except manipulate it in the service of "news" and, through this habit, instinctively get the truth wrong. And yet the mere presence of an Englishman sweating in the tropics, wounded eyes looking out over his pink gin, is enough to remind us that the British colonist is a more acceptable figure to Greene than the comfortable bourgeois stay-at-home.

One is impressed by Greene's own nostalgia for the Rider Haggard, Conan Doyle, John Buchan hero, pursuing the cause of British decency in some fever-ridden outpost. His most sympathetic character remains Scobie, the colonial government officer, who, like Aristides the Just, is traduced by the petty minds of men and women who have brought lending-library gossipy suburban England with them into the African darkness.

English Catholics, even converts, are tempted by more heresies than are the children of Mediterranean baroque Christianity. The greatest temptation is provided by the British heresiarch Pelagius, a monk who denied original sin, doubted the need of divine grace to achieve salvation, and thought that man could attain some sort of perfection by his own efforts. His doctrines, which flourish in our mild air, are the root of both the major political ideologies of this country, though they are at their more conspicuous in socialism.

If an English Catholic does not wish to be tainted by Pelagianism, he had better seek the exile either of Evelyn Waugh's "idiosyncratic Toryism," which can properly flourish only in a small manor cut off from the traffic, or of one of the barbarous places of the world. Surprisingly enough, such barbarous places take kindly to the heresies that have come out of France, a most civilized place; it is easy to be Albigensian or (which is not so bad) Jansenist in Cuba, Haiti or the Heart of Darkness. But once a Catholic lays open his soul to the corruptions of the great world of commitment, he must accept a kind of empiricism if he is not to be damned, drawing from the natural order what may conceivably further the terrestrial ends of the supernatural order.

In Greene's fiction, however, there is little flavor of empiricism (which, after all, has something of Pelagianism about it). There are instead paradoxes and anomalies—the sinner who is really a saint, the philanthropist who is really a destroyer. And there are dangerous epigrams like "There is always an alternative to the faith we lose." No significance need be attached to the fact that Graham Greene is now living not too many kilometers away from Port-Royal. His beliefs are his own affair; we are merely concerned with his fiction. And fiction, as we know, has to be stranger than truth.

FRANCIS STEEGMULLER
Apollinaire and Friends

Four years after attending the ceremony for Apollinaire described in the following essay, Francis Steegmuller was the author of "Apollinaire, Poet among Painters." He has also written a biography of De Maupassant, edited Flaubert's letters, translated "Madame Bovary." He is at work on a life of Cocteau.

ONE DAY late in May, 1959, when I was living in Paris, I received a card from the president and members of the Municipal Council, inviting me to attend, on Friday the 5th of June, at 11 A.M., the inauguration of a monument erected to the memory of the poet Guillaume Apollinaire "in the Square Laurent-Prache, at the corner of the Place Saint-Germain-des-Prés and the rue de l'Abbaye."

I had had advance word of this ceremony, and passing the Square Laurent-Prache recently (it is the familiar, charming little cluster of chestnut trees and traveled walks tucked into an angle of the Church of Saint-Germain-des-Prés, just to the left of the church as you face it) I had seen that just inside the gate a new stone pedestal had been set up, inscribed with the words "A Guillaume Apollinaire, 1880-1918." Atop it, thick folds of gray plastic concealed what I knew was a sculpture by Picasso. Someone had already decorated the pedestal, in pencil, with the word "*merde.*" Ordinarily that could be assumed to be the work of some nameless gamin or hoodlum, but since "*merde*" was one of Apollinaire's favorite words, I couldn't help wondering whether some admirer of the poet, a foe of officialdom like Apollinaire himself, hadn't passed by, and, aware of what was soon to take place, been inspired to add this happy touch in advance of the official ceremony.

As to Picasso's sculpture, I had heard a good deal about that, too. When Apollinaire died in 1918 (weakened by a war wound, he had succumbed to the influenza that was epidemic that year), he had left behind him a surrealist novel-autobiography called "Le Poête Assassiné," toward the close of which a memorial to the dead poet-hero of the book is constructed by a friend of his, an artist-genius who is both painter and sculptor. The memorial in the novel is a surrealist one: it consists of a hole in the ground that reproduces exactly the poet's bodily form. It is literally "pure form." Now the painter-sculptor in "Le Poête Assassiné" bears the nickname "L'Oiseau de Benin" ("The Benin Bird"): commentators have pointed out that for a number of years during Apollinaire's long friendship with Picasso, this genius painter-sculptor had in his studio a bronze Benin bird (a work of African sculpture), and after Apollinaire's death his friends and especially his widow, Jacqueline Apollinaire, had hoped that Picasso would provide some sculptured tribute to the poet's memory.

Indeed, Picasso himself had offered to do this, but, "having a morbid Spanish fear of anything connected with death" (at least, so went the story one usually heard), he had continually procrastinated, procrastinated for decades, for over a generation. It was only now, finally, badgered into action by Jacqueline, that he had come through, not indeed with a made-to-order hole in the ground or some other surrealist manifestation, not even with a bust of Apollinaire or some other work expressly created in memory of his friend, but at least with a sculpture, one of his more recent works (so it was said: I had not heard which one); and he had donated it to the city of Paris to serve as an Apollinaire memorial.

The only reason for my receiving an invitation to the unveiling of Picasso's gift was the fact that in connection with some work of my own I had been seeing, in Paris, a number of "Apollinairiens," people who either had been friends of the poet or had made him a subject of study. It was one of these, the author of a French biography of Apollinaire, who had kindly had the card sent to me.

Among the people I had been in touch with—in this case by correspondence—was Jean Cocteau, who was at that time living in the south of France. In a newspaper I had read a remark of Cocteau's to the effect that during the period of Cubism, Cubist artists had not been at all free to express themselves as they wished; they were "punished" when they disobeyed certain strict rules, and Cocteau and Apollinaire had both been "summoned to appear before a Cubist tribunal" on the charge of "stylistic deviation," Cocteau because of his daring, "non-Cubistic" use of a certain word in one of his poems, and Apollinaire because in the stage-set for one of his plays he had permitted the use of motifs "other than a bottle of anise and a guitar, or a pipe and a pack of cards." (Juan Gris, at the same moment, had been awarded official Cubist approval for his "introduction of the siphon into painting.")

"So Apollinaire and I came up for sentencing," Cocteau had ended his article, "and I assure you it was no laughing matter." I had wondered when I read that, what the grim sentence meted out by the Cubist tribunal might have been, and via a friend we had in common I wrote to Cocteau and asked him.

His reply, which came in an envelope postmarked "Saint Jean Cap Ferrat, Presqu'île de rêve," was a charming note written in brown ink. "Everything was serious at that time, the moment known as '*l'époque héroique de Montparnasse*,'" it read, in part, "and a tribunal was a tribunal. An artist was summoned before it for the slightest infringement of the Aristotelian rules of Cubism." That was the closest M. Cocteau came to answering my question. The letter was signed "*Votre poête, Jean Cocteau*," the signature being followed by a star, the Cocteau emblem. There was a postscript: "It is the dictators of art who make possible the disobedience without which art dies"— one of the better Cocteau aphorisms, I thought.

By the time M. Cocteau's answer came, the day of the inauguration of the Apollinaire monument was close at hand, and in the note
of thanks I mailed off to the *"presqu'ile de rêve"* I wrote that I looked
forward to seeing him at the ceremony on the 5th and hoped that
he would allow me to introduce myself to him that day. Privately, I
hoped I might be able to extract from him, when we met, the answer
I had asked him for. There was no doubt in my mind that he would
be present unless he were prevented by ill health (he had recently
been not very well, our friend had told me). As a young man Cocteau
had known Apollinaire; ever since, he had made much of that acquaintance; he was famous; and he was the only person even remotely
connected with Apollinaire to have become a member of the French
Academy. He would certainly be a guest of honor.

What was my surprise, therefore, to receive after a day or two a
second, briefer, note from M. Cocteau, this one addressing me with
flattering informality as a colleague and saying that due to his "various
addresses," letters sent to him sometimes went astray, and that he
had not heard about the ceremony on the 5th. "It would be very
good of you," he wrote, "to advise the organizers of this and to give
me a few details." It seemed to me that it would smack of impertin-
ence for me to write to M. Cocteau again, to give him details that he
should receive from an official source, so after I had "advised the
organizers" (that is, telephoned my biographer friend who had had
the invitation sent to me, and got his assurance that he would immediately telephone one of his friends on the Municipal Council:
something had certainly gone wrong he said), I sent a telegram to
M. Cocteau. I said that he would hear almost immediately from the
Council, which was counting on his presence on the 5th at 11 A.M.

By now there was only a day or two to go.

The morning of the 5th was fine, and inside the Square Laurent-
Prache I found that quite a few Apollinairiens had already shown
their cards at the gate and were waiting around the shrouded sculpture
on the pedestal (the word *"merde"* had been erased) for things to
begin.

Among them were a number of now-venerable writers who had
been friends or acquaintances of Apollinaire, including his truly close
friend, André Salmon, and there was a lady professor who gave a
course on Apollinaire at a French university. As we waited, a friend
introduced me to this lady, and I offered her a compliment that
proved to be anything but a success. I told her that I had recently

enjoyed reading not only the published text of the lectures she had given during the first semester of her course the year before, but also notes on her still unpublished lectures of the second semester— quite copious notes, made by one of her students, who had loaned them to me. *"Comment?"* the lady shouted at me—the entire conversation had to be carried on in shouts and shrieks, for a hearse had just pulled up at the portal of Saint-Germain-des-Prés a few yards away, and the bells in the old tower above us were tolling loudly— *"Comment? Mes étudiants font circular leurs notes? On pourrait me voler mes idées!"*

As I was yelling indignant words of self-defense, something foolishly bald, I fear, like *"Je ne suis pas voleur, chère Madame!"* the bells abruptly stopped, and the Apollinairiens in the square, quite numerous by now, turned as a man to stare at me in surprise. Luckily, the moment was cut short by the arrival of a cluster of important-looking gentlemen in morning dress, clearly the delegation from the Municipal Council. As most of the assembled guests moved back to let the new arrivals take a position close to the pedestal, the group separated to reveal a dapper figure until then hidden in their midst and whom they now respectfully gestured into a place beside the pedestal itself. I recognized Jean Cocteau.

Just as I was reflecting how curious it was that but for a chance remark in a letter from a stranger the guest of honor might not be present, and I was picturing M. Cocteau receiving first my telegram, then a wire or telephone call from the Council, then packing a valise and being driven to the Nice airport and taking a plane to Paris, I saw, outside the wire fence that encloses the square, someone crossing the Place Saint-Germain-des-Prés, quite alone. A slender woman with auburn hair, elderly, but with a still-pretty face and trim figure to make one think what a lovely young girl she must have been.

I recognized Jacqueline Apollinaire, the "pretty red-head" whom Apollinaire had married less than a year before his death, whom he celebrated in one of his most famous poems, "La Jolie Rousse," who still kept, unchanged, the apartment they had shared, and whose persistence, it was said, was responsible for the memorial we had gathered together to inaugurate. No one, apparently, had been sent to escort her.

She entered the square and made her way to the pedestal. The officials shook her hand; Jean Cocteau kissed her on both cheeks, and then she took her place a few yards away with her old friend André Salmon. Close to the pedestal but not at it, they formed a second-string pair.

It was a signal from the crew of a sound-truck from the Radio-diffusion Française, parked outside the fence, that started the ceremonies. The president of the Council briefly welcomed the principal guests and the assemblage in general; then, raising his voice—and perhaps remembering that André Salmon, though at the moment less known by the younger generation, was, in the opinion of many, a finer, though certainly less sensational, artist than the Academician guest of honor, besides having been a far closer friend of Apollinaire —loudly presented, to listeners both present and to be reached by airwaves, *"Monsieur* André *Cocteau, de l'Académie Française."*

Cocteau's aplomb was complete. Not by the slightest flicker or glance did he reveal that he had heard the gaffe; whipping out from his breast pocket a sheet of paper so neatly folded that I had supposed it was a handkerchief, he read a deft little speech that sparkled from beginning to end. "To salute Apollinaire is to salute Picasso, whom Apollinaire compared to a pearl"; "On Nov. 11, 1918, Paris was all beflagged in Apollinaire's honor"—a reference to Apollinaire's death a few days before the Armistice; "He augments the list of that sacred and glorious race of poets whose work so soon takes precedence over themselves." It brought to my mind again the speed with which I knew Cocteau had prepared himself: certainly within a few days, probably within a few hours, perhaps within a few minutes, he had written an elegant, if rather glib, little speech for an occasion of which so recently he had had no inkling.

André Salmon was introduced next. He was at that time 87 years old, from the start his voice trembled, soon his text about his old friend began to ramble, in a few moments tears began to trickle down his rugged, Semitic face, and shortly he burst into sobs and could read no more. Amid a hush, someone quickly took the paper from Salmon's hands, found the place, and finished the reading, as Salmon withdrew and was comforted by friends. Jacqueline Apollinaire kissed him, I noticed.

And then Jacqueline Apollinaire unveiled the sculpture. She was introduced, stepped to the pedestal, said nothing—or if she did murmur a few words, they were inaudible 10 feet away. She pulled a cord —the gray plastic once covering the sculpture had been replaced, for the ceremony, by a kind of white veil—and there stood, revealed, Picasso's gift. It was a handsome, bronze, more than life-size head of a woman. I recognized the sitter immediately. She was Dora Maar, a lady prominent in recent Picasso annals, whose double profile is seen in many a canvas of the 1940's: when Picasso knew Apollinaire, Dora Maar was probably not yet born. Certainly those rumors had been correct that had reported the "memorial" as having no express connection with Apollinaire. On one side of the pedestal, I now saw, were inscribed the words: "This bronze, the work of Pablo Picasso, is dedicated by him to his friend Guillaume Apollinaire, 1959."

At that moment, timed so perfectly that I wondered whether the crew of the radio truck had arranged matters with the curé, the bells of Saint-Germain-des-Prés once again began to clang: the requiem mass was over; the pallbearers with the casket emerged from the church, and a line of black cars was forming behind the hearse. The lady professor, seeing a policeman in the Place Saint-Germain-des-Prés asking people in a few parked cars to move, to make way for the funeral, began to screech: "*Mon chauffeur! Ou est-il? Quel est cet enterrement! O que c'est agaçant! Chauffeur! Chauffeur!*" Hastily bestowing a few handshakes, she rushed off. The ceremony was over.

From the Square Laurent-Prache most of the guests made their way across the Boulevard Saint-Germain to the Brasserie Lipp, where the Muncipal Council had invited everyone to an "*apéritif d'honneur.*" There, in an upper room, I saw André Salmon seated in a corner with a couple of friends, one of whom I heard order for him not the *porto* that waiters were offering all of us on trays, but a cognac: the old poet looked tired and depressed, shaking his head as though in dismay and self-reproach. Elsewhere in the room, Jean Cocteau was surrounded by a growing throng.

Going over to Salmon, I presumed to say something about his having paid a tribute to Apollinaire that was recognized by everyone present as the finest moment of the day, but although one of his friends said, "*Vous voyez, Maître? C'est ce que nous vous disions,*" he grasped my hand but feebly and shook his head. I took my leave quickly, fearing he might weep again.

I had hoped to be able to try once more for an answer to the question I had asked M. Cocteau in my first letter, and now I made my way over to the group around him—a cluster, chiefly of younger men, that seemed almost to constitute a separate little *apéritif d'honneur* of its own. It took me some time to penetrate it, and then I

found Cocteau speaking so vivaciously about the new Orpheus film
he was writing that I simply listened with the rest. As I stood there,
his frequent utterance of the name "Orpheus" vividly recalled a
feature of his speech that I had but fleetingly noticed during its de-
livery. It, too, had made prominent mention of Orpheus, and of stars
—"les astres." Somehow, although Apollinaire, too, like most poets,
loved to speak of the stars, those in Cocteau's speech now began to
associate themselves rather with those brown-ink stars appended as
emblems to the signature "Jean Cocteau" in the letters from St. Jean
Cap Ferrat; and his mentions of Orpheus in the speech—although
Apollinaire, too, had loved Orpheus—seemed in retrospect to relate
rather sharply to one or two Orpheus films by Jean Cocteau.

This impression—it was no more than that, strengthened no
doubt by the strikingly non-Apollinairian, purely Picassian, character of Picasso's "memorial"—had the effect of stiffening my resolu-
tion. After all, I told myself, grotesque as the fact was, Jean Cocteau's
presence today was partly due to me, and I would press for a reward.
So, when he eventually broke out of the surrounding circle, I accosted
him.

I murmured my name, identifying myself as the sender of the
telegram. "*Le télégramme?*" M. Cocteau inquired, suddenly cold—
almost, it seemed, suspicious. "*Quel télégramme?*"

"In reply to your asking me to tell the committee that your invitation for today had gone astray."

"*Ah, ça.*" There were just those two syllables uttered in a dry tone
of boredom and displeasure. Was I being told that mention of the
episode was in wretched taste? That like the gaffe about "M. André
Cocteau" it should be treated as though it never happened?

"What were those sentences meted out by the Cubist tribunals?"
I persisted. I felt surprised at how completely willing to make a
nuisance of myself I had suddenly become. "What punishment did
they inflict on you and Apollinaire?"

"*Ah, ça . . .*"

Once again, that was clearly going to be the only answer, and
M. Cocteau was moving on. But then something happened. Several
of the young men who had been clustered around him had followed
him, like students after a favorite teacher, and they heard my words
and seemed surprised and intrigued. "*Comment Maître? Des tri-
buneaux Cubistes? On était jugé? Comment jugé, Maître?*" Several
such questions were quickly put.

No longer the mere prey of a lone importunist, but once again the center of a sympathetic group, Cocteau freshened before my eyes. His expression lost its coldness, vibrancy returned to his voice. "*Ah, oui, je vous assure. . . . On était puni . . . Voyez-vous . . .*" And he launched into a charming little lecture, almost word for word what he had written in the article I had seen and in his first letter to me. "Oh, yes," he ended, "in those days a tribunal was a tribunal. It was no laughing matter, I assure you. Apollinaire and I were punished."

"But punished how?" I cried, again. "The penalties—what were they?"

There was no indication that M. Cocteau had heard me. He glanced at his watch, murmured "*Je regrette . . . un rendezvous . . . ,*" bowed to us all, and quickly disappeared.

What might the answer to my question be, I wondered, standing there momentarily alone in the midst of the *apéritif d'honneur,* Cocteau having left and his young admirers dispersed? What punishments could have been decreed by Cubist tribunals to deviating artists? And why had Cocteau not replied?

Now I thought I knew the answers: and some of my guesses have since been confirmed, I am pretty sure, in allusions to artistic quarrels of the day that I have seen in letters written by Apollinaire. "Tribunals": of what could those have consisted except a few dogmatic artists and theoretical critics, probably lesser fry in both cases, discussing so-and-so's latest work around tables in a cafe and deciding that it had "fallen off," that it "wouldn't do"? And the "punishments," the "sentences": what could they have amounted to except omission of a name from articles, verbal ostracism by a clique, waspish words of exclusion: "Apollinaire! Traitor! Unworthy of the name Cubist! Out with him!" And, finally, as to Cocteau's refusal to answer my question: why *should* a question be answered if the asker of it does not care or see that the answer cannot possibly be as brilliant or as interesting as the intriguing statements that led to the question in the first place?

One does not *have* to consent to dampen one's fireworks, just to satisfy the curiosity of a stranger.

One more little episode stands out in my memory of that day. After the *apéritif d'honneur* and after the excellent lunch that some of us stayed for, I was leaving the Brasserie Lipp when I saw, a few yards away in the Boulevard Saint-Germain, the figure of Jacqueline Apollinaire once again alone. In the past I had called on her in her apartment, today we had exchanged a few words at Lipp's, and now I hastened my steps and asked if I might walk her home. She said she would be glad to be accompanied—to this day I marvel that no one had offered, or had been detailed, to escort Apollinaire's widow to and from the ceremony—and we walked along together.

I congratulated her on the success of the day, and said that I thought Picasso's head of Dora Maar looked very well—as indeed it does—under the trees.

"Yes," she said, "it is very strong. It is made of bronze. *Ça durera plus longtemps que nous.*" And after those words— I couldn't decide how equivocal they were—she told me that she had hoped that Picasso would attend the ceremony—"He sent a telegram"—and that throughout the morning she had kept missing good friends of Apollinaire who should have been present and who might have been present had the inauguration taken place only a few years before—*"les disparus."* André Derain, Vlaminck, Max Jacob, Serge Férat —she named those and others.

"The principal thing," I said, impulsively, "is that *you* were—*are* present—and so very beautifully so."

"Confess, Monsieur," she said, gaily, "that you were surprised, astonished, to find that after all these years 'La Jolie Rousse' hadn't quite lost *all* her looks."

I did confess it and she gave me a smile that conveyed a coquetry whose charm I could well imagine enrapturing Apollinaire. "Don't worry about me," she said. *"Je mourrai en beauté!"*

About the Author (Editor)

A native of Amherst, Massachusetts, Francis Brown graduated from Dartmouth College in 1925 and taught there for three years before taking up graduate work at Columbia University. After receiving a Ph.D. from Columbia, he was in turn Associate Editor of *Current History*, a member of *The New York Times* Sunday Department for almost a decade, and a Senior Editor of *Time* for four years. In 1949 he became Editor-in-Chief of *The New York Times Book Review*. The author of several books, including the biography, *Raymond of the Times*, he is married and lives in New York City.